SEARCHING FOR STRUCTURE

An approach to analysis of substantial bodies of micro-data and documentation for a computer program

John A. Sonquist
Elizabeth Lauh Baker
James N. Morgan

Revised Edition

Survey Research Center • Institute for Social Research
The University of Michigan
Ann Arbor, Michigan
1973

ISR Code No. 3292

Library of Congress Catalog Card No. 73-620236
ISBN 0-87944-109-7 paperbound
ISBN 0-87944-110-0 clothbound

Published by the Institute for Social Research
The University of Michigan, Ann Arbor, Michigan 48106

First Published 1971
Revised Edition 1974, Second Printing 1975

Table of Contents

List of Tables

List of Figures

Preface

Some years ago, in rebellion against the restrictive assumptions of conventional multivariate techniques and the cumbersome inconvenience of ransacking sets of data in other ways, we produced a computer program entitled The $\underline{Au}$tomatic $\underline{I}$nteraction $\underline{D}$etector.[1] This program simulated what researchers had been doing with data for many years but with prestated strategy and in a reproducible way.

The Structure-Search program described here, termed AID3, is a new and elaborated version of the original AID algorithm. This manual is intended as a technical guide to using the program. In order to make the documentation more complete, parts of the original AID monograph, "The Detection of Interaction Effects," have been incorporated into the text.

This version of AID3 was designed and implemented by the authors in cooperation with other members of ISR's Survey Research Center Computer Support Group. The advice and help of Judith Rattenbury, Neal Van Eck, Laura Klem, Duane Thomas and Robert Messenger are especially acknowledged. Tecla Schrader aided in developing the final program by testing and retesting many combinations of options on several data sets. William Haney provided valuable editorial suggestions. Joan Brinser cleared up the worst obscurities. Maryon Wells, Tracie Brooks, Nancy Mayer and Alice Sano helped with the typing. Priscilla Hildebrandt and Ellen Bronson typed the completed manuscript.

The financial support of the National Science Foundation and the Shell Oil Company is gratefully acknowledged. Mr. V. Hwang, Mr. J. Viladas and Mr. A.

---

[1]The support of the National Science Foundation for development of both the original "AID" program and the new AID3 documented here is gratefully acknowledged.

Armitage provided valuable suggestions.

The data computation upon which this paper is based employed the OSIRIS computer software system, which was jointly developed by the component Centers of the Institute for Social Research, The University of Michigan, using funds from the NSF, the Inter-university Consortium for Political Research and other sources.

I
Introduction to the Program

1.1 Program Overview

In many social science research situations the problem in the data analysis is to determine which of the variables are related to the phenomenon in question (under what conditions and through what intervening processes) but may not necessarily involve the exact testing of specific hypotheses.

Data analysis consists of searching for the best model, combining theory and examination of data in the process, and then assessing the best model (or two) by well-known processes of statistical inference. The pure theory of statistical inference requires that the second step be done on a fresh set of data, not those used to select the best model. It also assumes that the model is properly specified. The choice among several competing and probably misspecified models creates unsolved problems in statistics.

The present program focuses on the first step--the searching of data for an optimal model. Theory is involved in the selection, explanatory variables, their hierarchical ranking, and in the interpretation of the results. The likelihood that another sample would give the same results can be estimated by looking at the competitive possibilities at each split, but the probability of replicating the full process is usually negligible, and a test of the final results requires a fresh, independent set of data. Hence no significance tests are provided in this program--they are inappropriate.[1]

The general principle of the AID3 program is an application of a prestated, if complex, strategy simulating the procedures of a good researcher in searching for the predictors that increase his power to account for the variance of the

---

[1]See J. Morgan and F. Andrews (1973).

dependent variable. Thus the basic principle of least squares is followed, and
the focus is on power in reducing error, i.e., on importance rather than on significance. In place of restrictive assumptions, reliance is on a prearranged
procedure which starts with the most stable and dependable finding (division of
the data set on that predictor which reduces the variance of the dependent variable the most) and works down to less and less dependable and powerful findings
on smaller and smaller subgroups.

The data-model to which the procedure is applicable may be termed a "sample survey model," in which values of a set of predictors X_1, X_2, ... X_p, and a
dependent variable Y, have been obtained over a set of observations, or units of
analysis, U_1, U_2, ... U_α ... U_n . A weight, W_α, may also be established for U_α
if the sample is not representative and self-weighting, or if one observation
is considered to be more reliable than another. Data may be considered "missing" or undefined on any of the X_i. In particular, this analysis situation is
defined to be one in which the X_i are a mixture of nominal and/or ordinal scales
(or code intervals of an equal-interval scale) and Y is a continuous, or equal-
interval scale. The X_i variables may consist of a mixture of "independent variables" and also "specifiers" (conditions) and "elaborators" (intervening variables).

The question "what dichotomous split on which single predictor variable
will give us a maximum improvement in our ability to predict values of the dependent variable?" embedded in an iterative scheme is the basis for the algorithm used in this program. The program divides the sample, through a series of
binary splits, into a mutually exclusive series of subgroups. Every observation
is a member of exactly one of these subgroups. They are chosen so that at each
step in the procedure, the two new means account for more of the total sum of
squares (reduce the predictive error more) than the means of any other pair of
subgroups.

A major advantage of this procedure is the transparency of the process
and the results. At each decision point, the printed output allows one to examine all the alternative divisions of the data set. If several predictors were
similar in importance, clearly another set of data might have produced different
results. At the end of the process, what one has is a set of subgroups whose
definition (pedigree) is clearly and easily defined by the process by which they
were isolated and whose characteristics (mean and variance of the dependent variable) are simple statistics.

It is always easy to explain any process by describing it in relation to
something else. But this process is <u>not</u> like stepwise regression, factor analy-

sis , or even analysis of variance. The only thing with which it is really comparable is the activity of a researcher investigating a body of data with a basic theory about what variables are important. Stepwise regression adds predictors, but every one has its effect measured over the whole data set. This new procedure measures the effect of each predictor on each subgroup. Variance analysis asks how much of the variance is accounted for by each predictor and by each interaction effect, but it insists that effects, main or interaction, are to be measured over the whole sample. It thus assumes what is often not true. In any case, variance analysis runs into statistical problems with survey data which are not orthogonal since a factorial design with equal numbers in all the n-dimensioned subcells is not possible. The basic additivity of the variances does not hold anyway with such real data.

The variance analysis in the present program is a sequential one-way analysis of variance that is simple, robust, and easy to understand. Factor analysis or smallest-space analyses ignore any dependent variable and merely attempt to reduce a set of things to a smaller set. Factor analysis serves a different purpose and may be necessary to develop a dependent or criterion variable for analysis. With the kind of flexibility in the use of predictors provided by the present program, however, the utility gained by reducing the number or dimensionality of predictors is questionable, particularly since those methods ignore the dependent variable and make a number of unnecessary assumptions of measurability, linearity and additivity. Indeed, one of the things that comes out of analysis using the present program is a new set of complex variables (defining subgroups) which have high explanatory power, and should lead to improved theory as well.

Finally, multiple discriminant functions, canonical correlation, and other "multivariate" procedures all impose restrictive assumptions, e.g. additivity, linearity. Of course, once the best set of non-linearities and non-additivities is decided upon, a linear model can be designed to include them, and fit to a fresh set of data for testing.

A warning to potential users of this program: Data sets with a thousand cases or more are necessary; otherwise the power of the search processes must be restricted drastically or those processes will carry one into a never-never land of idiosyncratic results. A well-behaved dependent variable without extreme cases or severe bimodalities is also assumed. A dichotomous dependent "variable" is usable if it takes one of its values more than 20 and less than 80 percent of the time. The predictors should be classifications, where each of the classes is in a single dimension; otherwise one really should make dichotomies out of each

4

of the categories. Finally, some theory must be applied, if only in the selection of the predictors. If all of them are at the same level in the causal process, they can be used simultaneously; but if they are at different levels, a
more complex strategy must be used.

1.2 Output Illustration for the Original Algorithm

The following results, contrived, but realistic, will illustrate the basic
output of the procedure. Suppose that Age, Race, Education, Occupation, and
Length of Time in Present Job, are used in an analysis to predict Income. Age
is an ordered series of categories represented by the numbers [1,2, ...,6].
Race is coded [1 or 2], Occupation is coded [1,2, ..., 5], Education is coded
[1,2,3], and Time on Job is coded [1,2, ..., 5]. We find the following mutually exclusive groups whose means may be used to predict the income of observations falling into that group:

Group	Type	N	Mean Income	σ
12	Age 46-65, white, college	8	$8777	$773
13	Age under 45, white, college	12	6005	812
10	Age 36-65, white, no college, nonlaborer	24	5794	487
11	Age under 35, white, no college, nonlaborer	16	3752	559
9	Age under 65, white, no college, laborer	10	2750	250
5	Age under 65, nonwhite	10	2010	10
3	Age over 65	10	1005	5
Total		90	4434	2263

A one-way analysis of variance over these seven groups would account for 95 per
cent of the variation in income.

These results are arrived at by the following procedure, as represented by
the tree of binary splits:

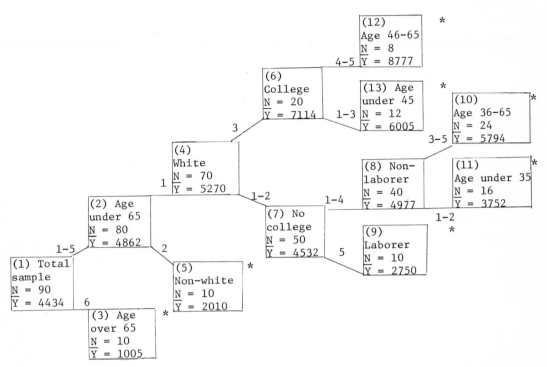

When the total sample (group 1) is examined, the maximum reduction in the unexplained sum of squares is obtained by splitting the sample into two new groups, "age under 65" (classes 1-5 on age) and "age 65 and over" (those coded 6 on age). Note that each group may contain some nonwhites and varying education and occupation groups. Group 2, the "under-65" people are then split into "white" and "nonwhite." Note that group 5, the "nonwhites" are all under age 65. Similarly the "white, under age 65" group is further divided, into college and non-college individuals, etc. A group which can no longer be split is marked with an asterisk and constitutes one of the above final groups. The variable "Length of Time in Present Job" has not been used. At each step there existed another variable which proved more useful in explaining the variance remaining in that particular group.

The predicted value Y_α for any individual α is the mean, $\overline{Y}_i$, of his final group. Thus $Y = \overline{Y}_i + \varepsilon$, where ε is an error term. Prediction of income on the basis of age, education, occupation and race would provide a considerable reduction in error. Variables which "work" are, of course, the most logical candidates for inclusion in a theoretical framework.

6

1.3 Capabilities and Differences from Previous Versions

The AID3 program is a generalized data analysis system, based on modifications of the original AID algorithm, and incorporating highly flexible capabilities for selecting subsets of variables and analyzing segments of the user's data file. It provides capabilities for controlling the way in which the variables are used in the automated sequential analysis, and provides for improved user intervention in this sequential partitioning process.

The analysis of variance model implemented in the original AID algorithm has been extended to include a covariate. Thus, an analysis can now be set up to maximize differences in group means, differences in the slopes of the regression of the dependent variable on the covariate, or differences in explained sums of squares due to regression (means and slopes). The sequential partitioning process of the procedure has undergone extensive modifications to make it more sophisticated in its search. The algorithm can now be set to examine the explanatory power of several sequences of prospective partitions before the choice of the first one is actually made. Thus, present explanatory power can be sacrificed temporarily in favor of even greater potential gains in subsequent partitions.

User controls over the behavior of the algorithm have been significantly improved, facilitating the exploration of interesting findings revealed in the course of the analysis. The analyst can request that the automated search procedure start from a particular point in a pre-specified partial tree structure. He can specify that certain predictors be used first in the partitioning process, or he can insist that statistics be computed for certain predictors, but that they not be actually used as the basis for a partition. The entire set of predictors can even be replaced in successive stages of a run. The analyst can use these capabilities to impose limitations on the partitioning process that are consistent with the kinds of causal explanatory assumptions he is willing to make about his data.

A further improvement is the capability to compute the potential explanatory power contained in the entire subset of predictors chosen for the analysis. This "configuration" rating is the upper bound of the statistical "usefulness" of this set of predictors, and represents the amount of variation that could be explained if the predictors were to be used in a model containing all possible interaction terms and main effects. It is essentially an analysis of variance using all the subgroup means in a k-way table if there are k different predictors.

The type of input acceptable to the program is basically the same as that acceptable to the original version, but with two important restrictions lifted. First, extremely powerful recoding and variable generation capabilities have now been provided. Thus, it is no longer necessary for the user to make expensive and time-consuming preliminary runs on other programs to recode or alter his input variables. He may even alter the coding scheme of his dependent variable and predictors in the course of one run, or he may generate new forms of any of his input variables. Secondly, this capability is used to provide an extremely powerful facility for selecting subsets of the input file for analysis, and for repeating analyses over several such groups. In addition, this recoding facility provides improved user control over the handling of missing data, either by assignment, exclusion, or randomization.

Improvements have also been made in the types of output supplied to the analyst. Information formerly scattered over many pages has been gathered together in more concise tabular form. The analyst may choose to receive an output file containing any or all of his input and generated variables as well as predicted values and residuals for each stage of his analysis.

It has been our experience that it takes time to examine the output, rethink over strategy, and that batch processing rather than an interactive mode is satisfactory. Indeed, the general principle of a prestated strategy rather than artistic ad hoc revisions of strategy at each local decision point appeals to us.

Two types of program operation modes are available: parameter definition (or redefinition), and execution. Three types of program functions can be requested in any sequence desired by the user. These are data input, computation, and output. A "run" on the program (to use computer batch-processing terminology) consists of an ordered sequence of parameter definitions and requests for execution of functions using then current values of the parameters. This series of macro instructions is executed in the order defined by the analyst in submitting his control information stream to the computer. After the execution of each function a query is made by the program to this control stream for information as to what function is to be performed next and what parameters are to be re-defined.

II
Analysis Strategy

2.1 Basic Procedure

The AID3 algorithm uses a repeated one-way analysis of variance technique to explain as much of the variance of a dependent variable as possible.

The simple conceptualizations given below should aid one's understanding of the program. If one thinks of the error in predicting the value of some variable in a small data set and its progressive reduction by knowing things about each case, the following holds:

(1) If one knows absolutely nothing about the variable, not even the sign, and can only predict 0:

Error variance is the sum of squares of the Y's = ΣY^2

(2) If one knows only the overall average, one predicts that for each case:

Error variance is $\Sigma(Y-\overline{Y})^2 = \Sigma Y^2 - \frac{(\Sigma Y)^2}{N} = \Sigma Y^2 - N\overline{Y}^2$

(3) If one knows the average $(\overline{Y})$ for each of two groups, and for each case knows which group it is in:

Error variance is: $\Sigma Y_1{}^2 - N_1\overline{Y}_1^2 + \Sigma Y_2^2 - N_2\overline{Y}_2^2 = \Sigma Y^2 - N_1\overline{Y}_1^2 - N_2\overline{Y}_2^2$

which is less than (2) by:

$$N_1\overline{Y}_1^2 + N_2\overline{Y}_2^2 - N\overline{Y}^2$$

Put another way, with one overall average, one explains $N\overline{Y}^2$ of the variance. With averages for two groups, one explains $N_1\overline{Y}_1^2 + N_2\overline{Y}_2^2$ of the variance.

Clearly the two group means must be different and the two groups not too different in size (both of some appreciable size) for maximum further reduction in error by knowing in which group individuals belong.

The present version of the program allows reduction in error not solely by using means but alternatively by using simple regressions for each group. By knowing which of two groups a case is in, one can do better if the two have either different means or different regression slopes (on the single covariate allowed) or both. The program allows either one or both sources of error reduction to be applied. (See Section 2.3 below.)

On the continuum between testing one pre-specified model (set of hypotheses) and completely flexible artistic data-searching, the approaches facilitated by this program fall in the middle. The program operates sequentially, imposes a minimum of assumptions on the data (selection of predictors, and the mode of classifying those with much detail), does a great deal of searching; but it does pre-specify the strategy of the search process so that it is reproducible. A rerun using the same specification for both the dependent variable and the predictors on the same data set will produce identical results. A similar run on another data set will probably produce something similar, at least for the first few steps.

The most common restrictive assumptions made by statisticians for easing the computational and analytical burden are those of linearity and additivity. With large data sets these restrictions are unnecessary. The use of categorical predictors representing subclasses of predictors (dummy variables) with multiple regression can deal with nonlinearities in the relationships quite adequately; hence it is the additivity assumption that is a problem. Additivity means the absence of any interaction effects, the effects of X_1 on Y being pervasive and independent of the levels of any other factor. It is cumbersome to handle interactions using regression. Either one runs separate regressions for subgroups, ending up with no overall relationships, or one introduces "interaction terms" which are themselves restrictive and limited. Suppose there are two predictors, each with three levels. Any one of the nine combinations of the two may reveal some non-additive effects, higher if the two are complements or lower if they are substitutes. Should one introduce separate terms (dummy variables) for each possibility, omitting the main effects, or what? If one omitted one level of each of the predictors in order to use usual regression programs (since the membership in a third class is a linear function of membership in the other two -- if you are in neither of them you must be in the third), then the cross-product terms would specify only four of the nine combinations, which particular four depending on which level of each predictor was omitted! The goal is not exhausting all the information in the predictors but discovering how they work.

Once one allows for higher-order interactions, the possibility of introducing variables for all of them in a simultaneous analysis dims rapidly. The real world, however, is full of examples of higher-order interaction effects. There are things which are substitutes for one another--any one of several handicaps can make a family poor. And there are some results which require that a combination of things be right. An interesting, if somewhat usual, example of this is the result of an analysis of time spent on do-it-yourself activities, shown in Figure 1. It indicates that any one of several things inhibit such activity or, put another way, only a combination of several favorable factors leads to a substantial amount of such activity. Read the right-hand boxes down the page.

There is so much confusion between interaction effects and intercorrelation among predictors that it may pay to distinguish them.[1] Multiple regression handles the problem of intercorrelation among predictors, so long as it is not too extreme. When the predictors are categorical, it simply means that one does not have a factorial design, i.e., equal numbers of cases for each of the possible combinations. The weighted means in any one dimension, as a result, reflect both the effect of that dimension and the hidden spurious effects of other factors disproportionately represented in the groups. In Figure 2 the intercorrelation shows up in the distribution of cases (Part A) and in the weighted means of Part B. With reasonably small errors around the subgroup means given in Part B, a dummy-variable regression will uncover the $4,000 education differential and the $2,000 age differential using only the intercorrelation data from Part A and the weighted means outside Part B. The investigator will then report that the negative correlation between age and education had hidden part of the effects of each--the simple weighted means differing by less than the true effects, i.e., by only $2,800 for education and $400 for age.

But if there is, in addition to the direct effects, an added $1,000 a year bonus to people with both education and experience (as shown in Part C), a regression would indicate somewhat larger effects of both age and education. Adding a cross-product term would locate the $1,000 interaction effect, but only if one happened to define it in the one way out of four possibilities that hit the correct corner. And with more complex combinations, and/or with more levels, the

[1]See also Appendix VII, James N. Morgan and John A. Sonquist, "Problems in the Analysis of Survey Data, and a Proposal," Journal of the American Statistical Association 58 (June 1963), 415-435, reprinted from Sonquist and Morgan, The Detection of Interaction Effects, Institute for Social Research, The University of Michigan, Ann Arbor, Michigan, 1964.

Or see John B. Lansing and James N. Morgan, Economic Survey Methods, Institute for Social Research, The University of Michigan, Ann Arbor, Michigan, 1971.

12

Figure 1

Hours of Home Production Done in 1964 by Heads of Families and Wives*
(For 2214 families)

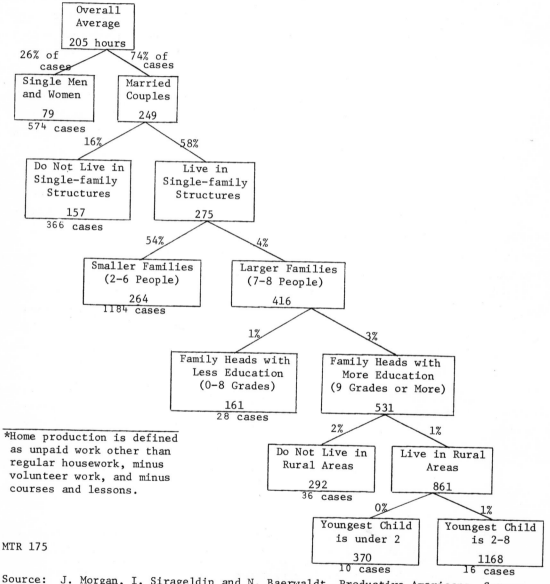

*Home production is defined
as unpaid work other than
regular housework, minus
volunteer work, and minus
courses and lessons.

MTR 175

Source: J. Morgan, I. Sirageldin and N. Baerwaldt, Productive Americans, Survey
          Research Center, Ann Arbor, Michigan, 1965, p 128.

Figure 2

A Simple Example of Intercorrelation and Interaction

Part A.

	Uneducated	Educated	
Youth	10	40	50
Old	40	10	50
	50	50	100% of Sample

Intercorrelation
(Negative)

Part B.

	Uneducated	Educated	Means*
Youth	$3000	$7000	$6200
Old	$5000	$9000	$5800
	$4600	$7400	$6000

No
Interaction
Effect
(But Weighted
Means are
Affected by
Intercorrelation)

Part C.

	Uneducated	Educated	
Youth	$3000	$7000	$6200
Old	$5000	$10,000	$6000
	$4600	$7600	$6100

Interaction
Effect
Added

*All means outside boxes
are weighted.

likelihood of finding interactions rapidly diminishes.

If one took the weighted means, one factor at a time, and used them to predict the interior of the table, one would see the large positive deviation of
actual from expected in the lower right corner.

How one describes an interaction effect is always arbitrary. In the present example one might say that the effect of education on earnings depended on
one's age, or that the effect of age on earnings depended on education. Either
may be true, but choice of a statement implying causal direction must be based
on other considerations, not the data themselves.

The crucial point is that not only are main effects not necessarily the
same or even present in all parts of the sample (or population), but interaction
effects themselves may be of various complex kinds affecting only some subgroups.

The theoretical importance of these considerations should be kept in mind.
Many theories of human behavior, whether from economics, psychology, sociology
or the new political science, deal with behavior of those who have a choice to
make, i.e., not dominated by other less interesting forces or constraints. Hypotheses are built on what affects those at the margin, to use the economist's
phrase. But if many people are not free to make choices or are dominated by other forces (which may not change over time, or be subject to policy, or even be
interesting), then the data may show that the overall effect of some important
theoretical variable is insignificant, when in fact it is quite powerful for the
relevant subgroup--something that this program will reveal.

If this program handles non-additivities better than regression, does it handle intercorrelations among predictors as well? The answer is that it handles
them differently. In regression a simultaneous estimate is made of the effects
of each of two correlated predictors, each effect adjusted for the fact that
those in a class on one predictor are distributed differently (from the rest of
the sample) over classes of the other predictor. The nature of this simultaneous solution can be seen best when it is described as an iterative adjustment
process.[1]

In contrast, the AID program divides the sample on the most powerful of
two correlated predictors, and searches the two subgroups to see whether the
other still matters. If the two are largely correlated and have similar effects
on the dependent variable, then the second usually loses most or all of its power and may well never appear in the branching diagram. Since rather few groups

---

[1]See F. Andrews, J. Sonquist and J. Morgan, Multiple Classification Analysis, Ann Arbor, Survey Research Center.

can exhaust the explanatory power of any one predictor, the pre-emption by one predictor is often dramatic. But this merely dramatizes the problem of inter-correlation. These may be situations where one wants a simultaneous estimation--then a regression model is required.

The program formalizes and makes explicit the exploratory nature of one's analysis so that it can be judged, repeated, and tested on other data sets. Most behavioral-science investigators have only a rudimentary theory, particularly in terms of the measured variables, as distinct from the theoretical constructs they hopefully represent. Even those who start with one model and test it usually end up testing several other alternatives, frequently by segregating subgroups for separate analysis.

To use the present program one must specify a dependent variable, a set of predicting characteristics, and some strategy parameters, which are discussed below. It examines the full data set using each predictor, and with each searches for the best single division according to that predictor. "Best" means the largest reduction in predictive error from knowing to which of two subgroups on that predictor each case belongs (and the means or simple regressions of those subgroups). The criterion is one of importance in reducing error, not statistical significance.

Where a predictor has a natural order (e.g., age) that order can be preserved, or the order can be left unspecified, in which case the categories are reordered according to the level of the subgroup means on the dependent variable. In either case, with k subgroups, there are k-1 possible ways to form two groups, and the division that makes the largest contribution to error reduction ("between sum of squares") is retained.[1] Among these best-for-that-predictor splits, the one (over all the predictors) which reduces the error variance the most is used to divide the data set into two groups.

Needless to say, the same predictor may be used again to divide the sample into several subgroups. Indeed, if there is one extremely powerful predictor, it may dominate the process and it suggests turning to a covariance search process.

A brief description of the splitting process is as follows:

(A) Choose the unsplit group L which has the largest sum of squares

$$SS_L = \sum_{\alpha=1}^{N_L} (Y_{L\alpha} - \overline{Y}_L)^2 .$$

The total input sample is the first group, i.e. L=1.

---

[1]The first versus the k-1 others, the first two versus the k-2 others, etc.

(B)   For each predictor P_i find that division of the classes in P_i that
      provides the largest reduction in the unexplained sum of squares.
      That is, split L (the "parent" group) into 2 non-overlapping groups
      (or "children") L1 and L2 so as to maximize the between sum of squares.
      For example, in a means analysis:

$$BSS_i = N_{L1}\overline{Y}^2_{L1} + N_{L2}\overline{Y}^2_{L2} - N_L\overline{Y}^2_L$$

where $N_{L1} + N_{L2} = N_L$, and N_{L1}, $N_{L2} \geq$ NMIN; NMIN is a minimum group size requirement (see (2) below). Note that if the order of a predictor with
k classes is maintained only k-1 possible splits are checked. If not,
one of k! possible orders is selected first (the one in order according
to the mean of the dependent variable), then k-1 computations made.
To avoid undue chances for idiosyncratic findings, it is wise to maintain the order of each predictor, or, if that is impossible, to convert it to a set of dichotomies.

(C)   Select that predictor P_j such that $BSS_j \geq BSS_i$, $j \neq i$, and if $BSS_j \geq$
      $P_e SS_1$ split L into the 2 groups L1 and L2 defined for the predictor
      P_j. The parameter p_e is an eligibility criterion (see (1) below). If
      $BSS_j < P_e SS_1$ then L is deemed a final group and is not split.

(D)   Return to step (A).

The process stops when one or more of the several criteria below are met:

(1)   The marginal (added) reduction in error variance if a split occurred
      would be less than some prestated fraction of the original variance
      around the mean; often the value .006 (0.6%) is chosen. This is the
      best criterion to use.

(2)   If a split on a group were to occur, one or both would have fewer than
      some prestated number of cases (e.g., 25) and the mean would be unre-
      liable. This is usually a dangerous rule, since (a) the least squares
      criterion being used is very sensitive to extreme cases, (b) cases in
      subgroups can appear extreme even if they don't in the full sample,
      and (c) the program can alert the researcher to their presence (and
      damage) by isolating a group of one or two cases that account for a
      substantial fraction of the variance if this criterion is not used.[1]

(3)   The total number of splits has already reached some prestated maximum

---

[1]See Section 2.8 for one method of treating extreme cases.

(e.g., 30), meaning that there are already that many final groups plus one and more than twice that many groups altogether. This is a useful secondary safeguard to prevent generating too many groups through inadvertence, e.g., in setting the first, main criterion too low. These criteria insure that the process stops before unreliable reduction in error variance occurs.

It should be obvious that if there are M different predictors of K subclasses each, even if all are maintained in some logical order, each split looks at M (K-1) possibilities and by the time twenty-five such splits have been decided upon, the program has selected from among 25M (K-1). With twenty predictors of ten classes each, this is 4,500. If any reordering of scales is allowed, the number explodes. Hence there is no point asking about statistical significance or degrees of freedom.

What can we say about the stability of the process? Each division selected is on the basis of an estimated "between sum of squares," a variance, as compared with similar measures for competing alternatives. The sampling stability (likelihood of producing the identical split on another sample) is clearly dependent on the sampling variance of the difference between the best reduction in variance and the reduction in variance occasioned by the use of each of the various competing predictors, which depends on differences between pairs of variances and their sampling errors. And of course the probability of getting the same sequence of splits is the product of the probability of getting the first (one minus the probability of getting any of the others) times the probability of making the same second split, etc., a product which diminishes in value rapidly. Of course it is possible to end up with the same breakdown of a sample with splits in different orders, i.e., one can split first on age and then on education, or the reverse, and end with the same final groups.

The examination of the predictors for competing alternative splits (two or more predictors where splits reduce the error variance about the same amount) for each subgroup provides a clear picture of the amount of intercorrelation among the predictors. If there are two competing predictors, and a split is made on one of them and the other retains no explanatory power over either of the resulting two groups, one sees clearly that they are alternative explanations and probably highly correlated with one another. Instead of a simultaneous process of "dividing up the credit" among correlated predictors, the sequential process used here selects one and reports that having once taken account of it (even in a single binary split) the other doesn't matter any more for that group. Once again, as with the extreme case problem, the results are transparent and face the researcher with his problems, rather than burying them in complex statistics.

Researchers accustomed to using numerical variables are often concerned with the use of binary divisions and with the possible loss of explanatory power when numerical predictors are converted into a few subclasses. The example below shows the potential loss of power from grouping a numerical predictor variable. It should be noted that when a predictor is used in several splits, dividing the sample into three or four subclasses on that dimension, the results are even better than in Table 1 because one has used only the best of the information. But even if one used all the classes available, as in dummy variable regression, it is clear that the losses in power are minimal, if the relation is actually linear. If the relationship is not linear, then one often does better by grouping a numerical variable in terms of explanatory power, to say nothing of the fact that one learns more about the real world.

Table 1

Percent of the Total Possible Explanatory Power Achieved
By Using Equal Sized Subgroups Instead of Regression[1]

Number of Subgroups	With: Uniform Distribution (▭)	Triangular Distribution (△)	Right Triangle (◿)	Bimodal Right Triangle (◠◠)
2	.75%	.67	.67	.89
3	.89	–	–	–
4	.93	.89	.91	.96
5	.96	–	–	–
6	.97	.95	.96	.98
7	.98	–	–	–
8	.98	.97	.98	.99
10	.99	.98	.99	.99

Source: Graham Kalton, <u>A Technique for Choosing the Number of Alternative Response Categories to Provide in Order to Coerce An Individual's Position on a Continuum</u> (Memos of Nov. 7, 1960, Feb. 10, 1967 and March 10, 1967), Sampling Section, Institute for Social Research, Ann Arbor, Michigan.

[1] If a regression gives r^2 and the squared correlation ratio using K subgroups of that predictor is η^2, the table gives $\frac{\eta^2}{r^2}$. A useful approximation is is $\frac{\eta^2}{r^2} = 1 - \frac{1}{K^2}$.

In fact, though, the comparison is not fair since the search process uses up many more degrees of freedom. A branching diagram with a dozen final groups usually accounts for as much of the variance of the dependent variable as a dummy-variable regression with sixty or more dummy variables (70 or more sub-classes of predictors).

Perhaps the most striking possible result from the program is the firm conclusion that some particular predictor may not matter. With an additive model, one is never sure about the possibility that a factor might matter for some subgroup of the population. But if that factor cannot account for any substantial fraction of the variance of the dependent variable over the whole sample or over any of the various different but homogeneous subgroups created by the program, then one can confidently dismiss it.

Results are independent of the order in which predictors are introduced, in spite of the sequential nature of the decisions made, but they are of course dependent on which predictors are used. Since there are often predictors which can affect other predictors but cannot be affected by them, the program allows for conducting the analysis in stages. One can introduce a set of basic background factors, remove their influence by calculating for each individual his deviation from the average of the final group to which he belongs, reassemble the full data set and analyze these residuals using another set of predictors. Since this process assumes no interaction between stages, one may want to reintroduce some of the initial predictors at the second stage. For instance, age, race, or education may be used in the first stage as background but can as well be used in the second stage. For example, the influence of moving to the city may depend on education.

It must be kept in mind that analysis of residuals, which is also done with ordinary regression, is not usually the best way to estimate the marginal or added power of certain predictors. The influence of the other things has been removed only from the dependent variable. True partial correlation requires removing their influence also from the predictor in question. (There also exists a concept called "part correlation" where the influence of other predictors is removed from the predictor in question, but not from the dependent variable.) It would be possible to derive two sets of residuals, using the present program, and correlate them as the tightest fair test of a nonspurious correlation.

The present program also provides evidence for marginal contributions of a predictor in the sense of their added effect on groups already freed from most of the effects of predictors already used to create them and free from the assumption of partial correlation coefficients that the marginal contribution is perva-

sive and universal, rather than restricted to a sub-part of the population. Or
it provides such evidence in the form of the second-stage analysis of residuals
from the first stage.

If the dependent variable is a dichotomy, the results are given in the form
of proportions which are on one side of the dichotomy. Even with numerical variables it is sometimes useful in analysis to _form_ two alternative dichotomies to
find out whether the factors which push many people toward one end of a scale are
actually the mirror image of those which push them toward the other end. This is
not a non-linearity issue but a substantive theoretical issue. For instance,
factors associated with increases in savings accounts are not the reverse of
those associated with decreases.[1]

The capacity to produce residuals from one analysis (and expected values--
the final group mean attached to each individual in the group), enables the program to identify and study extreme cases in more detail (cases deviant from their
own group), or to develop an expected value of a variable that could be used as
a predictor in a second analysis in the tradition of two-stage least squares or
instrumental variables, reducing the errors-in-variables problem.

The remainder of this chapter is an examination of the features and options
that are offered to the user.

2.2 Configurations

A rather special option unrelated to the main algorithm is a provision for
finding the explanatory power of the subcell means of all possible combinations
of a set of predictors. Instead of operating sequentially it subdivides the
sample factorially, even though some combinations have few or no cases, and does
a one-way analysis of variance components indicating what fraction of the total
variance (around the mean) is accounted for by the subgroup means, i.e., by
$\Sigma N_i \bar{Y}_i^2 - N\bar{Y}^2$.

It requires an extra prior step, sorting the data on all the predictors, in
ascending order, so that all cases with any given combination of predictor values
are together.

Meehl (1950) coined the term configuration and discussed what appeared to
be a paradox in which dichotomous items taken singly had no correlation with a
criterion, but their cross-product correlated. The use of configuration terms
in scaling was then discussed by Stouffer, Borgatta, Hays and Henry (1953).

---

[1]See Eva Mueller and Jane Lean, "The Savings Account as a Source for Financing Large Expenditures," Journal of Finance 22 (September 1967), 375-393.

Horst (1954) showed that Meehl's configurational techniques were a special case of multiple regression with all variables having values of 1 or 0 and including all possible cross-product terms in the equation. Lubin and Osburn (1957) developed the rationale even further, relating it to what they termed "pattern analysis" by presenting a method for analyzing the relationships between a set of dichotomous items and a quantitative criterion. Their general polynomial equation for the optimal prediction of a criterion in its configural form was shown to have maximum "validity" in the least squares sense. They defined a dichotomous configural scale as follows:

1. Given a test of "t" dichotomous items, there are 2^t possible answer patterns (configurations) and a mean criterion score associated with each.

2. Assign this mean as the predicted criterion value for all individuals in an answer pattern.

They showed that the zero-order correlation of the configuration scale with the criterion was equal to or greater than the correlation of the criterion with any other set of scores based on the answers to the "t" dichotomous items. This follows immediately from the formula for the mean, since, by definition, it produces the smallest sum of squared deviations. Consequently, the pattern means must explain more variation than any other set of means. Sonquist (1970) discusses this further. The extension to polytomous predictors is straightforward.

Computation of the configuration score provides the analyst with some indication of what his predictors are worth in explanatory power when all the "stops are pulled." It is suggested that if the variation explained by the configuration is undesirably small, the analyst had best spend his time obtaining hints as to what other variables he might undertake to include in a subsequent investigation.

Basically this option calculates a single one-way analysis of variance asking what fraction of the total variance is accounted for by the subgroup means if one defines a subgroup for each combination of predictor-classes.[1] The fraction is of the <u>sample</u>, not of the population, as is true of all the fractions of variance "explained" as used in this program. Extrapolations to the population are difficult and depend on the variation in subcell sizes.

There is a limit on the number of subgroups (possible combinations) that can

---

[1] For one predictor at a time the eta squared in the optional predictor summary table is equivalent to a one-way analysis of variance, again for the sample, not extrapolated to the population.

be handled, making it advisable to recode predictors into trichotomies in order
to use more of them. Five trichotomies produce 243 subcells. In any case, one
should not stretch the limits because with enough detail one could always make
the unexplained variance approach zero. The dependent variable should also have
its extreme cases truncated, to avoid erratic results.

The result is usefully compared with dummy-variable regression to see the
extent of the explanatory power lost with regression by assuming additivity. It
can also be compared with the usual output to see what the tree gains by not assuming total detail.

2.3 Analysis Types[1]

Perhaps the most promising new feature or set of features was developed to
deal with the problem of one dominant explanatory variable. Frequently in economic studies, income or education so dominates the dependent variable that the
data are split on little else. One may then want to remove that effect to see
what else matters. One could assume a particular relationship such as linear
through the origin and simply divide the dependent variable into groups by that
predictor. This often has the added advantage of improving the homogeneity of
variance where the variance of the dependent variable is related to its level.[2]

Moreover, with non-orthogonal survey data, one may want to search out subgroups in which there are different relationships between the dependent variable
and the "control." For instance, in much analysis of cross-section survey data,
the economist is often interested in the effect of income on some behavioral variable, and on whether that effect (as represented by its slope) varies with other
circumstances. The answer to this question will tell him whether it is necessary
to disaggregate the data in the models used for forecasting, and the optimal way
to do it.

Sociologists, psychologists and market analysts often face similar problems
in which the purpose of the investigation requires isolating the effect of a particular variable under a wide variety of combinations of circumstances. For instance, intelligence, alienation and authoritarianism have all been the subject
of repeated investigations in which the object has been to relate the particular

---

[1] Parts of this section are adapted from Sonquist, Baker and Morgan (1969).

[2] See L. R. Klein and J. N. Morgan, "Results of Alternative Statistical
Treatments of Sample Survey Data," Journal of the American Statistical Association 46 (December 1951), 442-460.

factor to specific consequences in such a way as to specify the form of the relationship under various conditions and for particular types of people.

Another illustration is in the analysis of changes taking place over time.
The initial value of a phenomenon under study clearly affects its value measured
at a subsequent time. This is why the residuals from the regression of its t_2
value on its initial t_1 value are often used as a measure of change, instead of
the raw increments.[1] However, this "initial value" effect may not be the same
for all subgroups in the population. If, then, a single equation is fitted, a
downward bias would be exerted on the correlations between change and those factors thought to be responsible for it. Thus, when residualizing a variable for
study, a search should be made to determine if this effect is homogeneous throughout the population. Where "regression" toward normalcy over time is powerful, a
two-stage analysis allows using the first analysis to estimate deviations from
expected first-year levels (from final group averages) and using a recoded set of
class intervals on them as the covariate or a predictor in a second-stage analysis of change.

To deal with these covariate problems, the AID algorithm has been expanded
from the original means analysis to include a regression analysis, where the sum
of squares is explained by differences in the two subgroup regression lines instead of the subgroup means.

In addition, one may ignore differences in the intercept and consider only
differences in the slopes. This slopes criterion differs from the other two sufficiently to warrant a more detailed description.

The difficulty with subgroup regressions (simple correlations) is that their
explanatory power is dominated by differences in the levels of the regression
lines rather than their slopes. And we may not even care to isolate groups with
a high level on Y, being interested rather in groups with differences in the
slope of the XY relationship (income elasticity, etc.). Hence a third option,
the covariance search, calls not for a criterion of explanatory power for two
separate regressions, but the power of two different regression slopes using the
parent group level.

Since there may be several subclasses on each side of a split, the criterion
is the power of the weighted average slope, not a pooled slope, on each side
since different subclass means on X and Y can distort the pooled slopes.

The search for differences in regression slopes only turns out to be more
complex than one might think. Suppose one wants to separate the K subclasses of

---

[1] For a thorough discussion of this problem see Lord (1950).

a characteristic into two groups, the first consisting of groups 1 through K_1 and the second consisting of groups K_1+1 through K. The first set may all have very steep slopes, the second very flat slopes, but if either their means on X or their means on Y vary, the pooled slopes of either of the two sets may have little resemblance to the subgroup slopes. A diagram may make this clearer. Suppose there are three subgroups in a set, forming separate clusters. While each of the

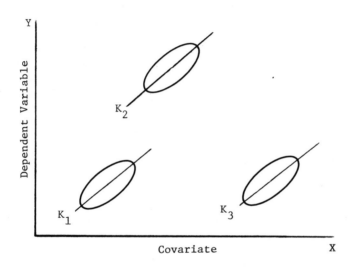

three groups has a regression slope of approximately 1.0, the regression slope pooling K_1 and K_2 would be approximately 2.0 and that pooling K_1 and K_3 would be approximately 0.0, and that pooling all three groups would be <u>negative</u>.

Hence, whether or not the subclasses are rearranged in order of their regression slopes, a criterion which uses the two pooled slopes from the two subgroups ($1 \rightarrow K_i$, $K_i+1 \rightarrow K$) would hide a great deal, <u>whenever the subclass means differ on X or Y or both</u>. So, we use the <u>weighted average slope</u> for each of the two children, both as a criterion for deciding which split to make and as the criterion for calculating residuals where they are to be used in a subsequent analysis.

As the formulas show, one can think of the remaining error variance around predictions using such a weighted average slope, instead of a pooled slope as originally proposed. Indeed, the terms subtracted from total sum of squares separate into one table attributable to subgroup means and one attributable to the weighted average slope. There are two such "explained sum of squares" terms, one for each of the two children. The criterion for selecting the best split is the maximization of that term (not of the total explained sum of squares, which includes terms for the subclass means). (See Table 2).

This is somewhat intuitive. For instance, there is no proof that where the

Table 2

Analysis of Covariance

Source of Variation	Sums of Squares	Degrees of Freedom
k individual slopes b_i about their average slope $\bar{b}$.	$$S_1 = \sum_i^k \left[\frac{\left[\sum_v^{n_i}(x_{iv}-\bar{x}_{i.})(y_{iv}-\bar{y}_{i.})\right]^2}{\sum_v^{n_i}(x_{iv}-\bar{x}_{i.})^2} - \frac{\left[\sum_i^k \sum_v^{n_i}(x_{iv}-\bar{x}_{i.})(y_{iv}-\bar{y}_{i.})\right]^2}{\sum_i^k \sum_v^{n_i}(x_{iv}-\bar{x}_{i.})^2}\right]$$	k-1
Deviations for each of k groups about their individual slope b_i.	$$S_2 = \sum_i^k \sum_v^{n_i}(y_{iv}-\bar{y}_{i.})^2 - \sum_i^k \left(\frac{\left[\sum_v^{n_i}(x_{iv}-\bar{x}_{i.})(y_{iv}-\bar{y}_{i.})\right]^2}{\sum_v^{n_i}(x_{iv}-\bar{x}_{i.})^2}\right)$$	N-2k
Deviations of the k group means about the regression line with slope b based on group means.	$$S_3 = \sum_i^k n_i(\bar{y}_{i.}-\bar{y}_{...})^2 - \frac{\left[\sum_i^k n_i(\bar{x}_{i.}-\bar{x}_{...})(\bar{y}_{i.}-\bar{y}_{...})\right]^2}{\sum_i^k n_i(\bar{x}_{i.}-\bar{x}_{...})^2}$$	k-2
Difference between $\bar{b}$ and $\hat{b}$.	$$S_4 = \frac{\left[\sum_i^k \sum_v^{n_i}(x_{iv}-\bar{x}_{i.})(y_{iv}-\bar{y}_{i.})\right]^2}{\sum_i^k \sum_v^{n_i}(x_{iv}-\bar{x}_{i.})^2} + \frac{\left[\sum_i^k n_i(\bar{x}_{i.}-\bar{x}_{...})(\bar{y}_{i.}-\bar{y}_{...})\right]^2}{\sum_i^k n_i(\bar{x}_{i.}-\bar{x}_{...})^2} - \frac{\left[\sum_i^k \sum_v^{n_i}(y_{iv}-\bar{y}_{...})(x_{iv}-\bar{x}_{...})\right]^2}{\sum_i^k \sum_v^{n_i}(x_{iv}-\bar{x}_{...})^2}$$	1
Deviations about the average slope $\bar{b}$.	$$S_w = S_1 + S_2$$	N-k-1
Differences between Y-means, adjusted for x=x, about $\bar{b}$.	$$S_b = S_3 + S_4$$	k-1
Deviations about the overall line (Error sum of squares)	$$S_E = S_w + S_b = \sum_i^k \sum_v^{n_i}(y_{iv}-\bar{y}_{...})^2 - \frac{\left[\sum_i^k \sum_v^{n_i}(y_{iv}-\bar{y}_{...})(x_{iv}-\bar{x}_{...})\right]^2}{\sum_i^k \sum_v^{n_i}(x_{iv}-\bar{x}_{...})^2}$$	N-2
Due to the overall regression line.	$$S_R = \frac{\left[\sum_i^k \sum_v^{n_i}(y_{iv}-\bar{y}_{...})(x_{iv}-\bar{x}_{...})\right]^2}{\sum_i^k \sum_v^{n_i}(x_{iv}-\bar{x}_{...})^2}$$	1
Total sum of squares	$$S_T = \sum_i^k \sum_v^{n_i}(y_{iv}-\bar{y}_{...})^2$$	N-1

subclasses are rearranged according to subclass slopes that one of the K-1 splits using that ordering will be the best.[1]

Not only must we use an average slope, rather than an overall slope, for the parent and for each child at any split, but we must calculate the net gain from using two different average slopes, one for each child, over using a single average slope for the combined parent, because the latter is not constant for changing predictors!

In the case of means, the explained sum of squares from knowing only the parent group mean is $N\bar{Y}^2$ regardless of the predictor, but with slopes, it is $\bar{b}\ N\sigma_x^2$ which will vary with the predictor classification since each one will produce a different $\bar{b}$.

Both with regressions and with slopes only, if the overall regression on the full sample accounts for much of the variance, the subgroup differences have less variance to account for, yet the criterion is a fraction of the original variance around the mean, hence the split reducibility criterion must be set lower. Slopes are also extremely sensitive to extreme cases, in X or Y or XY, and tend to become unstable very rapidly as subgroup sizes diminish. The different slopes may account for very little of the variance but may still provide some important information. And the procedure can be used to trick the computer into solving some other problems: One can use a dichotomous 0-1 covariate, like sex or race. The program then looks for groups with the largest differences in the racial or sexual differences, say in earnings. Or one can merge two separate surveys from different times or places, use a 0-1 covariate representing which time or place, and search for the groups with the largest differences between times or places.

The last possibility opens up vistas of powerful use of separate cross-section samples to search for social trends and their differences. The predictors, of course, should be things that do not change for individuals: race, sex, education, farm background, age (increases by one each year). The results should be far superior to the present system of finding groups that differ in one data set and looking for differentials among them in the differences with another data set. There is no reason to expect a correlation between the two, and we really need to search explicitly for the subgroups that differ on the differences.

Given the problems with weighted average slopes, however, it is advisable to reduce the number of categories of each of the predictors to five if the order is to

---

[1] See Appendix VI giving Ericson's proof for means which may or may not extend to slopes, reprinted from John A. Sonquist and James N. Morgan, The Detection of Interaction Effects, the Institute for Social Research, The University of Michigan, Ann Arbor, Michigan, 1964, pp. 149-157.

be maintained and three if it is not.[1] And it is particularly important to eliminate extreme cases in the dependent variable since they can have such a disturbing effect on estimated regression slopes. There may also be a problem if one of the two covariate groups is relatively small and is affected by something on which the majority group does not split evenly, so that not enough cases appear on one side of the split.

2.3.1 Means Analyses

If the total sum of squares for the parent group is

$$SS = \sum_1^N y^2 - N\bar{Y}^2 \quad ,$$

and the corresponding sums of squares for the two children are

$$SS_1 = \sum_1^{N_1} y^2 - N_1\bar{Y}_1^2 \quad \text{and} \quad SS_2 = \sum_1^{N_2} y^2 - N_2\bar{Y}_2^2 \quad ,$$

where $N=N_1+N_2$, then splitting the parent group such that the observations within each of the children are homogeneous is equivalent to minimizing the quantity SS_1+SS_2. Thus the reduction in the total sum of squares,

$$SS-(SS_1+SS_2) = \sum_1^N y^2 - (\sum^{N_1} y^2 + \sum^{N_2} y^2) - N\bar{Y}^2 + (N_1\bar{Y}_1^2 + N_2\bar{Y}_2^2) = N_1\bar{Y}_1^2 + N_2\bar{Y}_2^2 - N\bar{Y}^2 \quad (1)$$

is maximized. But this is simply the between sum of squares term in a one-way analysis of variance (Table 3).

2.3.2 Regression Analysis

The corresponding between-sum-of-squares term for a regression analysis (means and slopes) can be formed in a similar manner. Table 4 is an analysis of variance representation of the regression of Y on X. (The derivation of this table may be found in Brownlee, pp. 338-341.) The error or residual sum of squares from estimating the regression line in the parent group is

---

[1] See Kalton, Table 1.

$$SS_R = \sum_1^N y^2 - N\bar{Y}^2 - \frac{\left[\displaystyle\sum_1^N (y-\bar{Y})(x-\bar{X})\right]^2}{\displaystyle\sum^N (x-\bar{X})^2} \qquad (2)$$

By splitting the parent group so as to minimize the residual sums of squares for the two children, the reduction in using two regression lines instead of the original regression line for the group is maximized, i.e.

$$SS_R - (SS_{R_1} + SS_{R_2}) = \sum_1^N y^2 - N\bar{Y}^2 - \frac{\left[\displaystyle\sum_1^N (y-\bar{Y})(x-\bar{X})\right]^2}{\displaystyle\sum^N (x-\bar{X})^2}$$

$$- \left\{ \sum_1^{N_1} y^2 - N_1 \bar{Y}_1^2 - \frac{\left[\displaystyle\sum_1^{N_1} (y-\bar{Y}_1)(x-\bar{X}_1)\right]^2}{\displaystyle\sum^{N_1} (x-\bar{X}_1)^2} + \sum_1^{N_2} y^2 - N_2 \bar{Y}_2^2 - \frac{\left[\displaystyle\sum^{N_2} (y-\bar{Y}_2)(x-\bar{X}_2)\right]^2}{\displaystyle\sum^{N_2} (x-\bar{X}_2)^2} \right\}$$

$$= N_1 \bar{Y}_1^2 + N_2 \bar{Y}_2^2 - N\bar{Y}^2 + \frac{\left[\displaystyle\sum^{N_1} (y-\bar{Y}_1)(x-\bar{X}_1)\right]^2}{\displaystyle\sum^{N_1} (x-\bar{X}_1)^2} + \frac{\left[\displaystyle\sum^{N_2} (y-\bar{Y}_2)(x-\bar{X}_2)\right]^2}{\displaystyle\sum^{N_2} (x-\bar{X}_2)^2}$$

$$- \frac{\left[\displaystyle\sum^N (y-\bar{Y})(x-\bar{X})\right]^2}{\displaystyle\sum^N (x-\bar{X})^2} \qquad (3)$$

2.3.3 Slopes Analysis

In a slopes-only analysis the analyst is concerned only in maximizing differences in slopes without regard to means. Thus, for a given predictor, the parent group should be split such that class slopes within a given child are homogeneous. For example, if the parent group has three classes, the first and second with identical slopes $b_1 = b_2$ but different means. The overall or "pooled" regression line for a child with classes 1 and 2 will have a totally diverse slope b_p, and the group will be split between classes 1 and 2 rather than between classes 3 and 2.

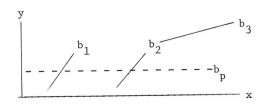

In the slopes-only analysis then, it is necessary to disregard differences in class means in estimating a group slope.

If for a given predictor there are k classes in the parent group with n_i observations in each class, then the average slope over the k classes can be shown to be: (see Brownlee, Chapter 11)

$$\bar{b} = \frac{\sum\limits_{i=1}^{k} \sum\limits_{\alpha=1}^{n_i} (y_{i\alpha}-\bar{y}_i)(x_{i\alpha}-\bar{x}_i)}{\sum\limits_{i=1}^{k} \sum\limits_{\alpha=1}^{n_i} (x_{i\alpha}-\bar{x}_i)^2} \quad ,$$

and the resultant residual sum of squares using $\bar{b}$ is:

$$R = \sum\limits_{i=1}^{k} \sum\limits_{\alpha=1}^{n_i} y^2_{i\alpha} - \sum\limits_{i=1}^{k} n_i \bar{y}_i^2 - \frac{\left[\sum\limits_{i=1}^{k} \sum\limits_{\alpha=1}^{n_i} (y_{i\alpha}-\bar{y}_i)(x_{i\alpha}-\bar{x}_i)\right]^2}{\sum\limits_{i=1}^{k} \sum\limits_{\alpha=1}^{n_i} (x_{i\alpha}-\bar{x}_i)^2} \quad (4)$$

Note that the essential difference between equations (2) and (4) is in the means. The regression analysis takes deviations from an _overall_ group mean while the slopes-only analysis takes deviations from _class_ means. This results in a different total sum of squares term for each predictor.

Splitting the parent group on a given predictor such that the reduction in the parent group residual sum of squares is maximized is equivalent to maximizing

$$R - (R_1 + R_2) = \frac{\left[\sum\limits_{i=1}^{k_1} \sum\limits_{\alpha=1}^{n_i} (y - \bar{y}_i)(x - \bar{x}_i)\right]^2}{\sum\limits_{i=1}^{k_1} \sum\limits_{\alpha=1}^{n_i} (x - \bar{x}_i)^2}$$

$$+ \frac{\left[\sum\limits_{i=1}^{k_2} \sum\limits_{\alpha=1}^{n_i} (y - \bar{y}_i)(x - \bar{x}_i)\right]^2}{\sum\limits_{i=1}^{k_2} \sum\limits_{\alpha=1}^{n_i} (x - \bar{x}_i)^2} - \frac{\left[\sum\limits_{i=1}^{k} \sum\limits_{\alpha=1}^{n_i} (y - \bar{y}_i)(x - \bar{x}_i)\right]^2}{\sum\limits_{i=1}^{k} \sum\limits_{\alpha=1}^{n_i} (x - \bar{x}_i)^2} \qquad (4a)$$

where $k = k_1 + k_2$, since the $\sum y^2$ and $\sum n_i \bar{y}_i^2$ terms cancel.

Clearly, selecting which of several subgroups are to go on one side of a split according to subgroup regression slopes and also allowing re-ordering of the subclasses of a predictor, is a doubly dangerous procedure, quite likely to produce idiosyncratic splits and results difficult to explain. Regression slopes are less stable than means, affected by extreme cases in either the covariate or the dependent variable but particularly by any cases extreme on both at the same time.

On the other hand, if one is searching for differences in regression slopes, not in levels of the dependent variable, the regression option is unsatisfactory, since different regression line levels account for so much more of the variance than differences in their slopes. Differences in level would dominate the selection of predictors in covariance search processes using regression.

The best policy if one is searching for slope differences, would seem to be to (a) be doubly careful to eliminate or truncate any extreme cases on the dependent variable, or on the covariate, and (b) recode the predictors to collapse each to three or four classes for those to be left "free" and four or five classes for those whose rank order is to be maintained.

2.4 Pre-Set Divisions

The program has a simple procedure for specifying a sequence of splits, after which the usual search procedure can attempt further splits. The purpose of allowing the analyst to force the first few splits is mainly to allow a prior division of the sample into some obviously different groups that are not expected

Table 3

Analysis of Variance for Differences
in Means

Source of Variation	Degrees of Freedom	Sum of Squares	Mean Square
Observations around grand mean $(Y - \overline{Y})^2$	N-1	$(N - 1)s_y^2 = SST$	s_y^2
Between group means $(\overline{Y}_j - \overline{Y})^2$	k-1	$\sum N_j(\overline{Y}_j - \overline{Y})^2 = SSB$	MSB
Within groups $(Y - \overline{Y}_j)^2$	N-k	$\sum_{i=1}^{N_j}(Y_{ij}-\overline{Y}_j)^2 = SSW$	MSW

Table 4

Analysis of Variance for Regression

Source of Variation	Degrees of Freedom	Sum of Squares	Mean Square
Regression estimates around $\overline{Y}$ $(\hat{Y} - \overline{Y})^2$	1	$(N-1)r^2s_y^2$	$(N-1)r^2s_y^2$
Observations around regression estimates $(Y - \hat{Y})^2$	N-2	$(N-1)(1-r^2)s_y^2$	$\frac{N-1}{N-2}(1-r^2)s_y^2$
Observations around $\overline{Y}$ $(Y - \overline{Y})^2$	N-1	$(N-1)s_y^2$	s_y^2

Where $r^2 = \dfrac{[\Sigma(X-\overline{X})(Y-\overline{Y})]^2}{\Sigma(X-\overline{X})^2 \, \Sigma(Y-\overline{Y})^2}$

$s_y^2 = \dfrac{\Sigma(Y-\overline{Y})^2}{N-1}$

$\hat{Y} = \overline{Y} + b_{yx}(X-\overline{X})$

$b_{yx} = \dfrac{\Sigma(X-\overline{X})(Y-\overline{Y})}{\Sigma(X-\overline{X})^2}$

to show the same patterns. But the procedure has other uses. One may want to take output derived from another set of data, or half the sample, and force it on a set of data to see how well it explains that data set (percent of variance explained). One cannot compare two different trees very well--they differ in too many ways. But the differences in the subgroup means and in the variance explained, when the same tree is imposed on a second set of data, provide important insights into the stability of the first findings. It would technically be possible to make estimates of the probability of arriving at the same tree with a different set of data, but it depends on the sampling errors of differences between variances--the sum of squares that are compared at each split in deciding which split to make. If there are other possible splits which would explain nearly as much variance, then the probability that in another sample they would actually explain more, is large. And the probability of arriving at the same whole tree is clearly the product of the probabilities of making each of the successive splits the same way--a number which falls rapidly as the tree grows.

Or one may want to look at a set of related dependent variables, for groups which differ a lot on one of them. Another use of the pre-set tree is to disaggregate a sample sequentially according to some logical order. Poverty, for instance, may be explained by some clearly exogeneous and irremovable forces: old age, physical disability, a single adult who has children or disabled people to care for, lack of education or job skills. Similarly, in looking at change in family income, one may want to remove sequentially those with a changed family head, a shift in marital status, changed number of adults, etc. Figure 3 gives an example of this, where the covariance option was used in order to provide two means for each group, income change and change in heads, by pretending that the latter was the covariate.

It is not always a good idea to force splits merely because there is some deviant group with an obvious explanation--such a group may often be found by the regular process of splitting.

A major purpose of the original program was to avoid the arbitrary selection of subgroups for separate analysis, and to allow the data to suggest the appropriate subgroups, divide the sample into them, and proceed. The criterion of power in reducing error variance used with the program assures that the groups so split off will be both different enough and large enough to deserve separate treatment.

There are, however, situations where some group is important out of all proportion to its frequency in the sample, for theoretical or ethical or public policy reasons. In this case one may want to force a subdivision at the start. But

Figure 3. Average Annual Change in Income and In Needs, by Groups with Changes in Family Status or Wife's Work Status (For 1967, 1968 and 1969 Incomes)

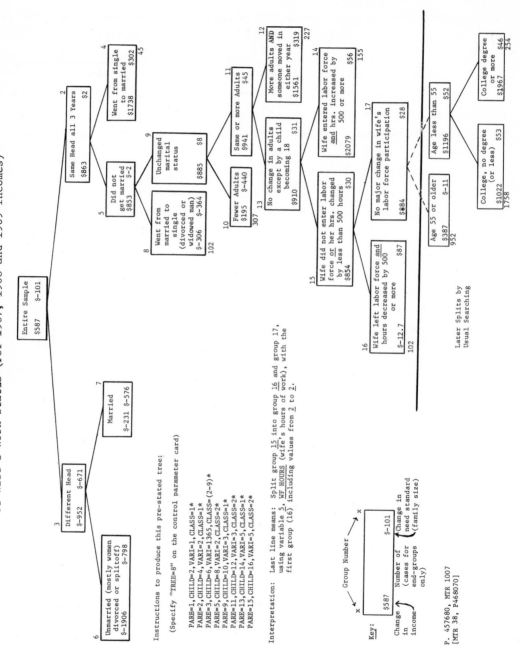

Instructions to produce this pre-stated tree:

(Specify "TREE=8" on the control parameter card)

PARB=1, CHILD=2, VARI=1, CLASS=1*
PARE=2, CHILD=4, VARI=2, CLASS=1*
PARE=3, CHILD=6, VARI=1365, CLASS=(2-9)*
PARE=5, CHILD=8, VARI=2, CLASS=2*
PARE=9, CHILD=10, VARI=3, CLASS=1*
PARE=11, CHILD=12, VARI=3, CLASS=2*
PARE=13, CHILD=14, VARI=5, CLASS=1*
PARE=15, CHILD=16, VARI=5, CLASS=2*

Interpretation: Last line means: Split group 16 into group 16 and group 17, using variable 5, WF HOURS (wife's hours of work), with the first group (16) including values from 2 to 2.

Key:

Group Number

$587 $-101

Change in income

Number of (cases for end-groups only)

Change in need standard (family size)

P. 457680, MTR 1007
[MTR 38, P468070]

one may also want simply to look at that subgroup within each of the groups generated by the analysis to see whether it differs from the majority anywhere in
the population. The difficulty with the forced procedure is that the group will
be so small that the criterion for allowing further splits may not allow any.

An alternative for examining such minority groups is to assign them weights
appropriate to one's values and proceed with a weighted analysis. If they have
been oversampled, and weights have been used to reduce the influence of that
group to its proper proportion in the population, one can simply run an unweighted analysis to allow the oversampled group more influence. The recoding
flexibility allows any complex generation of a new weight variable for an analysis without rewriting a new data tape.

2.5 Lookahead

Experimentation with the original AID algorithm to determine its behavior
under known conditions has been carried out using contrived data.[1] While the original procedure was found to be capable of dealing adequately with many two-way
interactions, others were identified as being difficult for it to deal with.
These were seen to consist of interaction relations characterized by consistency,
i.e., by balance or symmetry. One such example is the "exclusive-or" model shown
below. No main effects appear in these cases, so no split is made that would reveal the mutually offsetting interaction effect inside.

	B	Not B
A	High	Low
Not A	Low	High

"EXCLUSIVE-OR"

The obvious test is to take each predictor's best split on the group in
question and make one or two additional splits (the best possible) on one or both
of the resulting subgroups. One then asks which set of two (or three) splits provides the largest total sum of squares explained, makes the first split, and proceeds. It is possible that a weak first split would allow subsequent splits that
were sufficiently powerful to offset that fact. Certainly even a two-split sequence would uncover the offsetting interaction effect just described.

---

[1] An extensive discussion is presented by Sonquist (1970).

Although the frequency with which variants of this model actually occur in real data is not known, it is notable that at least one realization has received considerable attention in the recent sociological literature, the concept of status inconsistency.[1] Analysis techniques for dealing with this class of models are of importance for economic, educational and psychological research as well as for sociology and marketing.

It can be seen that the earlier sequential partitioning algorithm which examines only the zero-order effects of A and B separately could not discover the consistency effect in a number of these models. In some cases there are really two A effects and they cancel each other out in the total group. Of course, the additive assumptions required in regression or Multiple Classification Analysis would also tend to conceal the real state of the world.

However, the extended AID algorithm incorporated into this version of the program can be instructed to partition the sample tentatively, first on one explanatory variable and then on the other (as well as making tentative partitions on other variables). This makes it possible first to reveal the consistency effect to the analyst by means of profiles of means and differential changes in explanatory power, then to make an appropriate partition and, finally, to continue with the rest of the sequential search procedure.

In general, such a two-split scanning algorithm appears to provide complete and positive identification of all two-way interactions existent in the data. It will even provide leads or clues to the existence of three-way interactions. This is seen to be a simple extension of the way in which the present algorithm provides clues to the existence of two-way interactions. An algorithm which examines the cross-classification of p predictors simultaneously can identify completely terms composed of p raw variables regardless of the symmetry of the term. However, such an algorithm also appears capable of revealing a term involving p + 1 raw variables if the term is asymmetric.

For instance, if we have the three variable negative "and" model:

"If A and B and C, then Y = 0, otherwise Y = 4"

the algorithm using a two-split strategy would produce the sequence of partitions illustrated in Figure 4 and reveal the basic structure.

Of course the amount of computing required to search out combinations of three or more variables increases as an exponential function of the number of variables considered simultaneously. Hence constraints have to be put on the process to permit the elimination of unpromising leads and thus the examination

---

[1]For an example, see Blalock (1966).

Figure 4

A Three Variable Negative "and" Model

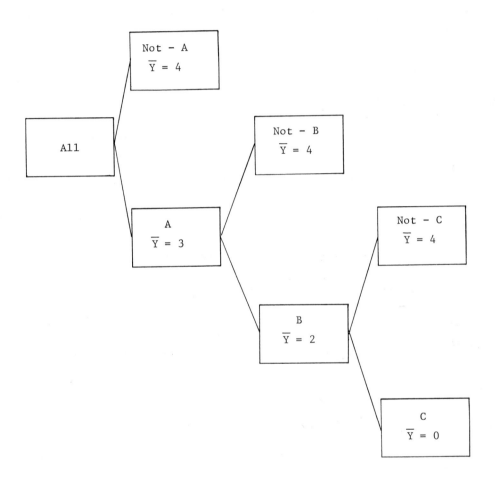

ABC Implies Y = 0, Else Y = 4

38

of the subsequent partitions.

2.5.1 Lookahead Algorithm

There are two parameters governing the lookahead process:

(1) the number of lookahead steps, i.e., partitions made <u>after</u> the tentative partition of the parent group; and

(2) the number of partitions for which all variables are to be permuted, i.e., where the algorithm "forces" the group to be tentatively split on each predictor.

Thus, in a 1-step lookahead, two successive partitions are made and the permute parameter must be 1; and in a 2-step lookahead, three successive partitions made and the permute parameter may be 1 or 2.

A 1-step lookahead with 1 forced split is executed in the following manner:

(A) Every predictor is examined as a possible basis for partitioning the candidate group. The "best" split definition is saved for each predictor.

(B) A tentative partition is made on the first predictor based on its best split from (A).

(C) The resulting new group with the largest unexplained sum of squares is the new candidate group, and the best split for each predictor is determined for this group.

(D) The predictor found to be the most powerful is selected as the partitioning variable for this second group, and the total amount of variation explained by the <u>two</u> partitions (three groups) is saved.

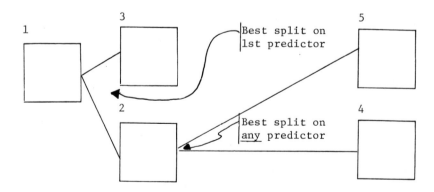

(E) Steps (B), (C), and (D) are repeated with each predictor in turn used at step (B) to create the first tentative partition.

Thus, if there are k predictors, the entire process is repeated k times;

each time the explained variation is recorded. At the end of the k repetitions, the k tentative levels of explained variation are compared. Then, that partition rule for group 1 which had been associated with the configuration providing the largest obtained level of explained variation is now actually used to split group 1 into two parts. At that point, the algorithm starts over again from the beginning.

2.5.2 Stopping the Lookahead Partitioning

Permitting the algorithm to wind itself so closely around the data as is done in, say, a three-step lookahead, runs the risk of spurious splits.[1] Hence this version of AID has had incorporated into it a series of controls that permit the user to reduce the probability of obtaining incorrect or unstable, unreproducible results. Provision has been made to require that if the lookahead option is exercised partitions based on it must explain proportionately more variation than a partition based only on permutations of the predictors in a single group.

When a lookahead of k splits is used, a parallel number of split reducibility parameters are submitted, one for each of the k tentative partitions. A split reducibility parameter is that percent of the total sum of squares which must be explained by the proposed partition in order for it actually to take place. These parameters, each consisting of a percentage (e.g., .6%, 1.8%, etc.) can be set by the user in such a way as to require that in order to be used, a partition based on a lookahead of length two would have to explain more variation than a partition of the same group based on a lookahead of length one, and that a partition based on a lookahead of length three would have to explain more than a partition based only on a lookahead of two, etc., etc. Further, the analyst is given control over how much more powerful a split based on a lookahead of length k + 1 must be in comparison to one of length k.

The analyst may require that any partition of length k explain P_k of the original total variation in the dependent variable. This is accomplished by setting P_k to a percentage between .01% and 100%; for instance, setting P_2 to 1.8 would mean that the three groups tentatively generated by a lookahead of two splits would have to explain at least 1.8 percent of the original total sum of squares for the partition associated with these three particular groups actually to be used. Each of the P_k are set by the user independently of each other. This means that the lookahead can be set to exhibit a preference for partitions

---

[1] See Sonquist (1970)

based on two or three tentative splits. These preferences are expressed as per-
centages of the total sum of squares.

It is recommended that in the absence of other guidelines, the first lookahead be required to explain at least twice (and that the second lookahead be required to explain at least three times) the variation required for a split to
take place at all. That is, lookahead steps should be required to explain at
least an additive function of the initial requirements.

The lookahead algorithm always works from the "top" down; that is, it attempts first to make a partition using the longest lookahead that has been permitted by the user. If it cannot make a partition using a lookahead of this
length (i.e., the reducibility criterion for that length lookahead cannot be met
or all of the resulting partitions would cause some of the new groups to be below the minimum size) it then tries to partition the group using a lookahead one
step shorter. It repeats this process if, at any given point, none of the resulting partitions meet the explained variation and minimum size requirements. Finally, if it cannot make a partition of the group under the requirements for no
lookahead, it marks the group as a final, unsplittable one.

We now give a more formal statement of the operation of the lookahead under
the reducibility criteria.

Let TSS_o be the total sum of squares for the dependent variable. Let S be
the lookahead length specified by the user. Let B_i (S) be the explained variation resulting from a proposed split on variable i with lookahead length S.

Then $B_i(o)$ is this maximization function for the original AID algorithm.
B_{max}(S) is the largest B_i of all those computed at lookahead length S--that is

$$B_{max}(S) \geq B_i(S)$$

where i ranges over all candidates resulting from the lookahead.

Then if

$$B_{max}(S) \geq P_S \times TSS_o; \quad S \text{ specified,}$$

the parent group is split on the original predictor i which yields B_{max}(S). If
no B_i(S) satisfies this inequality, then the maximum B_{max}(S-1) at the previous
step (S-1) in the lookahead is compared with the required minimum explanatory
power P_{S-1}.

Finally, if, upon examination, $B_{max}(0) < P_o \times TSS_o$, the parent group is
termed final and no further attempts to split it are made. The lookahead will
not continue beyond any step where a resulting group is smaller than the minimum
group size specification. Also, the process is stopped when the maximum number
of splits has been reached.

2.6 Predictor Constraints

The original AID algorithm provided for constraining the ordering of the classes of each predictor. The present variation of the program allows this constraint of ordering, and, in addition, allows the user to require that certain predictors be ranked so that some must be used before or after others in the partitioning process. Further, some variables may be inserted as predictors, but ranked so that statistics are obtained for them, but they are never actually used to partition the input sample.

2.6.1 Monotonic vs. Free

Any input variable may be used as a predictor, provided it is either read in as an integer in the range 0 to 31 or is recoded so that it falls in this range. Predictors are also classed either as Free or Monotonic. Monotonic predictors will have the order of their coded values $(0,1,2,\ldots,29,30,31)$ maintained during the partition scan. In this case, the classes of the predictor will not be rearranged by sorting them into ascending sequence using the within-class mean value of Y (means option), or the within-class slope of the regression of Y on X (slopes or regression option). Thus, this option is intended for ordinary use with predictors which are ordinary scales or which consist of class-interval codes established for a continuous variable.

The classes of a "free" predictor are rearranged to find that partition which maximizes the sum of squares between the two resulting groups. For a predictor with k classes, the partition of these classes into two sets with m classes in one and k-m classes in the other $(m=1,2,\ldots,k-1)$ that maximizes the between sum of squares, $n_1\bar{y}_1^2 + n_2\bar{y}_2^2 - n\bar{y}^2$, is that one where the m class means in the first group are less than or equal to the k-m class means in the second, i.e., $\bar{y}_1, \ldots, \bar{y}_m \le \bar{y}_{m+1}, \ldots, \bar{y}_k$.[1] Thus, one need only examine k-1 partitions, after arranging the k groups in ascending order according to their means on the dependent variable.

No proof exists that the correspondence between sum of squares in a covariate analysis is maximized by sorting on class slopes, however, it seems a reasonable assumption especially since it cuts the number of possible combinations to be examined considerably.

The usual use for the free predictor designation is for variables that are nominal scales, or for other cases in which it is desired not to constrain the

---

[1]See Appendix VI for a proof of this by W. Ericson.

42

classes which are to be placed together in the resulting two new groups.

The free option should be used sparingly, since it vastly increases the number of things looked at and the possibility of idiosyncratic splits. If a set of categories does not form a natural ordering, it is quite possible that it represents more than one dimension, e.g., occupation which contains elements of skill, white versus blue collar, managerial responsibilities, entrepreneurial activities, self-employment, etc. In such cases, it is better to convert the classification into a series of dichotomies, or even to maintain the order, not allowing splits with odd combinations on each side. It is better to recode, to put such codes as "inapplicable" and "missing information" in a reasonable place, than to leave a whole predictor free because of them.

Even non-monotonic relations can be handled unless they are symmetrical, and the output of a run that maintains order will reveal what reordering might be substituted.

2.6.2 Ranking

To facilitate user control over the order in which predictors are used in the partitioning process, two predictor ranking options have now been incorporated into AID3. These are termed "simple ranking" and "range ranking." In both cases, each predictor is assigned a rank. Ranks may range from 0 to 9.

Rank zero has a special significance; all variables assigned to rank zero will have statistics computed for them in every parent group that is selected for a partition attempt. However, rank zero variables are prevented from entering into the actual partitioning process and they are not examined in the look-ahead. This permits the user to insert one or more variables as predictors, and examine their effect profiles in various parts of his sample without permitting them to enter into the partitioning process. Rank 0 can be assigned to any number of variables whose effects it is desired to observe and it may be used with either of the ranking options. It is particularly useful for variables which may either affect or be affected by the dependent variable.

The user may elect to assign as few as two of the available ranks or he may use all ten. He may assign the same rank to several of his variables. He may or may not wish to use zero as a rank.

2.6.2.1 Simple Ranking

The objective of simple ranking is to permit the user to govern the order in which various sets of variables are permitted to enter the partitioning process.

The algorithm then uses the ranking assignments as follows. The total sample is partitioned using only those variables in the highest non-zero rank (smallest non-zero integer). Statistics are computed for all ranks, however, including such variables as may have been given rank zero. If none of these variables are capable of producing a partition rule that meets the split reducibility and minimum group size requirements supplied, then that rank is chosen which is next highest (i.e., which has the next assigned number). All of the variables which had been assigned this next highest rank are now eligible to be used as the basis for a partition and may now be used in the lookahead, and the first (highest) rank is abandoned. If, again, none of these variables can be used, the program abandons this rank and proceeds to the next one. This continues either until a rank is reached at which a successful partition can be made or until there are no more predictors.

When a successful partition is made, the program is said to be "at" this rank. All higher level ranks are abandoned. Variables in the abandoned higher level ranks are no longer eligible for being used as the basis for a partition, although the program will continue to compute statistics for them in the parent group. They will no longer continue to be considered in the lookahead computations, however. Lower level ranks have not yet become eligible.

Further partitions of the new groups that have been created as a result of a partition will be made "at" that rank provided they meet the reducibility and minimum group size requirements. Whenever the requirements are not met by any variables having the rank where the program is "at," it moves downward to the next highest rank (i.e., which has the next larger assigned rank number).

Note that various branches of the tree may work downward through the ranks at different speeds. Where the program is "at" in any given branch depends only on where it was "at" in the preceding node and on the ability of those and the next ranked predictors to produce a satisfactory partition.

This can be illustrated as follows: consider the following ten variables ranked as indicated in Table 5. Variable ten is ranked 0, variable one is ranked 1, variables two and three are ranked 2, etc. When the partitioning starts, variable one is the only predictor eligible for use, since it is the only predictor in the first rank. However, statistics are produced for variables in rank 0 and for the other ineligible predictors. The lookahead could not be used since several of the ranks have only one predictor and there must be at least k+1 predictors in every rank used if a lookahead of length k is used.

If variable one did not meet the reducibility and minimum group size criteria, the algorithm would move to rank 2, abandoning rank 1. Variables two and

44

Table 5

Ten Variables and Six Ranks

Variable	Rank
10	0
1	1
2 ⎫ 3 ⎭	2
6 ⎫ 7 ⎭	3
4	4
5 ⎫ 8 ⎬ 9 ⎭	5

three would then both be eligible for consideration, but variable one would not be. However, again statistics are produced for all input predictors. If a partition were made, say, on variable three, then the algorithm would start its next partition attempt again using the rank 2 variables, variable numbers two and three.

2.6.2.2 Range Ranking

The second ranking option, range ranking, provides somewhat more flexibility in the way in which variables are used in the partitioning process. In addition to the ranks themselves, two ranges of ranks and a preference are supplied.

The preference can be set "UP" so that the algorithm chooses its partitioning variables starting with the highest rank (provided they meet the reducibility and minimum group size criteria). Alternatively, it can be set to "DOWN" reversing the preference order, or to "AT" providing a third alternative. The preference is effective within the range of ranks specified by the user. Variables outside the range (either because of abandonment or because progression "downward" into the ranks that far has not occurred yet) are excluded from eligibility as in simple ranking, although, as above, they always have statistics reported for them.

As in simple ranking, the algorithm is initially "at" rank 1; subsequently, the "at" rank is determined by the last partition in that branch of the tree.

The eligibility range is defined as a certain number of ranks "up" and a certain number of ranks "down" from the rank where the algorithm is "at." Any variable in that range of ranks is eligible for use in a given partition.

The preference option can be set to cause the algorithm to <u>start</u> at one end or another of the eligibility <u>range</u>. Alternatively, the preference option can be set to cause the selection of variables to start where the algorithm is "at." In each case, the algorithm first determines whether or not according to the reducibility criteria a split could be made on the basis of one of the variables in the preferred rank. If there is at least one that meets these eligibility and minimum group size requirements, the actual selection of a variable to use as the basis of the partition is made from the variables in the preferred rank. If there are none that meet the criteria, the algorithm attempts to make its selection from the variables in the next preferred rank. If, after failing the entire length of the range (no variable has been found which works) the algorithm moves "down" one rank, bringing the next lower rank within the range.

If the preference is for higher ranked variables, the algorithm will start at the highest (1,2,3, etc.) end of the ranking range. If the preference is set for lower ranked variables, the algorithm starts at the lowest (8,9) end of the ranking range moving back upward if not successful. When the preference is set for lower ranked variables, and the unsuccessful attempts to find a split variable have caused a progression back upward all the way to the end of the eligibility range, the algorithm again moves downward so a new rank is brought in at the "downward" end of the eligibility range and an attempt is made to use these newly eligible variables in the partition.

If the preference is set for variables at the rank where the algorithm is "at" and the search is unsuccessful, then both adjacent ranks are made available for scanning and, if possible, a variable is chosen from a higher rank, i.e., towards 1. If the variable eventually chosen for use is in one of the adjacent ranks, the algorithm progresses upward or downward accordingly, and is then "at" a new rank. A summary of the various possible options is given in Figure 5.

A separate range is provided to govern the lookahead operation, i.e., tentative splits of other than the parent group. The operation of the lookahead range is the same as that of the parent group except that statistics for variables at rank zero or outside the current range are not reported. The lookahead range must be at least equal in width to the range used for the partition, and it may be wider. More specifically, the number of ranks "up" must be equal to or greater than the number of ranks "up" specified for the parent group range. Similarly, the number of ranks "down" must be a number greater than or equal to the corresponding "down" range specified for the selection of variables for the parent group.

2.6.2.3 Using the Ranking Options

The purpose in providing these types of ranking is to permit the analyst to impose whatever theoretical considerations he may have on the order of the splitting process.

The simplest use is to look at the effects of a variable but not split on it (assigning it rank 0). This allows looking at its relationships without allowing it to make divisions, an especially useful procedure if a variable is not clearly either cause or effect of the dependent variable. This is particularly true of attitudes, where one may want to know their relation to the dependent variable without assuming that they cause it, rather than result from it. In covariance analysis (see above), one may want to use classes of the covariate in order to see whether there are non-linearities which the covariance analysis assumes away (assigning the bracket rank 0). The print-out will provide means of the dependent variable within groups according to the covariate at the same time it is computing the regression slopes. It is always possible that a relationship that is linear overall is not linear within some subgroups, and this procedure

Figure 5

Results of Alternative Rank Specifications

RANK	Range UP (L) "AT-L"	Range DOWN (K) "AT+K"	Eligible Rank Numbers, in Order of Preference (Low number = high rank)
SIMPLE RANKING			
ALL	0	0	1, 2, 3, ... M (if M ranks specified)
	L	0	
	0	K	Not allowed
	L	K	
RANGE RANKING (see NOTE below)			
UP	0	0	Equivalent to "ALL"
	0	K	A, A+1, A+2,...A+K (Preference for A)
	L	0	A-L, A-L+1,...A (Preference for A-L)
	L	K	A-L, ..A, A+1, ... A+K (Preference for A-L) i.e., always tries lower rank numbers and works up (down the the ranks) to A, then on to A+K.
AT	0	0	Equivalent to "ALL"
	L	0	A, A-1, A-2, ... A-L
	0	K	A, A+1, A+2,...A+K
	L	K	A, A+1, A+2, ...A+K,A-L
DOWN	0	0	Equivalent to "ALL"
	L	0	A, A+1, A-2,...A-L (Preference for A)
	0	K	A+K, A+K-1,...A+1, A (Preference for A+K)
	L	K	A+K,...A,... A-L (Preference for A+K)

(AT rows L,0 / 0,K / L,K grouped with brace: Preference for A)

NOTE: If "A" denotes the AT rank, "L" the number of ranks UP, and "K" the number of ranks DOWN, then the eligible range is [A-L, A+D].

On the first split, A=1. A-L is bounded by 1, and A+K is bounded by 9, e.g., if A=4, L=5, K=6, then the eligibility range is still only 1-9.

"UP", "AT", and "DOWN" refer to rank numbers, so "UP" the numbers means down the ranks, the usual procedure.

"UP, L, K" tries the full set of ranks at each split, starting with A-L which can be set equal to 1, but in practice the results are likely to be the same as "ALL".

will reveal the problem.

But perhaps the most important use of ranking is in the situation where the explanatory variables are not all at the same stage in the causal process-- some being clearly logically prior to others.[1] Then one may want to give Rank 1 to the exogeneous, background, and constraint variables, and only then allow variables that represent the current situation, motives, opportunities, and recent changes, to come into play at Rank 2. Such a procedure is an alternative to a two-stage analysis using pooled residuals from one stage as the dependent variable in a second analysis. If one feels that there are interaction effects between variables at the two levels, that is, that the groups according to background variables will respond differently to current situational variables, then it would be better not to pool. But pooling does have advantages in providing larger groups, more stability, and more degrees of freedom.[2] Finally, one may want to put at a last and highest rank, variables which may be either cause or effect, but whose relationship to the dependent variable is of interest.

A minor option with ranking is a choice whether one allows only the predictors at that rank (UP, 0, 0), or allows all those already tried and exhausted to come back in if they can (UP, L, 0). It is minor because the chance that they will do so is small.

For range ranking, a preference must be stated for UP, AT, or DOWN. The best eligible predictor in the preferred rank will be chosen over predictors in other ranks regardless of explanatory power. Simultaneous inclusion of all previous ranks can be achieved by redefining the predictor ranks.[3] Using the previous example of Table 5:

STEP	rank 1 variables	rank 0 variables
1	1	2-10
2	1-3	4-10
3	1-3,6,7	4-5,8-10
4	1-4,6-7	5,8-10
5	1-9	10

---

[1]For example, see Sonquist and Morgan (1964), pp. 105-109.

[2]For extensive use of pooled residuals in two- and three-stage analysis, see Morgan, Sirageldin and Baerwaldt, _Productive Americans_, 1966.

[3]See section 2.9 and Appendix III (an analysis step).

2.7 Premium for Symmetry

Particularly when there are several predictors in close competition for splitting on the dependent variable, it is tempting to suggest that one would prefer a symmetric tree if forcing that symmetry did not result in loss of too much explanatory power. The advantage of a symmetric tree or section of a tree is that it is simpler. Indeed, a totally symmetric tree implies an n-dimensioned table where all the subcells are important and different. What is meant by symmetry? It means that if one of a pair of groups has already been split on particular classes of a predictor, the other of the pair is split in the same way. A looser definition would be that the second is split on the same predictor, but not necessarily with the same sets of subclasses on each side of the split. The advantages in simplicity of this partial symmetry seemed minor, so we use the complete symmetry.

One can, of course, set the premium at 100 percent, forcing symmetry, but still leaving open the decision about the first split made on each of a pair. This will still not force total symmetry; since once one has two pairs of groups, the first splits on each of the pairs can be different!

The option allows selection of a loss-function specifying how much one is willing to lose at any splitting decision, relative to the best split, in order to achieve symmetry. In other words, one might end up with some symmetric splits in an otherwise nonsymmetric branching diagram. A ten percent premium for symmetry (penalty for assymetry) means that the symmetric split will be made if its power is at least 90 percent that of the best split. For example, the symmetric split is made if its BSS satisfies:

$$\text{BSS for the symmetric split} \geq (1 - \frac{\text{Premium for symmetry}}{100}) \times (\text{BSS for best split}).$$

When the symmetry option is specified, the algorithm selects the symmetric branch of the tree to split on next (as opposed to that group with the largest unexplained sum of squares) whenever possible. Symmetry takes precedence over ranking, provided the symmetric split is an eligible one.

If one really wants to know the total loss from total symmetry, then the configurational option gives the explanatory power of a total tree using all the details of a set of predictors and can be compared with dummy-variable regression using the same predictors, which is total symmetry.

We have not found very many places where this feature was useful, and it borders on another problem--the dominant variable. If each of several groups splits on the same predictor because it is dominant, a better solution may be to go to the covariance approach described above in Section 2.3.

Even perfect symmetry does not imply additivity. Just because each of two

50

groups can be split in the same way on the same predictor does not mean that the differences between the resulting pairs will be the same, absolutely or relatively.

Additivity of effects (absence of interaction effects) is a sufficient but not necessary condition for symmetry of a branching diagram. It is possible for the same predictor to be the most powerful for subsequent splits of each of a pair of groups, but not to have a uniform effect on the two groups. The branching diagram below is a real case, hence makes the point only weakly (Figure 6a). The data produced a symmetric tree but an interaction effect clearly exists.

If we take the weighted means for whites and nonwhites, and for young and old, to estimate the interior of the table assuming additive effects, we have Figure 6b, where the first entry is the actual proportion, the second the expected proportion, and the third the difference.[1] It is clear that the older nonwhites are more likely and the younger less likely, to approve of mothers' working, than an additive model would suggest.

Actually, one could also take the unweighted means for whites and non-whites, and for young and old, to estimate the interior of an additive table, though such data are unavailable unless one has the detailed table in the first place. In this case we get Figure 6c, which says that older nonwhites and younger whites are more likely to approve, and the other two groups less likely.

2.8 Elimination of Extreme Cases

The least squares criterion almost universally used in statistics, and in this program as well, is very sensitive to extreme cases. In much real data, moreover, the extreme cases are likely to involve either errors of measurement or conceptual problems. In any case, we may not want our findings to be dominated by a few cases, or to face the likelihood that another sample would produce widely different results because of them. One can use the recode capability either to truncate extreme cases or to give them a zero value on the filter variable so they will be excluded. However, this requires defining extreme cases uniformly regardless of their situations. In the population as a whole, a house value greater than $75,000 may not be extreme, but among lower income families where the head is less than 65 years old, such a value might well be extreme.

---

[1] One estimates the expected values in the subcells as follows: Take the deviations of the means by age or race from the grand mean as estimates of age or race effects. For any subcell, add the appropriate age and race effect to the overall mean to estimate that subcell mean.

Figure 6a

Proportion of Husbands Approving of Mothers' Working*
(For all 1640 married heads of families)

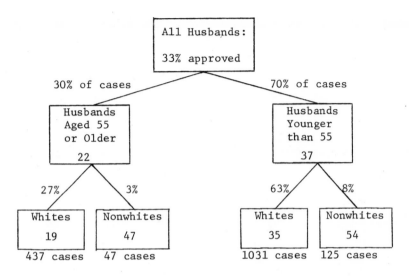

*The question was: "Suppose a family has children but they are all in
school--would you say it is a good thing for the wife to take a job
or a bad thing or what? Source: Morgan et al. Productive Americans,
p. 330.

Figure 6b
Deviations from Weighted Expected
Values

	Nonwhite	White	
Youth	54-56=-2	35-34=+1	37
Old	47-41=+6	19-19=0	22
	52	30	33

Figure 6c
Deviations from Unweighted
Expected Values

	Nonwhite	White	
Youth	54-56=-2	35-33=+2	45
Old	47-44=+3	19-21=-2	33
	50	27	39

The user defines "extreme" in terms of the number of standard deviations from the mean in either direction, where the mean and standard deviation are those for the group in question. If the identification numbers of the extreme cases are needed in order to look them up, that variable must be read in with the other data, and its "variable number" specified on the set-up forms.

Extreme cases are dealt with in two stages. Initially, the entire data set is read and recoded (only cases filtered with the global filter are excluded). The mean and standard deviation are calculated on the dependent variable for the sample, and any cases lying outside of $\bar{y} \pm n\sigma$, where n is specified by the user, is considered an outlier. These cases may be removed from the data, or simply cause a warning to be printed. At this stage, one would hope to find the gross errors in the data.

Subsequently, extreme cases are defined by the mean and standard deviation of each group as it is being split. These outliers may be removed before making the split. After each group, including the first, has been searched and the best split decided, the extreme cases are located and removed so that they do not appear in the two resulting subgroups. Note that the data given for each group are before the extreme cases in that group are removed. This allows extreme cases to affect one split before they are taken out, and to affect the total sum of squares and hence the actual value of the split reducibility criterion. This is unlikely to be a problem, except at the beginning, and the extreme cases for the full sample could be taken out by the filter anyway.

Experimentation with this feature on a regression analysis of house value on income, throwing out cases more than five standard deviations from each group mean, showed that twelve cases were thrown out, in four different places, and the resulting tree was different--at the third split on one branch and the fourth split on the other. The results were, however, very much the same as when we truncated house value at the beginning.

Since the purpose is to eliminate the rare extreme cases, no more than twenty-five cases can be eliminated from any group, and if more are eligible, only the first twenty-five encountered will be eliminated. However, the others would almost surely be eliminated from the two subsequent subgroups before they were split (but after the split had been selected).[1]

This feature could be used for cleaning data of errors, in an effective but biased way (increasing the apparent fraction of the variance explained). Or one could isolate small groups of deviates for special analysis.

---

[1]This does not apply to the initial outliers treatment.

2.9 Multi-stage Processing

AID3 operates in three modes: input, compute, and output. The input mode is executed automatically at the beginning and again after an output mode. However, the user specifies compute and output commands. By not specifying the output command, once the partitioning process has stopped the user may re-define certain parameters (e.g., maximum number of splits, symmetry) as well as defining forced splits and continue the partitioning under the new definitions. This type of user control would be most useful in an interactive system, but it may be useful when the analyst has some concept as to the structure of the partitioning process. For example, it might be used in conjunction with ranking to allow greater control over the algorithm.[1]

---

[1]See section 2.6.2.3.

III
Input Features

This chapter details the requirements and options for the input data file. The input setup, i.e., parameter cards, is described in Appendix III. The reader is referred to other publications for more extensive treatment of research uses.[1]

3.1 Data Structure

The program assumes a rectangular data structure: each logical record is one data observation containing all variables to be transmitted to the program, plus any other variables which may also be contained on the file.

This file may or may not be pre-sorted on one or more variables used as keys.[2] Pre-sorting requires a separate job-step using a sort-merge program, but is only necessary if the configuration option (section 2.2) is used.

The data file is read in integer fields. Scale factors are provided for the dependent variable, covariate, residual, and predicted value. Predictors must be integers in the range $0 \leq p \leq 31$.

Since the recoding routines operate in integer mode, decimal places are truncated, and variables must therefore be appropriately scaled before dividing to obtain the desired accuracy (e.g., by multiplying by 1000).

Decimal points within data fields are not allowed, but may be bypassed in the following manner: a 4-character field AB.C may be read as two fields, AB

---

[1]See Morgan and Sonquist (1963), Sonquist and Morgan (1964), Andrews, Morgan and Sonquist (1967), Sonquist, Baker and Morgan (1969), Sonquist (1969), Sonquist (1970), Sonquist (1970b).

[2]A parameter setting permits computation of "configuration" statistics for sorted files. See section 2.2.

56

and C and converted back by 10xAB+C.

3.1.1 Weighting the Data

In some sampling designs for collecting data, multi-stage probability designs are used that require "weighting" the resulting observations. AID3 has been designed to accommodate those types of designs where the resulting "weight" attached to each resulting observation is a positive integer. If the user designates one of his input variables as a "weight," the program treats the data as though it were receiving multiple copies of each observation, the number of such copies being determined by the associated weight. Non-integral values of the weight variable are not permitted. The range that may be taken on by a variable designated as a weight is $1 \leq V_w \leq 999$. However, users with weights larger than 99 and sample sizes of 1000 or more are cautioned that floating-point arithmetic rounding errors may occur. Such users are encouraged to seek local individual advice on rounding errors in sums of squares. Users with one- or two-digit weights, dependent variables in the range 0 to 999,999 and samples not greater than about 3000 should experience no difficulty with rounding problems.

3.1.2 Multiple Response Variables

AID3 will only accept single-valued variables. So-called "multiple-response" variables must be read as separate variables and the recoding routine used to create as many single-valued variables as desired from them. For instance, if, in response to the question "Which magazines do you read regularly?" a respondent says "Time, Life, and Progressive," the analyst might wish to reserve five or six 2-column fields in his file for up to that many answers, recording as successive positive integers those mentioned (e.g., 01, 08, and 27 for those mentioned above). This might be coded 0108270000 if five fields were reserved as a 2-digit "multiple response" variable. If this configuration is to be used in an analysis using AID3, then the analyst would have to create one or more variables each of which has a single value (e.g., 1 if person reads any magazines of a certain type, 0 if not).

3.1.3 Scale Factors

Although all variables must be supplied to the program in integer form using implied decimal places, it may be desirable to shift decimal points on the dependent variable and the covariate for readability and compatibility with other program output. This is true also if residuals are computed for output. Consequently, input scale factors have been provided for the dependent variable and the covariate. The user simply indicates in "powers of ten" notation where he wishes the program to place a decimal point for that variable. By using a positive scale factor, the decimal point is moved to the right by the number of places indicated. A negative scale factor causes it to be moved to the left. For example, if the integer field supplied as the dependent variable has three implied decimal places, the user may supply an associated scale factor of -3, causing the variable to be multiplied by 10^{-3}, or 1/1000 and be properly scaled and rounded.

The use of an appropriate output scale factor causes the desired number of significant digits to be retained during the computation of residuals. Generally two more decimal places than used on input are sufficient for accuracy in generating residuals. If the dependent variable is dichotomous (one or zero), the user may wish to round these residuals back to either 1, 0 or -1, however.

3.2 OSIRIS vs Formatted Data Files

Input data files may be described with an OSIRIS dictionary or with a Fortran IV format statement.

For data sets without a dictionary, up to three cards of format information must be supplied.[1] The format statement describes an input (or output) data case. All variables transmitted to the program from the data file, whether used in the analysis or not, must have a format code or field descriptor (e.g., I10). The transmitted or input variables should be in integer mode (non-integer variables may be transmitted if they are only to be carried along, i.e., not used in the analysis, and later outputted in a formatted residual file). The variables are read in the order listed on the input variable list card.[2] In addition, field descriptors for each variable created during execution, i.e., with the internal recode or the residual options, must also be supplied if a formatted output file is requested. These "output" variable fields will naturally follow the "input" fields.

The OSIRIS multivariate recode, bad data option, and global filter cannot be used with formatted data files.

A detailed account of OSIRIS dictionary and data files may be found in

---

[1] See the IBM System/360 and System/370 FORTRAN IV Language Manual for information on formats.

[2] See Appendix III and the OSIRIS/40 User's Manual for a description of variable list cards.

Appendix D of the OSIRIS/40 CSF User's Manual.

3.3 Recoding

It is recognized that users of complex statistical programs often need a built-in capability for transforming their variables at the time a statistical run is made. This has been found to be particularly true in the case of research tasks to which AID is frequently addressed. Predictor variables typically involve nominal scales (classifications) which reflect several dimensions and should be converted into separate dichotomies, as well as continuous variables which must be converted into sets of ordered classifications to be used as AID predictor variables. Also, AID users typically wish to generate interaction terms for later use in a Multiple Classification Analysis.[1] In addition, if distributions are skewed, dependent variables may need transformations using square roots or logarithms. Users may wish to locate and re-assign missing values, the assignments sometimes being made on a probability basis. Users may wish to exclude certain observations from their analysis. The reasons for exclusion may include the presence of missing values of the dependent variable or covariate, the analyst's desire to analyze only a subset of his data, or the presence of some observations which have so much missing information that they must be excluded from the analysis. Or extreme values of the dependent variable may be reduced to some limited value.

AID3 provides capabilities for accomplishing these tasks of recoding and selection of subsets of observations. A powerful, newly-developed recoding language is appended to the input section of the program, permitting the user to generate almost any type of new variable he chooses.[2]

The recoding control language is actually a kind of special purpose programming language; that is, it operates sequentially. The user submits a series of instructions which are executed in order. Execution is initiated once for each observation in the user's input data file. Each instruction consists of a logical clause, an operational clause, or both.

A logical clause is a simple proposition about the arithmetic relationship (equality, inequality, larger than, etc.) between two input variables or between a variable and one or more constants. When values of the variables are supplied

---

[1] See Sonquist (1970a).

[2] A complete description of the AID3 internal recode including examples is given in Appendix II.

from an observation that has been read in and altered as desired by any preceding computation this proposition acquires a defined "value." It is either "true" or "false" for the values given. This result is then recorded as the value of a "truth switch." Any number of logical clauses may be concatenated to form a compound logical clause.

Similarly, any number of operational clauses can be concatenated to form a block of ordered computational instructions. These instructions are used to establish values for new (or old) variables, and to perform arithmetic operations. In addition, one instruction, GO TO, enables the user to control the sequence of computation any way he wishes. In a block of contiguous operational clauses, individual instructions are always executed in the order submitted, except where the sequence is altered by execution of a GO TO command. A print instruction PRNT allows the user to look at 1 or 2 variables.

Logical control over actual execution of the recoding instructions is accomplished by use of the "truth switch." When the recoding routine starts it executes operational clauses until it encounters a logical clause. When it encounters the beginning of a logical clause, it determines whether the proposition represented by the clause is true or false and records the results in the truth switch. If the following clause is also a logical clause, it is concatenated with the results of the previous one using the Boolean operator, and a new value for the truth switch is computed. Other logical clauses immediately following are treated similarly. On the other hand, if, after encountering the beginning of a logical clause, the next instruction is found to be an operational command, the truth switch is interrogated to determine whether the operational clause should, in fact, be executed.

If the truth switch is "true," then execution of the operational clause is initiated, and all successive operational clauses are also executed. Then when the beginning of the next logical clause is encountered, the program returns to logical mode and starts computing a new value for the truth switch. However, if the truth switch is "false" when an operational clause is encountered, the operational clause is not executed nor are any other operational clauses that may be concatenated to it; the program does nothing until it encounters the next logical clause. What it does then depends on the type of logical clause it finds.

Logical clauses are of two types--"initial" and "subsequent." A subsequent clause cannot act as the "beginning" of a logical clause, either single or compound. Upon encountering a subsequent clause not concatenated to an initial clause, the program simply returns to logical mode, but it does not evaluate this clause and hence a new value for the truth switch is not computed. The program is now in "limbo" since a return to logical mode also means that no further operational clauses can be executed until a new value for the truth switch has been established. Yet this cannot happen until the program encounters an "initial" clause and has evaluated it, whereupon the whole logical process is re-initiated from scratch. As a result, encountering a "subsequent" clause after computation simply turns off all activity until a subsequent "initial" clause starts it again.

This organization permits the user to write down a set of conditions (compound logical clause) under which a specified block of computation is to be done. He then simply writes the block of computations. If the conditions are not fulfilled the computation is not performed. He may then write an alternative set of conditions and specify a second alternative computational block. If the first set of conditions is "true" for a given observation and the second set is "false," the first block of computations is performed and the second suppressed. (If both conditions are true then both blocks of computations are executed. If neither, then there is no computation.) Thus, alternatives can be set up to accomplish the various kinds of assignments that are to be made during the recoding process.

Provision is made for the user to supply a residual, or "alternative" condition which corresponds to a "none of the above" condition (i.e., true if and only if previous conditions were all false), completing the logical capability.

The sixteen Boolean operators that are permitted for concatenating logical clauses include "and," "or," and "exclusive or," "not," and "implication" as well as all of the less well known operators. The arithmetic operations that can be performed include establishing a value for a variable, all four of the elementary arithmetic operations, as well as square root, logarithmic, modulo and arcsine functions, and the generation of random numbers. The relational operators include less than, greater than, equality or inequality and membership in a closed interval. For error reduction and simplicity, all operations are integer, implied decimal points being assumed in the input. Four-digit statement labels and the GO TO operation provide complete user control over computational sequences.

To facilitate sophisticated use, a simple form of indirect referencing of input variables is provided, enabling user-written subroutines which can be inserted and applied to several variables as desired, as well as facilitating repetitive operations.

Instead of eliminating cases with extreme values on the dependent variable, one can truncate them, converting all values larger than some amount to be equal to that amount, or combine several items (sum, ratio, etc.) into a new variable and then truncate it. Since this is done case-by-case as the data are read in, one cannot calculate within this program the distribution of a new variable and then decide how to truncate it.[1]

Given the earlier warning about maintaining the order of predictors in order to reduce the possibility of idiosyncratic splits, it may be necessary either to alter the scale value of the 0 or the missing information code, especially if they are at the wrong end of a scale; or a set of categories which do not form a scale can be converted into a set of dichotomies. Unless one is willing to assume that a variable such as religious preference or occupation forms an ordinal scale, it is advisable to convert it to a set of dichotomies, one per class.

Another warning: Complex recoding is easily done incorrectly, and a substantial analysis can be done before one discovers the error. The usual safeguards against incorrect specifications do not operate in this program. The best hedge against expensive mistakes is to have a small data-tape like the main one but with only 25 or 100 cases with a listing available of all the data on those cases. One can then do the analysis with these few cases, which takes very little computer time, and make sure all the newly created variables and filtering have been done correctly.

The same recoding capacity is available during each input stage of a multistage run, and there are several recoding possibilities that exist before doing a second or later-stage analysis. One can take the residuals from a first analysis (after taking account of background factors) and transform or truncate them to make a better dependent variable for use in the next analysis. Or they can be converted to a set of categories and used as a predictor in a second analysis as in studies of regression to normalcy; or one can take the expected values (means of final subgroups), convert them to a set of categories, and use this as one of the predictors in a second analysis. This is an application of the principle of two stage least squares, where the expected values are considered freer of measurement error and provide a less biased estimate of the effect sought. Or one can take the actual identification number of a group (only some of which remain) and transmute that into a set of categories which produce a new predictor, namely the final groups identified in the first run. Of course the second-stage analysis would be very likely to split on that predictor most often (though not necessarily), and one could assign it a low or zero rank to suppress it altogether (see Section 2.6.2) in the second analysis. This makes it available for observation but allows other predictors to make the splits. Or one could use the group numbers to generate a filter variable to select only certain

[1]An alternative method is to allow the program to throw out extreme cases in each parent group; see Section 2.8.

groups to use in a second analysis.[1]

3.4 Culling the Data

Several methods for eliminating or subsetting the data are available to the user. If a residual file is to be generated, any data cases eliminated from the analysis step will be outputted with missing data values generated for the residual, predicted value, and group number. The exception to this is, no observation will be outputted for data eliminated with a global filter or the bad data options.

3.4.1 Bad Data Treatment

With OSIRIS dictionary defined data sets, the standard bad data option is available: eliminate the case; substitute a missing data value; or terminate the run. With formatted data sets, records which cause a reading error are ignored. Cases discarded as bad data are not outputted on the residual file.

3.4.2 Missing Data on the Dependent Variable

Cases which have missing data codes for the dependent variable may be eliminated from the analysis (see Appendix C of the OSIRIS/40 User's Manual). This option may be used with all data files, however, missing data are not defined for formatted input variables.

3.4.3 Illegal Predictor Values

The user specifies a maximum allowable code for each predictor. Any predictor value greater than the specified maximum will be eliminated from the analysis.

3.4.4 Filters

The OSIRIS global and local filters are described in Appendix H of the OSIRIS/40 User's Manual. The global filter may only be used with OSIRIS data files.

The program also provides for the optional interrogation of a subset selector variable. Since the decision to include or exclude a given observation is made after the recoding routine operates on that observation, the analyst can

---

[1] But one would probably want to see the first analysis results before deciding which groups to use in the second analysis to save some elaborate recoding.

simply use his first few recoding instructions to generate a new variable according to whatever specifications he wishes, indicating what classes of observations to include or exclude. He then designates this as the subset selector variable. If the value of this selector variable is zero when interrogated after the recoding, the entire observation is simply excluded from input.

3.4.5 Outliers

The mean and standard deviation of the dependent variable are calculated on the sample after global filtering and elimination of bad data. Any cases lying outside n standard deviations from the mean (n specified) will cause a warning message to be printed. These cases may also be excluded from the analysis.[1]

---

[1]See section 2.8.

IV
Interpretation of Output

4.1 Basic Output and Notation

Output from AID3 is generated during each of the three control modes. General sample statistics are printed during the input mode and include the optional 1-way analysis of variance on the predictor configuration. Also, data cases excluded from the analysis will be outputted onto the residual file.

During execution of the compute mode, a record of the partitioning process including statistics on the parent group may be printed (i.e. , the trace). Groups which cannot be split will be outputted onto the residual file.

During the output mode, a 1-way analysis of variance is computed on the final groups. Groups which have not been split are considered final and outputted onto the residual file. Summary tables are then generated.

Data is input to the program after global filtering or exclusion of cases using the bad data option. These input cases constitute the sample. For each analysis packet, the data are culled using local filters, missing data options, etc. All formulas pertain to this culled sample[1] and conform to the following basic notation:

$$w = \text{weight value}$$
$$Y' = \text{unweighted value of the dependent variable}$$
$$Y = wY' = \text{weighted Y value}$$
$$Y^2 = wY'^2 = \text{weighted Y-squared value}$$
$$X = wX' = \text{weighted value of the covariate}$$
$$X^2 = wX'^2 = \text{weighted X-squared value}$$
$$YX = wY'X' = \text{weighted cross product (also denoted Z)}$$

---

[1]The exception to this is the mean and standard deviation of the dependent variable calculated on the full sample and used to calculate the initial boundaries defining an outlier. See section 3.4.5.

4.2 Initial Statistics

The program lists the total number of cases read, how many cases were excluded, and the number of cases used in the analysis. These remaining cases make up the total sample for the analysis packet and are therefore the first group to be split. Totals for the sample are:

N = Total number of observations in the sample

$$W = \sum_{\alpha=1}^{N} w_\alpha = \text{sum of weights}[1]$$

$$MW = W - \frac{W}{N}$$

$$\Sigma Y = \sum_{\alpha=1}^{N} w_\alpha Y'_\alpha = \text{sum of Y}$$

$$\Sigma Y^2 = \sum_{\alpha=1}^{N} w_\alpha Y'^2_\alpha = \text{sum of Y-squared}$$

$$\overline{Y} = \frac{\Sigma Y}{W} = \text{mean of the dependent variable}$$

$$TSS = SS = \Sigma (Y - \overline{Y})^2$$

$$\sigma^2_Y = \frac{SS}{MW} = \text{variance of Y}[1]$$

$$\Sigma X = \sum_{\alpha=1}^{N} w_\alpha X'_\alpha = \text{sum of X}$$

$$\Sigma X^2 = \sum_{\alpha=1}^{N} w_\alpha X'^2_\alpha = \text{sum of X-squared}$$

$$\overline{X} = \frac{\Sigma X}{W} = \text{mean of the covariate}$$

$$\sigma^2_X = \frac{\Sigma (X - \overline{X})^2}{MW} = \text{variance of X}$$

$$b_{y.x} = \frac{\Sigma (Y - \overline{Y})(X - \overline{X})}{\Sigma (X - \overline{X})^2} = \text{slope of Y on X.}$$

---

[1]If W is small, say W < 50, and the run is unweighted, then it may be advisable to correct for small sample sizes and $\alpha_{adj} = \sqrt{N/(N-1)}$ where N is the number of observations over which summation has taken place.

4.3 Trace

Trace statistics include parent group as well as resultant group statistics for each possible partition. The parent group totals

$$N, \ W, \ \Sigma Y, \ \Sigma Y^2, \ \Sigma X, \ \Sigma X^2, \ \Sigma Z, \ SS$$

correspond to the quantities given in the preceding section for the sample, but are summed only over the parent group.

For each predictor, the non-empty classes are listed in the order in which the tentative partitions are made. If classes 5,1,4,2,6 appear, then

$$\text{BETWEEN} \quad 4$$
$$\text{AND} \quad 2$$

denote the partition results in one group with classes (5,1,4) and the other with classes (2,6). The statistics

$$N, \ W, \ \overline{Y}, \ \sigma_Y^2, \ \overline{X}, \ \sigma_X^2, \ b \ \text{(slope)}$$

are given for both of the two resulting groups as well as the between sum of squares (BSS) corresponding to the split. If L1 and L2 are the group numbers for the children, then formulas for the slope and BSS terms are[1]:

(1) Means Analysis

$$b \qquad \text{undefined}$$

$$BSS = W_{L1}\overline{Y}_{L1}^2 + W_{L2}\overline{Y}_{L2}^2 - W\overline{Y}^2$$

(2) Regression Analysis

$$b = \frac{\sum_{\alpha=1}^{N_i} (y_\alpha - \overline{Y}_i)(x_\alpha - \overline{X}_i)}{\sum_{\alpha=1}^{N_i} (x_\alpha - \overline{X}_i)^2} = \text{pooled slope, } i=L1, \ L2$$

---

[1] See section 2.3 for the derivations.

68

$$BSS = W_{L1}\,\overline{Y}_{L1}^2 + W_{L2}\,\overline{Y}_{L2}^2 - W\,\overline{Y}^2 + \frac{\left[\displaystyle\sum^{N_{L1}} (y - \overline{Y}_{L1})(x - \overline{X}_{L1})\right]^2}{\displaystyle\sum^{N_{L1}} (x - \overline{X}_{L1})^2}$$

$$+ \frac{\left[\displaystyle\sum^{N_{L2}} (y - \overline{Y}_{L2})(x - \overline{X}_{L2})\right]^2}{\displaystyle\sum^{N_{L2}} (x - \overline{X}_{L2})^2} - \frac{\left[\displaystyle\sum^{N} (y - \overline{Y})(x - \overline{X})\right]^2}{\displaystyle\sum^{N} (x - \overline{X})^2}$$

(3) Slopes Analysis

$$b = \frac{\displaystyle\sum_{k=1}^{M_j}\sum_{\alpha=1}^{n_k} (y_{k\alpha} - \overline{Y}_k)(x_{k\alpha} - \overline{X}_k)}{\displaystyle\sum_{k}\sum_{\alpha} (x_{k\alpha} - \overline{X}_k)^2}$$

= average slope of group i for classes k=1,...,M_j of predictor j,
   i=L1, L2

NOTE: There is a different average slope of group i for each predictor.

$$BSS = \frac{\left[\displaystyle\sum_{k=1}^{M_{i_j}}\sum_{\alpha=1}^{n_k} (y_{k\alpha} - \overline{Y}_k)(x_{k\alpha} - \overline{X}_k)\right]^2}{\displaystyle\sum_{k=1}^{M_{i_j}}\sum_{\alpha=1}^{n_k} (x_{k\alpha} - \overline{X}_k)^2} + \frac{\left[\displaystyle\sum_{k=1}^{M_{2_j}}\sum_{\alpha=1}^{n_k} (y_{k\alpha} - \overline{Y}_k)(x_k - \overline{X}_k)\right]^2}{\displaystyle\sum_{k=1}^{M_{2_j}}\sum_{\alpha=1}^{n_k} (x_{k\alpha} - \overline{X}_k)^2}$$

$$- \frac{\left[\displaystyle\sum_{k=1}^{M_j}\sum_{\alpha=1}^{n_k} (y_{k\alpha} - \overline{Y}_k)(x_{k\alpha} - \overline{X}_k)\right]^2}{\displaystyle\sum_{k=1}^{M_j}\sum_{\alpha=1}^{n_k} (x_{k\alpha} - \overline{X}_k)^2}$$

Also note that the focus is on the explanation of the sample variance, not that of the population. The searching operations make the specification of degrees of freedom necessary for extensions to the population difficult.[1]

---

[1]See Lansing and Morgan (1971), pp. 304-306, or Snedecor and Cochran (1956), p. 274, or Anderson and Bancroft (1952), p. 327.

The user may suppress any or all of the trace. The options are:

    (1)   Suppress the entire trace;

    (2)   Print only parent group statistics and the <u>best</u> eligible split on each predictor;

    (3)   Print parent group statistics and all eligible splits on each predictor;

    (4)   Same as (3) but include partitions which do not explain sufficient variation, i.e. , the BSS does not meet the reducibility criterion;

    (5)   Same as (3) but include partitions whose resulting groups do not meet the minimum group size criterion;

    (6)   Print the entire trace.

Option #5 is recommended if some minimum group size is used because splits with BSS large enough to qualify but splitting off very few cases will then be visible even if the split is not made, warning the user of extreme case problems.

With use of the lookahead option, option #4 or #6 should be used here since an actual split may be made even though its BSS does not qualify in cases where it is optimal when combined with one or two subsequent splits.

Option #6 is often useful, however, in allowing one to force the tree one split further beyond any final group, or to see the actual effect (not just the power) of some predictor on <u>each</u> of the final groups.

4.4 Final Tables

One of the design objectives in this version of AID was improvement of the form in which information was presented to the analyst. In previous versions of the program much of the useful information was scattered throughout the trace of the partitioning process. In the present version this detail has been collected and placed in several tables specifically geared to the decisions the analyst must make about the explanatory power of his predictors and their effect profiles in various parts of the sample. The analyst uses information about explanatory power and its changes throughout the partitioning process to make judgements about the presence of interaction effects. He uses effect profiles in a similar fashion.[1]

The final table printed as part of the basic output is an analysis of variance table over the final groups generated by AID. The within- between- and total sums of squares are presented, together with the proportion of variation

---

[1]For a discussion of display techniques see Sonquist (1969) and Sonquist (1970a), (1970b).

"explained" by the entire branching process.[1] (Tables 2 and 3 give the terms for covariate and means analyses respectively.) The total proportion of variation explained is

$$\frac{\sum\limits_{i} BSS_i}{TSS}$$

, where BSS_i is the between sum of squares term for the appropriate analysis type (defined in section 4.3) resulting from the partition of group i, i.e., the reduction in unexplained variation from splitting group i.

In addition, there are four types of summary tables which may be printed.

1. GROUP SUMMARY TABLE: Number of groups and number of final groups, followed by a recapitulation of the actual splits made and the fraction of the original total variance explained by each split. Branching diagrams can be made expeditiously using just this table.

2. (a) 100*BSS/TSS TABLE FOR N-STEP LOOKAHEAD: For each predictor used for the first split for each group, the explanatory power of that plus one or two more splits. Tagged with < if less than N+1 splits were made (because of other criteria). Replaced with **** if a resultant group too small. If a minimum group size rule excludes a particular division by a predictor on a group, but another division on the same predictor and group is allowable, the "second best" split's BSS/TSS will appear.

   (b) 100*BSS/TSS TABLE FOR 0-STEP LOOKAHEAD: Gives the results of a single best eligible split on each predictor for each group. Only eligible splits are reported as with previous table even if "second best," and replaced by **** if a resultant group did not contain enough cases.

   (c) 100*BSS/TSS TABLE FOR 0-STEP LOOKAHEAD, MAXIMUM BSS REGARDLESS OF ELIGIBILITY: Gives the power of the best split for each predictor with each group, except the final groups, even if group size or criterion makes that an ineligible split. Provides a warning of extreme cases even if minimum group size prohibits their isolation.

3. PROFILE OF CLASS MEANS AND SLOPES: Gives means of Y (and of X, and slopes if covariance), and N for each predictor subclass for each group. Useful for getting detailed profiles, since the trace tables give only the two pooled groups for each split. Arranged by predictors and for each predictor gives the ETA for its full subclass detail over the whole sample, that is, the explanatory power of that predictor over the whole sample using all its subclasses.

4. PREDICTOR SUMMARY TABLE: Gives more detail on each subclass of each predictor over each subgroup, including ETA, ETA (NSTEP), and ETA(0).

---

[1]This may be compared with the configuration analysis of variance, since the latter represents the total variation that could be explained by all main effects and interactions for the given set of predictors and as such is the upper bound on explained variation (see Lubin and Osburn, 1957).

The first uses all the detail, the second is the power of the binary splits, and the third of the first binary split.

The least useful is the Predictor Summary Table, most of which is elsewhere in the output. If no lookahead is used, and a small minimum group size, only one of the BSS/TSS tables is needed. The group summary table is essential and the profile of class means and slopes very useful.

4.4.1 Group Summary Table

The Group Summary Table provides a record of the actual partitions that took place during the analysis and summarizes the statistical effects of the co-variate. The following quantities are printed for each group:

1. Group number and children into which the current group is split.
2. Predictor number, name and class identifiers forming the basis for the split.
3. Percentage of the total variation explained by the split and percentage of the total variation remaining in this group: BSS/TSS and SS/TSS.
4. Number of observations in this group; sum of weights in group.
5. Statistics for the dependent variable; $\overline{Y}$ and σ_Y^2 .
6. Statistics for the covariate, where applicable;

$$\overline{X}, \ \sigma_x^2, \ r_{xy}, \ b_{y \cdot x}, \ a, \ a(norm)$$

(where $b_{y \cdot x}$ is the pooled or average slope depending on whether a Regression or Slopes-only analysis was used--see section 4.3)

$$r_{xy} = \frac{\sum (y - \overline{Y}_L) \ (x - \overline{X}_L)}{\sqrt{\sum (y - \overline{Y}_L)^2 \sum (x - \overline{X}_L)^2}}$$

= the correlation coefficient between x and y

$a \quad = \overline{Y}_L - b_L \overline{X}_L \ ,$

$a(norm) = \overline{Y}_L - b_L \ (\overline{X}_L - \overline{X}_1) \ ,$ where L denotes the current group and $\overline{X}_1$ is the original sample mean. Hence a(norm) is the expected value of Y for a member of the group whose X-value is equal to the overall sample mean; it is a measure of the _level_ of the subgroup regression line.

4.4.2 BSS/TSS Tables

Three BSS tables are available and may be printed when the BSS options are activated and a lookahead is used. The lookahead BSS table shows the explanatory power of the groups resulting from the partitioning of the parent group and the successive lookahead results. For instance, if a two-step lookahead is used, creating a total of four groups, the BSS shown in the table for the i-th predictor for this parent group is the explanatory power of all four of the groups resulting from the lookahead.

The entries in the lookahead BSS/TSS table are

$$\frac{BSS_{ijm}}{TSS} \ \text{x} \ 100 = xx.x$$

for the best partition on each predictor in each group. In the formula above the references are to the i-th predictor for the j-th parent group using a lookahead of length m. The partition may use other variables out in the lookahead splits after the maximizing action taken by the lookahead is attached to that variable forming the initial split in the parent group. Each variable has the maximum BSS associated with its initial use attached to it.

In each column of the table (one column per parent group) a flag appears if the partition was eventually based on less than the maximum lookahead permitted. Final groups are flagged also. Each entry is replaced with asterisks if that predictor was constant in that group, and it is replaced with a zero if the corresponding partition had been too small to meet the minimum group size requirement. Thus, the nonzero elements of the table are all valid, though possibly very small indications of explanatory power. Each variable has the maximum _eligible_ BSS associated with its initial use attached to it. If the STARTING TREE option is specified, the entries in the BSS table may not correspond to the actual BSS's from pre-specified splits, since the former are governed by the FREE/MONOTONIC predictor parameter and are based on a 0-step lookahead. Should the ordering of classes differ from that in the trace, then the entry in the table is based on that of the trace.

The BSS/TSS table with no lookahead corresponds to the lookahead table with m=0, the explanatory power of each predictor in the parent group.

The BSS/TSS table regardless of eligibility contains the maximum BSS/TSS regardless whether that BSS was obtained from an eligible split.

4.4.3 Profile of Class Means and Slopes

The means/slopes profile is broken down into separate tables, one for each predictor. The mean of the dependent variable (Y) is shown for every class of every predictor in every group, together with the number of observations upon which that mean is based.

In the case of a Regression/Slopes analysis, the mean of the covariate (X) is also given for each class in addition to the slope for that class. For Group 1 only (whole sample) ETA is also printed, showing the explanatory power of the full detail of each predictor.

$$\text{ETA} = \frac{\sum_{k=1}^{M_j} W_k \overline{Y}_k^2 - W \overline{Y}^2}{\text{TSS}} \quad , \text{ for classes } k = 1, \ldots, M_j \text{ of predictor } j.$$

4.4.4 Predictor Summary Table

Data for each predictor's behavior during the partitioning process are collected and organized in this table. One set of statistics for the predictor as it behaves in each group is printed. Data are presented for each class of the predictor.

For each class the following statistics are printed:

1. Number of observations and sum of weights for that class.
2. The sum of weights expressed as a percent of that group and a percent of the total sample.
3. The sum of Y (ΣY); and this sum expressed as a proportion of the total ΣY for the sample and of the total (ΣY) for the parent group.
4. The mean and variance of Y ($\overline{Y}$ and σ_y^2).
5. The sum of X (ΣX), and this sum expressed as a proportion of the total ΣX for the sample and of the total X for the parent group.
6. The mean and variance of X ($\overline{X}$ and σ_x^2).

In addition, three summary statistics are printed, showing the explanatory power of the predictor in the group in question.

1. ETA--the proportion of variation that can be explained by this predictor in this group, using all the classes of this predictor. This is the variation in this group that would be explained if a one-way analysis of variance were run on the observations in this parent group, using as grouping all of the classes of the predictor in question.

$$\text{ETA} = \text{BSS}_i/\text{SS}_i$$

for the i-th parent group, where

$$SS_i = \sum^{N_i} (y - \overline{Y}_i)^2$$

and

$$BSS_i = \sum_{k=1}^{M_j} W_k \overline{Y}_k^2 - W_i \overline{Y}_i^2$$

where the summarization is over the M_j classes of predictor j in the i-th group. It is the <u>square</u> of what is called the correlation ratio or η.

2. ETA (LOOKAHEAD)--The proportion of variation that can be explained by the specified lookahead groups based on a partition of the parent group using this predictor. The computation is the same as ETA, above, but the summation is over the N-step lookahead groups created from binary splits instead of the k classes of one predictor, i.e., summed over N+1 groups.

$$ETA (n) = BSS_{ijn}/SS_i$$

for a lookahead of length n using parent group i and variable j as the initial partitioning variable for the parent group.

3. ETA (NO LOOKAHEAD)--The proportion of variation that can be explained by a partition of the parent group using this predictor summed over the two resulting groups. This is the proportion explainable by the single split, itself.

In addition, components of sums of squares of Y about the fitted regression lines are printed.[1] These components are described in Table 2. They provide an analysis of covariance over the subclasses of each predictor separately, for each <u>group</u> created.

4.5 Residual Files

This version of AID can compute residuals, and predicted values, and can tag each observation with the group number of the final group into which it was placed. In addition, all input and generated variables can be transferred to the file containing the residuals, predicted values and group tags. All of these quantities are incorporated into the input data vector for each observation initially received by the program and are transferred along with this vector into a new data file. Residuals and predicted values may be appropriately scaled by separate output scale factors, and their field widths must be specified for the output file. The final group number is always put out as a 3-column field, hence

---

[1]See Walker and Lev (1953), p. 396, and Brownlee (1965), p. 378.

no field width specification is necessary.

The output file may be generated as a standard OSIRIS data file with a dictionary or as a format described file. In the latter case, output fields for all generated variables must have been included (following input fields) in the input FORMAT cards: Generated variables are outputted in the order they appeared in the parameter setup (Appendix III). A complete variable list is printed before the analysis begins and the user would do well to try a test run to insure his format fields correspond to the correct variables.

The scratch data file (ISR01) used by the program is updated with all generated variables and used as the data file in subsequent analysis packets. This allows the user to specify residuals without generating an output file.

Formulas used in calculating the residuals and predicted values are:

Means analysis:
$$\tilde{Y}_\alpha = \overline{Y}_i$$

$$R_\alpha = \tilde{Y}_\alpha - Y_\alpha$$

for individual α as a member of final group i.

Slope or Regression analysis:

$$\tilde{Y}_\alpha = a_i + b_i\,(X_{i\alpha} - \overline{X}_i)$$

$$R_\alpha = \tilde{Y}_\alpha - Y_\alpha \qquad \text{for individual } \alpha$$

in final group i.

4.6 Structure of the Trees[1]

The results of the program can show a series of different characteristic tree patterns. Each tree has sections that can be described as a combination of two configurations, based on the useful convention of showing the group with the highest mean as the uppermost branch. One may be termed a trunk-twig structure, the other a trunk-branch structure.

The trunk-twig structure is a main branch from which small groups are split off and are not themselves split again. This may take three forms: top-termination, bottom-termination, and alternating-termination. The top-termination structure may be termed an "alternative advantage" model. Group B consists of those observations possessing the "advantage" represented by that characteristic which split group A into groups B and C. Once group B has been

---

[1]The following sections were extracted from the original monograph, The Detection of Interaction Effects.

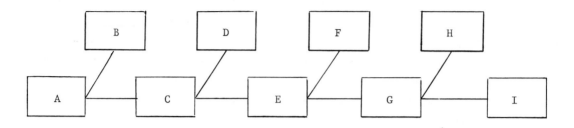

TOP TERMINATION

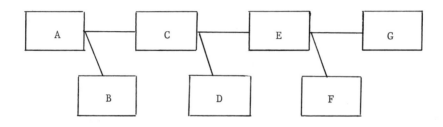

BOTTOM TERMINATION

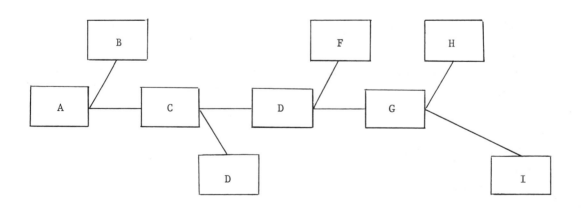

ALTERNATING TERMINATION

established, it cannot be split further by the program.

The bottom-termination structure may be termed an "alternative disadvantage" model, and is analogous. The possession of any one of a number of characteristics is enough to prevent an observation from achieving a high value on the dependent variable.

The interpretation of the alternating termination configuration is similar. In all three types, the interpretation to be made depends on the characteristics of the final groups themselves, especially on the number of observations in the group, its variance, and whether or not there existed predictor variables which "almost worked" in the attempt made by the program to split it.

Another property of the tree is its symmetry or nonsymmetry in terms of the extent to which the same variables are used in the splits on the various trunks. Nonsymmetry implies interaction, i.e., effects of combinations of factors. If a variable is used on one of the trunks, and if it shows no actual or potential utility in reducing predictive error in another trunk, then there is clear evidence of an interaction effect between that variable and those used in the <u>preceding</u> splits. The utility of a predictor in reducing predictive error is evaluated by statistic $(BSS_{mpr}/TSS)_i$ for each predictor at each branch in the tree. This output is produced by the program and represents the proportion of the variation <u>in the group to which the predictor is being applied</u> that would be explained if it were used in a binary split of that group.

Trees may, of course, be symmetrical with respect to the way in which top-termination, bottom-termination and alternating-termination configurations appear in the main trunks.

The trunk-branch structure is usually typical of the first few splits of any tree. In this case, each group produced by a split is further subdivided.

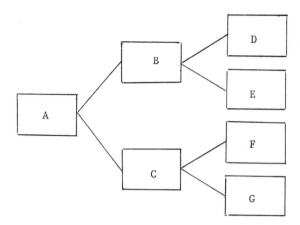

TRUNK-BRANCH STRUCTURE

Some of the early groups may remain unsplit. If this is so, then the most important aspect of the interpretation of this structure has to do with the fact that
there remains within-group variation which can be explained. At each step, the
analytic question that should be asked is, "What are the reasons why there is as
much variation in each of the groups as there is?" This question will be discussed below in more detail.

A further property of each tree is the number of final groups that result
from the analysis. This is, of course, a function of the input sample size, the
statistical properties of the algorithm, and the relationships between the characteristics of the predictor variables and the dependent variable.

Based on the present characteristics of the algorithm, we can distinguish
three types of final groups: small groups, explained groups, and unexplainable
groups. A small group is one containing too few observations to warrant an attempt to split it. An explained group is over this minimum size, but has too
little variation in it (less than, say, 2 per cent of the original variation) to
warrant an attempted split. An unexplainable group is sufficiently large and
spread out, but no variable in the analysis is useful in reducing the unexplained
variation contained within it. Each tree will generally have some of each of the
three types. But the total number of final groups is heavily dependent on the
rules used to stop the splitting process.

4.7 The Behavior of the Variables in the Trees

The analysis of the behavior of the predictors and their relationship to
the dependent variable during the partitioning process can be approached through

a series of questions, asked with reference to each partition.

4.7.1 Chance Factors

The first question is, "Given the minimum group size rule and split eligibility rule used, what is the likelihood that this split occurred by chance?"
This problem may still occur even if the above-suggested rules have been used for
minimizing the probability of its happening. If a variable actually used in the
split is the only one which shows up as important, according to the criteria used,
then the probability of its predictive power being based largely on sampling variability is relatively slight, unless it is an unconstrained variable with a
large number of classes. When several variables are almost equally good as predictors, in any given split, then the likelihood is greater that sampling variability has had a hand in selecting one, rather than another, as that variable
to be actually used in the split. The $(BSS/TSS)_i$ tabulation provides a guard
against basing an interpretation only on those variables actually based in the
partition process, since the explanatory power of the unused predictors is presented in all its detail.

The overall structure of the tree provides a clue as to the probability
that sampling variability is operating together with a skewed distribution.

In the case where the dependent variable is badly skewed and has a tail ex-
tending toward the right (positive skewness), a top-terminating trunk-twig structure is likely to appear in several main branches of the tree. These terminal
groups will have large, positive means, and will contain few (1-5) observations.
Typically, they will result from splits on several different variables. Sooner
or later the program will find some predictor which enables it to split out these
extreme cases from the group in which they happen to be.

A careful re-reading of interviews may turn up a variable, certain values
of which most of these extreme cases will have in common. This variable may then
be inserted into a subsequent analysis. One may be reasonably confident that
these observations will then be placed together in one group via a split on this
variable. Good strategy would, therefore, dictate a preliminary investigation
of the skewness of the dependent variable before the main analysis starts.

One might construct a dummy variable which has the value one if an observation is out in the skew tail and zero if it is not. A preliminary AID analysis,
using this as the dependent variable, together with the predictors to be used in
the main analysis will provide information as to which classes of the sample are
out in the tail, rather than being in the main body of the distribution. It may
be that one set of variables will be found optimal to explain being out on the

tail of a distribution. Another set might prove best for explaining overall variation or variation in the main body of the destruction. This possibility would,
of course, be of considerable theoretical importance.

Of course this technique need not be confined to observations out in a skew
tail of the dependent variable distribution. For some analytic purposes it may
be desirable to use this technique to determine what combination of variables are
associated with an observation's being, say, in the second quartile of the distribution, or less than some specified value.

It should be noted that a variable which is not skewed in the total sample,
may become skewed during the partitioning process. This cannot be caught in advance. Hence even when a preliminary investigation of skewness has been made,
the analyst should be on his guard for the appearance of this particular trunk-
twig structure. A bottom-terminating trunk-twig structure with small terminal
groups would provide a signal for negative skewness. The provision for identi-
fying and tagging and/or eliminating outliers should be of help here.

4.7.2 Conceptualization Problems

A second question that should be asked is, "Does this split reflect concep-
tualization problems in applying the framework of predictor variables to the sample, or sections of it?" A number of interpretation problems in the trees may
stem from measurement or coding errors, or from the use of variables that were
designed for other statistical purposes. This technique is at its best when the
predictors have a clear, uni-dimensional reference. We have found an example of
a conceptual problem that looked, initially, like a somewhat contradictory finding, until coding decisions were uncovered which appeared to misclassify unedu-
cated people living on the fringes of cities of 50,000 and over, with respect to
the rural or urban nature of their surroundings. Indices having several components also tend to behave in a somewhat peculiar fashion. Presumably, this is because the items in these indices, though related both theoretically and statistically, may affect the dependent variable in different ways, particularly if
some of them interact with other variables in the tree and others do not. Splits
involving such variables may or may not "make sense." See Coombs (1964) for a
thorough discussion of scaling problems.

Perhaps the most important point to be made here is that problems like
these are often revealed only by large standard errors that may accompany a multiple regression analysis. They tend to stand out quite clearly in the tree display of the AID results.

4.7.3 Manipulation of Variables

A further question which should be asked with reference to any given split is, "Are there competing predictors correlated with the one actually used in the split? If so, does their explanatory power increase, decrease, or stay the same in subsequent splits?" The logic to be employed here is developed extensively by Hyman in his discussion of spuriousness, and in his presentation of M- and P-type elaboration. He presents a formalization of the logic of examining the relationship between two variables when a third factor is introduced. The two factors under examination are referred to as x and y, and the third is called t. In our notation, x is the variable used to split group i into groups j and k; y is the dependent variable, and t is multiple and consists of each of the other predictors in the analysis. We are interested in the relationship between variable t and variable y, as represented by the statistics $(BSS/TSS)_i$, $(BSS/TSS)_j$ and $(BSS/TSS)_k$ for each predictor t. If, in addition, we consider whether or not there is a logical, theoretical justification for a correlation between x and t, and if so, whether x can be conceptualized as antecedent to t in a causal chain, we have a systematic application of the analysis strategies of:

1. Interpretation (t is an intervening variable)

2. Explanation (t is antecendent to x and is logically related to it)

3. Control for spuriousness (t is antecendent to x and cannot be related logically to it)

4. Specification (t is neither antecedent to x nor subsequent to it, but is logically related. Here x is a circumstance that affects the extent to which t is related to y.)

The reader is referred to Hyman and to Blalock (1961) for the details of the logic.

We note that we have reverted to a form of the analysis question, "Other things being equal, how does x affect y?" but in a somewhat different form. We now have the question, "When we extract variation associated with predictor x, how do the relationships between t_1, t_2, ..., t_p and y change?"

In providing an answer to this question that is meaningful, the question of the substitutability of variables in the analysis must be taken into consideration. This is the problem of intercorrelations between the predictors.

Another consideration related to the above question is, how does one decide whether to rank predictors, allowing some clearly exogenous or background variables to work first, and then asking whether certain intervening or attitudinal or environmental variables add anything, or to pool the residuals after allowing the background variables to work, and running them against a new set of predictors? The first alternative allows the second set of variables to operate differently in different subgroups, i.e., allows for interaction effects between the two sets of predictors. The second allows none, or allows only those built into the analysis by including first-stage predictors also in the second stage. The second option is also more economical of degrees of freedom, of course, and may be necessary if the sample is only of middling size (1000 or so).

For example, one might, in explaining earnings, want to put education, age, race, sex, farm background in a first analysis, and then go on, with or without pooling, to introduce mobility, occupational choice, current environment, etc. But even if one pooled residuals, one might want to reintroduce education and race in the next stage, in case the effects of mobility are dependent on one's education or race.

It is impossible here to consider all the problems associated with the relationship between a variable and the concept(s) it purports to represent, but a few points should be emphasized.

Some intercorrelations are built into the data by the coding process. Other high correlations may result because two predictors may themselves be the results of a third factor which may or may not be represented in the analysis by a variable. Still others are there because things go together in the real world. But it is on exactly this structure of relations that we are trying to get a grip. What is required is a strategy for minimizing the interpretation problems.

One way to deal with this is to put in the most clearly exogenous, most orthogonal and uni-dimensioned variables into a first-stage analysis or ranked highest, together with a relatively high reducibility criterion and fairly large minimum group size, and then use the richer matrix of predictors for an analysis of the residuals. Where a tight test is desired as to whether a variable which is of considerable theoretical importance has effects, this variable may be held out of the first-stage analysis and entered in the second stage to see whether it enables the explanation of residual variance. If a low eligibility criterion is used, the present algorithm will make a final sweep over all the final groups before dropping them from consideration, thus providing information on how all of the predictors are distributed within each group. These distributions can be used to provide information as to whether the group occupies its present place because of its actual pedigree or because of some other factor(s) correlated with the ones used to form it.

Moreover, it would certainly be desirable to obtain information on the zero-order correlations among the predictors in the sample. Since they are classifications, this is not easy. A complete set of bivariate frequency distributions provides a general impression. Further improvements in the algorithm itself should provide for a satisfactory method of computing the intercorrelation matrix of predictors at each branch of the tree.

If there are some variables which, because of high intercorrelations or low logical priorities, must be put into a second-stage analysis, one will not know (and has decided not to ask) what their influence would have been in the formation of the first-stage groups. The second stage, however, will show whether or not their influence on the dependent variable has already been accounted for. Re-introducing the first-stage variables into the second stage will also provide an answer to the question of whether there is a small, but universal, effect across all groups which will appear when they are pooled for the residual analysis.

In some cases, the first-stage analysis will identify groups which are clearly constrained in some special way, and explained so clearly that they really should be eliminated from the subsequent analysis.

Concentrating on explaining the level of the dependent variable may tend to obscure other information contained in the tree which may be extremely important. The homogeneity of the final groups, especially if some of them appear after only a few splits, and are large in size, may be more interesting and important than their average on the dependent variable. Since the program produces the standard deviation as well as the mean of each group, one can examine the variance, or relative variance of each final group. If any group has a larger variance than the others, it raises the question of whether there is some other factor which affects this group, or varies more over it, but which was not included in the analysis.

The use of the tree strategy calls one's attention to the possibility that one or two variables may be sufficient for explaining the variation associated with some of the observations, whereas, additional theoretical sophistication may be required for an adequate explanation of the remainder of the sample.

Appendix I
References

Anderson, R.L. and Bancroft, F.A. Statistical Theory in Research. Mcgraw-Hill, New York, 1952.

Andrews, F.M., Morgan, J.N., and Sonquist, J.A. Multiple Classification Analysis: A Report on a Computer Program for Multiple Regression Using Categorical Predictors. Institute for Social Research, The University of Michigan, Ann Arbor, Michigan, 1967.

Blalock, H.M. "Evaluating the Relative Importance of Variables," American Sociological Review, XXVI, No. 6 (December 1961).

Blalock, H.M. "The Identification Problem and Theory Building: The Case of Status Inconsistency," American Sociological Review, 31 (1966), pp. 52-61.

Blatt, J.M. Introduction to Fortran IV Programming, Ch. 15. Goodyear, 1968.

Brownlee, K.A. Statistical Theory and Methodology. Wiley, New York, 1965.

Coombs, C.H. A Theory of Data. Wiley, New York, 1964.

Hastings, C., et al. Algorithms for Digital Computers. Princeton University Press, 1955.

Hohn, F.E. Applied Boolean Algebra. Macmillan, New York, 1966, p. 48.

Horst, P. "Pattern Analysis and Configurational Scoring," Journal of Clinical Psychology, 10 (1954), pp. 3-11.

Hyman, H. Survey Design and Analysis, Chap. VI and VII. Glencoe, Free Press.

IBM Corp. System/360 Operating System Fortran IV (G and H) Programmer's Guide. File S360-25, Form C28-6817-1, p. 36.

Klein, L.R., and Morgan, J.N. "Results of Alternating Statistical Treatments of Sample Survey Data," Journal of American Statistical Association, 46 (December, 1951), pp. 442-460.

Lansing, J.B. and Morgan, J.N. Economic Survey Methods. Institute for Social Research, The University of Michigan, Ann Arbor, Michigan, 1971.

Lord, F.M. Efficiency of Prediction When a Regression Equation from a Sample is Used in a New Sample. Educational Testing Service, Res. Bulletin No. 50-40, Princeton, New Jersey, 1950.

Lubin, A. and Osburn, H.G. "The Use of Configurational Analysis for the Evaluation of Test Scoring Methods," Psychometrika, 22 (1957b), pp. 359-371.

McGee, V. and Carleton, W.T. "Piecewise Regression," Journal American Statistical Association, 65 (September, 1970), pp. 1109-1124.

Meehl, P.E. "Configurational Scoring," Journal Consult. Psych., 14 (1950), pp. 165-171.

Messenger, R. "Subroutine URDMN," OSIRIS III Subroutine Manual (See below).

Morgan, J.N. and Andrews, F.M. "A Comment on Mr. Einhorn's 'Alchemy in the Behavioral Sciences'," Public Opinion Quarterly, 37 (Spring 1973), pp. 127-129.

Morgan, J.N. and Sonquist, J.A. "Problems in the Analysis of Survey Data: And a Proposal," Journal American Statistical Association, 58 (1963), pp. 415-434.

Morgan, J.N., Sirageldin, I., and Baerwaldt, N. Productive Americans. Institute for Social Research, University of Michigan, Ann Arbor, Michigan, 1965.

Mueller, E. and Lean, J. "The Savings Account as a Source for Financing Large Expenditures," Journal of Finance, 22 (September, 1967), pp. 375-393.

OSIRIS User's Manual. Institute for Social Research, The University of Michigan, Ann Arbor, Michigan. (COMPREHENSIVE USER'S MANUAL FOR THE OSIRIS PACKAGE OF PROGRAMS FOR STATISTICAL PROCESSING)

OSIRIS III Subroutine Manual. Institute for Social Research, The University of Michigan, Ann Arbor, Michigan, July 1973. (TECHNICAL DETAILS OF 360 ASSEMBLY LANGUAGE AND FORTRAN SUBROUTINES USED IN ALL OSIRIS PROGRAMS INCLUDING AID AND MCA)

Snedecor, G.U., and Cohran, W.A. Statistical Methods. Iowa State University Press, Ames, Iowa, 1952.

Sonquist, J.A. "Finding Variables that Work," Public Opinion Quarterly, 33, No. 1 (Spring, 1969), 83-95. Reprint. (STRATEGY FOR USING AID AND MCA TOGETHER).

Sonquist, J.A. Multivariate Model Building: The Validation of a Search Strategy. Institute for Social Research, The University of Michigan, Ann Arbor, Michigan, March, 1970.

Sonquist, J.A. "AID in Use: 'Data-dredging' Cannot Be an End in Itself." Paper presented at Midwest Sociological Society, St. Louis, April 17, 1970, (22 pp. mimeographed).

Sonquist, J.A. and Morgan, J.N. The Detection of Interaction Effects. Survey Research Center Monograph No. 35, Institute for Social Research, The University of Michigan, Ann Arbor, Michigan, 1964. (DESCRIBES THE AID ALGORITHM AND ITS USES)

Sonquist, J.A., Baker, E.L., and Morgan, J.N. Recent Developments in Sequential Data Analysis Strategies. Proceedings of the Social Statistics Section, American Statistical Association, 1969, pp. 74-90.

Stouffer, S.A., Borgatta, E.F., Hay, D.G., and Henry, A.F. "A Technique for Improving Cumulative Scales," Public Opinion Quarterly, 16, No. 2 (1952), pp. 273-291.

Walker, H.M. and Lev, J. Statistical Inference. Holt and Co., New York, 1953.

Appendix II
Recoding

This section contains the detailed instructions for using the recoding routines that have been incorporated into AID. The recoding instructions consist of a series of clauses. One or more clauses constitute an instruction. The instructions are executed once for each observation read by the program during the input. They are executed in sequence, except as altered by GOTO instructions and those that are skipped because of the operation of the logical clauses and the truth switch. This is explained below.

A. Instruction Format

Each instruction consists of a statement label (optional) and one or two clauses. There may be a relational clause and/or an operational clause. An optional comments field is included with the statement but is merely printed on the user's output, having no effect on the computations.

All four parts of a single statement are punched on a single IBM card.

(1) Statement Labels

A positive integer may be attached to a statement. This is ordinarily optional and merely serves to identify the statement. It is required if the statement is to be referenced by a GOTO instruction. Not every statement need have a statement label and statement labels may be used in any order. A given positive integer may not be used as the label for more than one statement.

(2) Relational Clauses

A relational clause consists of a logical tag and, depending on the tag, it may also have a test variable reference, a relational operator, and A or (A and B) operands. If the logical tag used does not require the use of the remaining fields, their contents will be ignored. If there is no logical tag, no test variable number, no relational operator and no A and B operands, the instruction is deemed to have no relational clause as part of it. If at least one of these fields exists, blank tags, test variable references and relational operators are assumed to be the same as those in the immediately preceding logical clause. (Note: A and B operands must always be supplied when needed.) This permits the user to avoid excessive repetition in writing commands. If there is no logical clause, the instruction is deemed to consist only of computation. Logical clauses may be written without subsequent computational clauses, and thereby concatenated into a compound logical expression. This compound expression is of the form:

$$((((A)op\ B)op\ C)op\ D)\ \ etc.\ etc.$$

The user may make use of this nesting in adapting the commands to construct an expression reflecting the logical structure of his problem. A compound logical expression must begin with an Initial Clause. This is discussed in detail below.

The testing part of the relational expression uses four fields, a test variable reference, a relational operator and either one or two operands. The B operand is used only for the IN or OUT relational operators. It is ignored otherwise. When the logical clause is executed, the test is performed according to the requirements of the tag and the relational operator. The current values of the referenced variables are used. The result is a new value for the truth switch (see below), which is dependent on the old truth switch value as well as the test. The rules for referring to test variables and A and B operands are discussed below.

The test variable field may contain a test variable reference. This may be direct or indirect, but it must be a reference to a variable, not a constant.

An A or B operand may refer either to a variable, directly or indirectly, or it may contain a constant. Rules for forming A and B operands are discussed below.

Any relational operator may be combined with any legitimate test variable reference and any legitimate A (and, when appropriate, B) operand to form a test. The test should be formed by the user only if the tag requires a rest--and then it must be present.

(3) Operational Clauses

An operational clause may or may not be present in a given statement. When present its form depends on the type of operation to be performed. If the operator used does not require certain of the available fields, they will simply be ignored (see below). As with the logical clauses, the complete absence of all values in any of the fields indicates the absence of the clause.

If at least one is present, the clause is deemed to exist. Missing values of the Resultant Variable and the Control Operator are then supplied automatically from the previous operational clause. Values for operands must always be supplied if the operand is to be used. The Result Variable, where required, must be a direct or indirect variable reference. The C and D operands may be either direct or indirect variable references or integer constants.

Figure A2.1 illustrates the format required.

B. The Interpreter and Executor

The instructions supplied by the user are interpreted and stored by "the interpreter." The executor is a two-state machine. It operates either in logical mode or in computational mode. It initiates execution of the instruction sequence supplied to it once for each data-unit read by the computer. It starts in computation mode, executing operations in the order submitted by the user, except where the sequence of computation is altered by the execution of a GOTO instruction. Computation is its ordinary mode of operation.

When any logical clause of any kind is encountered, the machine exits immediately from computational mode and no further computational operations can be executed until a return from logical mode has occurred.

When this exit from computational mode takes place the value of the machine's "truth switch" first becomes undefined. Then the machine reenters logical mode and the only operation that can be executed is the evaluation of logical expressions and the establishment of a new value for the truth switch. When in logical mode and with an undefined truth switch the only type of operation that can be executed is one which can define a new value, either true or false, for the truth switch. Then, after the truth switch has been defined an exit to computational mode is possible. This can occur when the truth switch has the value "true" and a computational operation follows. Upon detecting this condition, the machine reverts to computational mode and the computation is executed. If subsequent instructions contain only computational clauses, the machine remains in computational mode.

The truth switch can become defined only through assignment or through evaluation of an Initial Clause. There are two logical constants (T, true, and F,

Figure A2.1

MULTIVARIATE RECODING FORM

Coder: _____   Job: _____

Date: _____   Data: _____

STATE-MENT NO.	LOG. TAG	TEST VAR. NO.	REL. OPER.	A OPERAND	B OPERAND	RESULT VAR. NO.	CONTROL OPER.	C OPERAND	D OPERAND	COMMENT
5 xxxx	10 xxxx T	15 xxxxx	20 xxxx	30 VPxxxxxxxxx	40 VPxxxxxxxxx	45 VPxxxx	50 xxxx	60 VPxxxxxxxxx	70 VPxxxxxxxxx	80 xxxxxxxx TRUNCATE
1	IF	V0005	GT	100000		V0005	=	100000		
2	IF	V0010	LE	-25	-5	V0010	=	1		BKT V10
	ØR		IN	-24	4			2		
				-4	24			3		
				5				4		
				25				5		
			GE	100	99			6		
3	IF	V0020	IN	0	2	V0100	=	1		
30	AND	V0021		0	2		=	0		
31	ALT									
4	IF	V0030	EQ	1		V0101	=	1		
	ØR	V0031	IN	2	9			GOTO	100	
	IF	V0040	EQ	1		V0101	=	2		
	AND	V0041	IN	2	9			3		
	ALT									
100	T									

false) which can be used to assign a value to the truth switch.

An Initial Clause is the first (and may be the only) part of a relational proposition. In other words, a relational proposition must begin with an Initial Clause or Assignment and may (or may not) be followed by one or more Subsequent Clauses. An Initial Clause is <u>always</u> headed by the tag IF (if) or NIF (if not). It is never headed by another type of tag. Subsequent Clauses are always headed by one of the other types of tags (e.g., OR, NOR, EXOR, etc.), and are <u>never</u> headed by IF, NIF, T, or F. The truth switch acquires a defined value as soon as an initial clause has been evaluated or it is assigned T or F. Its new value is dependent only on the current operation, not upon past values. The new value is established accordingly on the basis of the truth tables associated with IF, NIF, T, or F (see Table A2.1).

Since the truth switch has a new value defined after the evaluation of the Initial Clause, computational statements may be placed between the Initial and Subsequent Clauses or between Subsequent Clauses. If such statements are encountered in logical mode when the value of the truth switch is T, the machine will exit to computational mode and any number of <u>logically</u> consecutive statements can be executed. However, if such computational statements are encountered when the machine is in a logical mode, when the value of the truth switch is still F, then the machine will remain in logical mode. The computational statement(s) will then be passed over and the machine will proceed to evaluate the next Subsequent Clause. If, while in logical mode and seeking a Subsequent Clause, the machine encounters another Initial Clause, the truth switch will simply be reset according to the tag associated with this new Initial Clause. Then the machine will proceed in logical mode as above, again seeking a following Subsequent Clause or exiting to computational mode if the truth switch happens to be T when a computational statement is encountered.

When in computation mode the only instructions the machine can execute are another computation operation or the evaluation of an Assignment or Initial Clause, the latter two causing a change to logical mode and immediate redefinition of the truth switch. Encountering a Subsequent Clause when in computation mode also causes an immediate exit to logical mode, but with the value of the truth switch undefined.

When in logical mode the machine can do nothing but evaluate an Initial Clause or an Assignment, until its truth switch acquires a defined value. After that, it can evaluate Subsequent Clauses and can exit to computational mode if a computational instruction is encountered at the time the truth switch is T. If the truth switch is defined but equals F, and the machine is in logical mode, it

Table A2.1
Truth Tables for Boolean Operators

	Test	
	1	0

s w i t c h	1	0	0
	0	0	0

F

	1	0
1	1	0
0	0	0

AND

	1	0
1	0	1
0	0	0

NIMP

	1	0
1	1	1
0	0	0

ALSO

	1	0
1	0	0
0	1	0

BIF

	1	0
1	1	0
0	1	0

IF

	1	0
1	0	1
0	1	0

EXOR

	1	0
1	1	1
0	1	0

OR

	1	0
1	0	0
0	0	1

NOR

	1	0
1	1	0
0	0	1

CONS

	1	0
1	0	1
0	0	1

NIF

	1	0
1	1	1
0	0	1

NBIF

	1	0
1	0	0
0	1	1

ALT

	1	0
1	1	0
0	1	1

IMP

	1	0
1	0	1
0	1	1

NAND

	1	0
1	1	1
0	1	1

T

NOTE: The Test values appear across the top as indicated and the current value of the truth switch appears at the left side. The resulting value of the truth switch appears in the body of the table.

can only evaluate relational clauses, either Initial or Subsequent (all computational instructions being passed over and ignored). Note that Subsequent Clauses which follow computation and which are not preceded by an Initial Clause can <u>never</u> be evaluated and that computation which follows them can <u>never</u> be executed.

(1) The Truth Switch

Computation is started with the truth switch equal to T. Then when the first exit to logical mode occurs, the value of the truth switch becomes undefined. Later, when an Initial Clause is evaluated or an Assignment takes place, the truth switch acquires a defined value of T or F.

Each logical tag has associated with it a truth table for relating the current value of the switch and the results of the current test to a new value for the switch. Thus, when the machine is in logical mode and an expression is evaluated (as we have seen expressions are not always evaluated), a new value for the truth switch is defined. The truth tables for all of the logical tags were presented in Table A2.1.

(2) Logical Tags

The truth switch and the truth value of the current test are used together to establish a new value for the truth switch. The way in which these two quantities are used together to establish this new value is determined by the logical tag associated with the relational expression.

Each logical tag has associated with it a truth table (see Table A2.1). The truth switch has a defined value either T(true) sometimes represented by a "1" or F (false), sometimes represented by a "0." Similarly, the relational expression has a value of true or false, depending on the values of the variables that are supplied to it when the test is made. The new value of the truth switch is simply obtained from the corresponding row and column of the appropriate truth table.

The tags correspond to the sixteen unique elementary Boolean operators.[1] They are:

    1. T   -- The Boolean constant, "true."
    2. F   -- The Boolean constant, "false."
    3. IF   -- A univariate operator dependent only on the value
                of the test.
    4. ALSO-- A univariate operator dependent only on the value
                of the truth switch.
    5. AND -- Corresponds to set intersection. True only if
                both conditions are true.

---

[1]Hohn, 1966.

6. NAND-- The negative of AND. False only if both conditions are true.
7. OR -- Corresponds to set union. True if either or both conditions are true.
8. NOR -- The negation of OR. True only if both conditions are false.
9. NIF -- "If not true that"--the negation of IF, a univariate operator, dependent only on the value of the test. True only if the test is false.
10. ALT -- "Alternatively," a univariate operator dependent only on the value of the truth switch. It is true only if the truth switch is false; thus, it reverses the value of the truth switch.
11. IMP -- "Implication" operator, false only if the first condition is true, but not the second.
12. NIMP-- "Does not imply," the negation of implication. True only if the first is true, but not the second.
13. BIF -- "But if." True only if the first condition is false and the second one true.
14. NBIF-- The negation of "but if."
15. CONS-- The consistency, or biconditional operator, requiring both true or both false for the result to be true.
16. EXOR-- Exclusive OR. True if one or the other is true, but not both.

Not all tags will be found to be equally useful, especially since many are simply negations of the others. However, providing all of them makes it possible for the user to express the logical aspects of his problem in a manner most convenient for the way in which he thinks of it.

The tags likely to be found to be of most use are IF, AND, OR, ALT and T, and the user is directed toward an understanding of these first.

Well-formed logical expressions begin with an Initial Clause and end with a Subsequent Clause, usually headed by an ALT. This insures that the truth switch is "true" when subsequent operations are attempted. It is good practice to head a block of computation with a T to avoid possible earlier paths that arrived at this point with the truth switch undefined.

C. Operands

All operands are assumed to be integer in mode. There are three kinds of operands permitted: variables, constants and pointers.

(1) Variables

An understanding of the notation used is facilitated by considering the vector form of the data that is supplied to the program. All of the variables for a single unit of analysis (person, interview, transaction, automobile) are stored as a vector of integers. The file consists of a sequence of these vectors.

The program reads one vector at a time during its input phases. After this vector has been read, execution of the variable generation instructions is initiated, starting with the first instruction. The path taken through the instructions depends on the values of the input variables for that particular vector and the relational tests and computations that are performed upon them.

The variables are simply numbered using integers up to 9999, and there are up to 300 permitted in the current implementation of the program. Fewer than that may actually have been read in, but the user is free to use any of the others. They will all have been set to zero before the first analysis vector is read. Only those actually read in each time will have new values for each vector. The others are under the subsequent control of the user.

A variable is ordinarily referred to by placing it in the operand position of an instruction. This reference is of the form

Vnnnn

where V is a capital letter which is placed in the indicated column in the operand field, and nnnn is a positive integer. The positive integer must be right-adjusted in the 4-column space reserved for it. Some examples are:

V0005   (variable five)
V0019   (variable nineteen)

(2)   Constants

If the V is not present, and the column usually containing it is blank, the operand will be interpreted as an integer constant which may be as much as eight digits in width, or seven digits and a minus sign. The constant must be right-adjusted in the 8-column space provided in the operand field for it. Some examples are:

5

05

+5

−5

Minus signs must be punched and are to be placed just to the left of the most significant digit. Plus signs may be punched but are not ordinarily used. Use of leading zeroes is optional. Constants must be positive or negative integers, not alphabetic characters or real numbers containing a decimal point.

Several simple examples are given on Figure A2.1. The two lines starting with statement 1 first turn the truth switch to true. They are not really necessary

98

since the next statement starts with IF, but a reminder. The next line truncates variable 5 so that all values over 100,000 are changed to 100,000 (to keep extreme cases from dominating things, without omitting them altogether).

The six lines starting with statement 2 change variable 10 from a numerical field to a bracket or interval code. Note that the ranges go from the smallest real number up, e.g., from -24 to -5. Note also the economy in the implied ditto signs when OR, IN, etc. are repeated automatically.

The three lines starting with statement 3 illustrate the logical (AND) which means "both A and B," i.e., the new variable is coded 1 only if both things are true. ALT reverses the truth switch so that the remainder (only A, or only B, or neither) can be coded 0.[1]

The seven lines starting with statement 4 illustrate the GOTO, used to skip one group past the ALT statement so they will not be recoded to 3 after having been recoded to 1. The implied code created is:

Code	Meaning
1	V30 = 1 and/or V31 = 2-9 (either or both)
2	V40 = 1 and also V41 = 2-9
3	Remainder (neither of the above are true)

Statement 100 turns the switch to True just in case the next operations are not to start with IF.

(3)   Indirect References and Pointer Variables

A variable may also be referred to in an operand by means of a pointer. A pointer is established and given a value by setting any variable so that it contains a positive integer. This is accomplished using an arithmetic operation with the variable to be used as the pointer as a result, e.g., V101 = 26.

Subsequently, the pointer variable is referred to in an indirect reference and identified as a pointer by the reference. If this occurs, the operand is interpreted as a reference to the variable whose number is contained in the pointer.

Any variable can be used as a pointer. A positive integer can be placed in it using arithmetic operators. The contents of any pointer can be modified at any

---

[1] NOTE: The operational clause in statement 31 must have a non-blank field for either the result variable or the operator since the C and D operands are NOT non-zero or blank, e.g., without the = the clause is ignored and V100 is never set to 0.

time using arithmetic operations and referring to it by ordinary variable references to it. It can be subjected to relational tests. In fact, the only difference between a pointer and a regular variable is what happens when the pointer
variable is used as an indirect reference in an operand. When this occurs, the
pointer is used simply to find out which <u>other</u> variable is to be used as the oper-
and.

The difference between direct and indirect references to variables using
pointers is best elucidated by giving an example.

```
01      V0051 = 111
02      V0016 ADD P0051      V0015
```

In instruction 01 the constant 111 is placed in variable 0051. A direct reference
is made to V0051 to put it there. In statement 02, an indirect reference is made
to variable 0051. It is used as a pointer, as indicated by the reference P0051.
The pointer points to variable 111. Thus, instruction 02 really reads "add the
contents of that variable whose number is contained in V0051 to the contents of
V0015 and put the result into V0016." But V0051 already contains the number 111
because of instruction 01. Thus instruction 02 is interpreted as though it actually read

```
02      V0016 ADD V0111      V0015
```

Thus, variable 111 is added to variable V0015 and the results placed in variable
V0016.

If we had the set of instructions shown in Figure A2.2, we could obtain the
sum of those variables in the sequence V0011, V0012, V0013,..., V0030, V0031 which
did not have the value 9. The results would be placed in V0044. For instance,
one might want to build an index adding the code values for a number of different
variables except where they are 9 (for not ascertained).

Instructions 1, 2 and 3 establish the initial conditions desired, i.e., the
new variable to be generated (V0044) is set to zero and the pointer is set to the
first of the sequence of variables to be added, V0011. Then control is passed to
instruction 6. This instruction adds the variable "pointed to" to the partial sum
being developed in V0044 and puts the results back in V0044. However, the operation is performed only if the variable "pointed to" does not have 9 as its
value. (Let 9 be the "missing-data-code" for each of this series of variables
V0011-V0031.)

If the value of the variable currently being pointed to is not equal to
9, its contents are added to V0044. But if its value is equal to 9, the

Figure A2.2

MULTIVARIATE RECODING FORM

Sum Variables 11 to 33

Coder: _____

Date: _____

Job: _____

Data: _____

STATE-MENT NO.	LOG. TAG	TEST VAR. NO.	REL. OPER.	A OPERAND	B OPERAND	RESULT VAR. NO.	CONTROL OPER.	C OPERAND	D OPERAND	COMMENT
□xxxx (5)	□ xxxx (10)	xxxxx (15)	□ xxxx (20)	V Pxxxxxxxxx (40)	V Pxxxxxxxxx (30)	V Pxxxx (45)	□ xxxx (50)	V Pxxxxxxxxx (60)	V Pxxxxxxxxx (70)	□xxxxxxxxx (80)
1						V0044	=	0		Set
2						V0101	=	11		initial
3							GOTO	6		values
4						V0101	ADD	V0101	1	Increment
5	IF	V0101	GT	31			GØTØ	9		and test
6	IF	P0101	NE	9		V0044	ADD	V0044	P0101	Perform
7	ALT						NØØP			task
8	T						GOTO	4		
9				next instruction						

addition does not take place and the alternative (instruction 7) is executed instead. This results in nothing being added to V0044 from the current variable being pointed to. Then, after one of these two paths has been taken, instruction 8 sends control back to instruction 4.

The purpose of instructions 4 and 5 is to increment the integer in the pointer by 1 and then to check it to determine if the value of the integer in the pointer has now exceeded the subscript of the last variable we wished to add. Then either an exit takes place to the remainder of the work to be done (statement 9) or the next variable pointed to is checked and, if appropriate, is added and the loop repeats once more. In instruction 4 the constant 1 is added to the number in the pointer. (This started at 11 and thus eventually will take on as its value in turn all the integers between 11 and 32 inclusively.) Its value at the time statement 9 is executed is 32. Note that when the number in the pointer is larger than 31 we have completed our task. At this point, the relational expression in instruction 5 will be true and the operational clause will be executed, taking control to statement 9 in computational mode.

On the other hand, if the integer in the pointer is equal to or less than 31 this expression will be false; consequently, the operational clause will not be executed and control will pass in logical mode to statement 6. Statement 6 starts with an Initial Clause so logical mode is re-entered and the truth switch acquires a value based only on statement 6. If it is true, the operational part of statement 6 will be executed and computational mode will be assumed. This will prevent the ALT tag in statement 7 from being executed, since ALT heads a Subsequent Clause. Since the program is in logical mode, the operational part of statement 7 also is not executed. However, statement 8 contains an Assignment; hence the truth switch is set to T and the operational part of the statement is executed, sending control to statement 4 via the GOTO.

In the case where the test for a value of 9 is met, computational mode will be entered at statement 6 and the operational part of statement 6 executed. The occurrence of a logical clause in statement 7 causes a return to logical mode, but the tag is a Subsequent Clause and is ignored as above. The truth switch remains undefined until statement 8.

Eventually the value of the pointer variable reaches 32; but we do not wish to add V0032 to V0044. However, the relational expression in statement 5 would be true when the pointer reached 32. This would cause control to be transferred out of the loop upon execution of the operational part of instruction 5. On the other hand, if we had not yet finished our task, this relational expression would still be false and the operational part of instruction 5 would not be executed. Consequently, control would pass to instruction 6, which is what we desire since this would process the next variable in its turn.

This procedure would examine each variable in turn, adding it to V0044 if its value were not 9. Then, when variables V0011 through V0031 inclusively had been inspected (and added where appropriate) the pointer, V0101, would have the value 32 and control would pass to statement 9.

It can be seen from the above example that the benefits to be derived from using pointers are associated with repetitive operations that would take a great many instructions if written out once for each case. These benefits increase with the size of the block of "work" instructions that are to be applied repetitively.

A second example illustrates another kind of use of the pointer variable. (See Figure A2.3.) Here, a complex bracket code is applied both to variable 0061 and to Variable 0062, replacing each with the appropriate bracketed value. The reader is encouraged to proceed through the example in some detail, following out alternative paths that follow from different values of V0016 and V0062.

D. Operators

All "a" and "b" operands are assumed to be in integer mode, as well as the test variable, Vn.

(1) Relational Operators: IN, OUT, NE, EQ, LE, GE, LT, GT

Vn	IN	a	b	True if Vn lies <u>inside</u> the closed interval where "a" is the lower bound and "b" is the upper bound. The lower bound must always be placed as the "a" operand.
Vn	OUT	a	b	True if Vn lies <u>outside</u> the closed interval, where "a" is the lower bound and "b" is the upper bound. The lower bound must always be placed as the "a" operand.
Vn	NE	a		True if Vn is <u>not equal</u> to "a" algebraically.
Vn	EQ	a		True if Vn is <u>equal</u> to "a" algebraically. (Note that EQ Is used here; = for arithmetic operation)
Vn	LE	a		True if Vn is <u>less than or equal to</u> "a" algebraically (e.g., −6 is less than −5).
Vn	GE	a		True if Vn is <u>greater than or equal to</u> "a" algebraically (e.g., −1 is greater than −2).
Vn	LT	a		True if Vn is <u>less than</u> "a".
Vn	GT	a		True if Vn is <u>greater than</u> "a".

Figure A2.3

MULTIVARIATE RECODING FORM

Applying a Bracket Code to Two Variables Using Pointers

Coder: _____   Job: _____

Date: _____   Data: _____

STATE-MENT NO. (5)	LOG. TAG (10)	TEST VAR. NO. (15)	REL. OPER. (20)	A OPERAND (30)	B OPERAND (40)	RESULT VAR. NO. (45)	CONTROL OPER. (50)	C OPERAND (60)	D OPERAND (70)	COMMENT (80)
□xxxx	□xxxx	xxxxx	□xxxx	VPxxxxxxxxx	VPxxxxxxxxx	VPxxxx	□xxxx	VPxxxxxxxxx	VPxxxxxxxxx	□xxxxxxxx
1						V0201	=	61		
2						V0202	=	901		
3							GOTO	9001		
901						V0201	=	62		
4						V0202	=	902		
5							GOTO	9001		
902					next instruction					
					procedure to be applied					
9001	IF	P0201	LE	2499		P0201	=	1		
	OR		IN	2500	4999			2		
				5000	7499			3		
				7500	9999			4		
				10000	14999			5		
				15000	999998			6		
								9		
9002	ALT						GOTO	V0202		
9003	T									

103

(2) Arithmetic Operations: =, SET, ZAD, ZSB, ABS, ADD, SUB, MPY, DIV, MOD

All operands and results are assumed to be in integer mode. Note that the relational operator for equals is "EQ" but the arithmetical operator is "=". The first is a logical test, the second is an instruction that a variable assume a certain value.

Vn	=	c		
Vn	SET	c		The contents of "c" are placed in Vn. Note "=" is used, not "EQ".
Vn	ZAD	c		

Vn	ZSB	c		The contents of "c" are placed in Vn and the sign is is reversed (plus becomes minus, and vice versa).
Vn	ABS	c		The contents of "c" are placed in Vn and the sign of Vn is set to +.
Vn	ADD	c	d	The contents of "c" and "d" are added together algebraically and the result is placed in Vn. The largest result is 2^{31}. Overflows will not be detected.
Vn	MOD	c	d	This is a modulo operator. The contents of "c" are divided by the contents of "d" using truncated integer division (without rounding). The remainder is placed in Vn. The quotient is lost. The sign of the number placed in Vn is the same as the sign of the c/d quotient.
Vn	SUB	c	d	The contents of d is subtracted from c algebraically and the result stored in Vn.
Vn	MPY	c	d	The contents of c are multipled by the contents of d algebraically and the results are placed in Vn. Ordinary rules apply as far as the sign of the result. Overflows will not be detected.
Vn	DIV	c	d	The contents of c are divided by the contents of d using integer division. The integer part of the result is placed in Vn. The remainder is lost. There is no rounding; rather, truncation takes place. The sign of the resultant is according to regular algebraic conventions. If the result is between zero and 1 in absolute value, then Vn will have the value zero.

The acceptable range of integers is 2^{31} to -2^{31} and customary rules apply to all signs; e.g., -10 multiplied by -2 = +20.

(3) Functions: NRAN, FRAN, LOGT, LOGE, SQRT, ASIN

Arguments are assumed to be integer in mode. Results will appear as integers with the appropriate number of implied decimal places as indicated by the d operand.

Vn NRAN c d   A normally distributed random number with mean 0 and variance 1 will be stored in Vn with d implied decimal places. If c is not equal to zero or blank, then Vn will always be in the range $-c \leq r \leq + c$. All generated numbers outside this range will be rejected and another number generated until one meets the requirements; this is then stored in Vn. On the other hand, when c = 0, then the first number generated will be used. Numbers will be rounded to d implied decimals.[1]

Vn FRAN c d   A random number from a flat distribution in the range $0 \leq r \leq c$, and having d implied decimals will be stored in Vn. Numbers will be rounded to d implied decimals.[1]

Vn LOGT c d   The logarithm to the base 10 of c is stored in Vn. The number located at c is assumed to have d decimals. The logarithm stored in Vn always has three implied decimal places. If $c \leq 0$, Vn = 0.

Vn LOGE c d   The natural logarithm of c is stored in Vn. The number in c is assumed to have d decimal places. The result stored in Vn always has three implied decimal places. When $c \leq 0$, then Vn = 0.

Vn SQRT c d   The square root of the number stored in c is stored in Vn. This number stored in c is assumed to have d implied decimal places. The result stored in Vn will have d implied decimal places. If $c \leq 0$, Vn = 0.

Vn ASIN c d   The arcsin of c is stored in Vn. The number in c is assumed to have d decimal places. The result stored in Vn always has three implied decimal places. The function applies to all values of c such that $-1 \leq c \leq 1$. For all other cases Vn = 0.

---

[1]The pseudo-random number generation used is due to Hastings (1955). The methods were programmed and tested by Messenger (1970). A flat random distribution is generated by a non-overflow modulo type of algorithm using a call to the clock to obtain a starter number. A transformation is applied to produce a normal distribution. The cycle length is greater than 10,000 (cycle length is the number of random numbers generated when the first exact duplication occurs). Other tests of randomness have been examined (Messenger, 1970) and show satisfactory results, including Chi-square tests of fit to uniform (0,1) at the .05 level based on 10,000 observations, no statistically significant serial correlations in tests varying lags from 1 to 16, and 95% confidence intervals of the sample mean and standard deviation allowing acceptance of the null hypothesis that the sample was drawn from a uniform (0,1). About 350 random numbers/sec are drawn on a 360/40.

(4) Control Operators: GOTO, EXIT, NOOP, PRNT

GOTO c   Control is transferred to the statement number whose integer identifier is referred to by the c operand. Statement numbers are positive integers in the range $1 < c < 9999$. The truth switch is not affected (its value is "on" at this time anyway). If there is no such statement number control will pass to the next sequential instruction.

EXIT   Control is returned to the calling program in which the recoding statements are imbedded. No further recode statements will be executed. An EXIT statement is generated automatically when an END statement is encountered.

NOOP   No operation. Used as a "landing field."

PRNT Vn Vm   Causes variables n and m to be printed. The latter, Vm, may be omitted.

(5) Pseudo Operators: END

END   This operator is used to mark the physical end of the recoding statements, indicating that no more follow, even on the same physical IBM card. Its appearance causes transfer of control to the calling program, since all recoding statements have been read and processed. During execution of the recoding, an END statement will be treated like an EXIT.

All of the operators, operands, tags, comments and statement labels are illustrated and listed in Figure A2.4.

Figure A2.4

MULTIVARIATE RECODING FORM

Summary of Recoding Instructions

Coder: _____

Date: _____

Job: _____

Data: _____

STATE-MENT NO.	LOG. TAG	TEST VAR. NO.	REL. OPER.	A OPERAND	B OPERAND	RESULT VAR. NO.	CONTROL OPER.	C OPERAND	D OPERAND	COMMENT
5	10	15	20	30	40	45	50	60	70	80
□xxxx	□xxxx	xxxxx	□xxxx	V Pxxxxxxxxx	V Pxxxxxxxxx	V Pxxxx	□ xxxx	V Pxxxxxxxxx	V Pxxxxxxxxx	□ xxxxxxxx
0001	T	Vxxxxx	IN	Vxxxxx	Vxxxxx	Vxxxx	=	Vxxxx	Vxxxx	COMMENTS
9999	AND	Pxxxxx	ØUT	Pxxxxx	Pxxxxx	Pxxxx	ZAD	Pxxxx	Pxxxx	
	NIMP		NE	xxxxxxxx	xxxxxxxx		SET	xxxxxxxx	xxxxxxxx	
	ALSØ	V0001	EQ	-9999999	-9999999	V0001	ZSB	-9999999	-9999999	
	BIF	V0300	LE	99999999	99999999	V0300	ABS	99999999	99999999	
	IF		GE				ADD			
	EXØR	P0001	LT	V0001	V0001	V0001	SUB	V0001	V0001	
	ØR	P0300	GT	V0300	V0300	P0300	MPY	V0300	V0300	
	NØR		EXIT	P0001	P0001		DIV	P0001	P0001	
	CØNS		END	P0300	P0300		MØD	P0300	P0300	
	NIF						NRAN			
	NBIF						FRAN			
	ALT						LØGT			
	IMP						LØGE			
	NAND						SQRT			
	F						ASOM			
	END						GØTØ			
							NØØP			
							EXIT			
							PRNT			
							END			

Appendix III
Set-up Instructions

A. General Description

AID3 is a generalized data analysis program which uses analysis of variance techniques to explain as much of the variance of a given dependent variable as possible.

The AID3 search algorithm makes successive dichotomous partitions on the sample, using independent variables to "predict" the dependent variable, in such a way as to maximize differences among the split groups.

The algorithm may be set

(1)   to maximize differences in group means, slopes, or regression lines;

(2)   to examine the explanatory power of 1, 2, or 3 successive splits before selecting the "best" split;

(3)   to rank the predictors, weighting them as to preference in the partitioning;

(4)   to sacrifice explanatory power for symmetry;

(5)   to start after a specified partial tree structure has been generated;

(6)   to run in successive stages, e.g., redefining predictors, or creating and then pooling residuals in a 2nd stage analysis.

B. Input

1. Data file

2. Dictionary file (optional)

3. Control cards

C. Output

1. Initial printout

(a) statistics for the sample

110

        (b)   analysis of variance on predictor configuration (optional)

   2. Trace printout (split statistics)

        (a)   all splits for each predictor

        (b)   best split for each predictor

   3. Final tables

        (a)   analysis of variance on final groups

        (b)   group summary (optional)

        (c)   BSS/TSS with lookahead (optional)

        (d)   BSS/TSS no lookahead (optional)

        (e)   BSS/TSS regardless of eligibility (optional)

        (f)   profile of class means/slopes (optional)

        (g)   predictor summary (optional)

   4. Output residual file (with optional dictionary)

D. Restrictions

   1. Maximum number of predictors: $NP \leq 63$

   2. Largest valid class value for a predictor: 31

   3. Sum of largest class values for all predictors: 400-NP

   4. Maximum number of partitions: 89

   5. Maximum number of variables: 300

   6. R-type variables (see OSIRIS Recode) should not have the same variable number as V-type variables if an output dictionary is requested.

E. Missing Data Treatment

   1. Missing data on the dependent variable may be excluded.

   2. Missing data defined in the input dictionary is passed on to the output dictionary.

   3. Missing data is generated for the residual and predicted value as a field of 9's.

   4. Missing data is generated for the group number as '000'.

   5. Missing data may be excluded on the predictors by specifying maximum class values less than missing data values.

F. Setup Summary

   JOB cards

   // EXEC ISRSYS

   //FT07F001 DD parameters describing input data file
               (omit if using an OSIRIS dictionary)

   //FT08F001 DD parameters describing output data file
               (omit if not generating a FORMATTED residual file)

```
//DICTx     DD  parameters describing input dictionary
                (omit if on cards or if a FORMATTED data file)

//DATAx     DD  parameters describing input data file
                (omit if on cards or if a FORMATTED data file)

//DICTy     DD  parameters describing output dictionary
                (omit if residual file not created or a FORMATTED output
                file)

//DATAy     DD  parameters describing output data file
                (omit if residual file not created or a FORMATTED output
                file)

//SETUP     DD  *

$RUN   AID3

$RECODE card          )
   Recode statements   }    optional (may be used only with OSIRIS
                      )                  data files)

$SETUP card
```

   1. Global filter card (optional - only used with OSIRIS data files)

   2. Label card

   3. Global parameter card

   4. Format cards (optional)

   5. Input variable list card

   6. Local filter card (optional)

   7. Local label card

   8. I/O parameter card

   9. AID3 internal recode cards (optional)

 10. Predictor cards

 11. Control parameter card   Analysis Step

 12. Predefined split cards (optional)

(5-12 = Analysis Packet)

```
$ DICT        )
   dictionary }    If dictionary on cards

$ DATA        )
   data       }    If data on cards

/*
```

G. Description of Control Cards - defaults are underlined.

1. Global Filter (optional): See OSIRIS User's Manual
   For use with OSIRIS data files only

2. Global card: 1-80 columns used as a heading

3. Global parameter card:

   INFILE=IN/xxxx

   For OSIRIS data files only. Up to 4 characters used as the input ddname suffix

   PRINT=DICT/NODICT

   For OSIRIS data files only. Option to print or suppress printing of the input dictionary file

   BADDATA=TERM/MD1/MD2/SKIP

   For OSIRIS data files only. When non-numeric characters (including embedded blanks and all blank fields) are found in numeric variables:

   TERM: Terminate the run

   a message indicates
   the number of cases
   so treated

   MD1: Convert the value to the 1st missing data code and fields of &'s and -'s to nines + 1 or 2 respectively

   MD2: Convert the value to the 2nd missing data code and fields of &'s and -'s to nines + 1 or 2 respectively

   SKIP: Skip the case

   FORMAT=0/n

   For FORMATTED data files only. The number ($1 < n < 3$) of Format cards needed to describe the input data file FT07F001

4. FORMAT cards: If FORMAT=n, n>0, was specified on the global parameter card, n cards of format information. This should include all input fields, and if a formatted output file is requested the input descriptors should be followed by output fields for all generated variables (see section H for the order in which variables are generated), i.e., AID3 recoded, residual, predicted value, and group number variables. Each item constitutes one variable. Variables are read in the order listed on the variable list card, e.g., if the format is (I6,2I5,I4) and the variable list is V10, V6, V20, V1 * then the first format (I6) is for variable 10, the second (I5) is for variable 6 etc.

5. Input Variable List card: a list of all variables from the input data file plus OSIRIS recode variables (R-type) to be used in the run. (See OSIRIS User's Manual).

ANALYSIS PACKET

6. Local Filter (optional): See OSIRIS User's Manual

7. Local Label

8. I/O Parameter card:

YVAR=(n,m)	n=dependent variable number, no default m=scale factor. The y-values are multi-plied by 10 to the scale factor, i.e., 10^m default: 0.
NOWEIGHT/WEIGHT=n	Weight variable number (optional).
ANALYSIS=MEANS/SLOPES/REGRESSION	
	Type of analysis to be used
XVAR=(n,m)	n=covariate number, no default if a SLOPES or REGRESSION analysis is specified m=scale factor, default: 0.
SUBSEL=n	Subset selector variable number (optional). If a subset selector variable is given, all zero values of this variable are fil-tered from the analysis.
MDOPTION=BOTH/MD1/MD2/NONE (optional)	
	Missing data option: (See OSIRIS User's Manual)
	NONE: Ignore missing data.
	MD1: Eliminate cases with missing data 1 values for the dependent variable (Y=MD1).
	MD2: Eliminate cases with missing data 2 values for the dependent variable Y>MD2 , MD2>0 Y<MD2 , MD2<0.
	BOTH: Eliminate cases with MD1 or MD2 val-ues for the dependent variable.
NORECODE/RECODE	Internal AID3 recoding option. If RECODE is specified, then internal recode cards must be supplied (See 9. below).
OUTLIERS=INCLUDE/EXCLUDE	Option to include or exclude outliers from the analysis. An outlier is defined by the OUTDIST parameter.
OUTDIST=5./n	Number of standard deviations from the par-ent group mean defining an outlier (punch decimals).
IDVAR=n	Variable number for the identification var-iable printed with each case flagged as an outlier.
NOCONF/CONF	Analysis of variance on predictor configur-ation option.
TABLES=(BASIC/NONE,NOBSS/BSS,NOEL/ELIG,NOPR/PRED,NOME/MEANS)	
	Final tables options
	BASIC: Print Group Summary and BSS/TSS with lookahead tables.
	BSS: Print BASIC tables plus BSS/TSS with no lookahead.

	ELIG: Print BASIC tables plus BSS/TSS of maximum split regardless of eligibility.
	PRED: Print BASIC tables plus predictor summary.
	MEANS: Print BASIC tables plus class means/ slopes profile.
RESID=(n,m,w)	Omit if residuals are nót to be generated. n=residual variable number, no default. m=residual scale factor, no default. w=residual filed width, needed for OSIRIS output files only, no default. This should include a space for a sign character (+,-).

The following parameters are ignored if the residuals option is not specified:

RESNAME='name'	1-24 character name for the residual. Default: 'AID3 RESIDUAL'.
CALC=(n,m,w)	Omit if the predicted value is not to be generated. n=predicted value variable number m=predicted value scale factor w=predicted value field width, needed for OSIRIS output files only.
CALNAME='name'	1-24 character name for the predicted value. Default: 'PREDICTED VALUE'.
GROUP=n	n=variable number for the final group to which each case belongs. Omit if not to be generated.
GRONAME='name'	1-24 character name for the group numbers. Default: 'GROUP NUMBER'.
NOFILE/FILE	Option to generate an output file. The current data set which is stored on a scratch data file is updated within the program enabling the user to use residuals in a multi-stage analysis even if NOFILE is specified.
OUTFILE=OUT/ xxxx/FORM	For OSIRIS output data files, 1-4 characters used as the output ddname suffix (see section I). For Formatted output files: specify 'FORM'. FORM=n, n>0 must have been specified on the global parameter card. The same format is used for the output file as for the input file (see 4. FORMAT cards and section H). The output file is generated onto unit FT08F001.
NOSTAN/STANDARD	Option to standardize residuals. If STANDARD is specified residuals will be divided by the standard deviation of the final group to which they belong.

9. AID3 RECODE cards: RECODE must be specified on the I/O parameter card (8). The RECODE option is turned off after the INPUT mode is completed. See Appendix II for RECODE specifications.

ANALYSIS STEP

10. Predictor cards:

PRED=$(p_1,p_2,...)$ List of predictor variable numbers (up to 63) carrying the characteristics specified below.

PRENAME='name'   1-24 character name used for all predictors listed. Default: input dictionary name.

M/F   Monotonic or Free characteristic
M: do not sort on predictor class means/ slopes before executing the algorithm
F: sort on class means/slopes

MAXCLASS=9/n   Maximum class value allowed for the predictors. Values greater than the specified maximum are eliminated from the analysis.

RANK=1/n   Predictor rank, $0 \leq n \leq 9$.

END   Must be specified on the last predictor card.

11. Control Parameter Card

LOOKAHEAD=(n,m)   n=the number of lookahead steps (0-2)
 =the number of splits - 1.
m=the number of permuted steps.
 If n is non-zero, m must be greater than zero. Default (0,0).

REDUCIBILITY=(for parent group; for 1st lookahead step; for 2nd lookahead step)

Reducibility criteria for each step in the lookahead expressed as a percentage e.g., .8%=.008. Default (.8;na,na) (Punch decimals).

MIN=25/n   Minimum allowable number of cases in a group. If a SLOPES or REGRESSION analysis is specified then n must be at least 3. Otherwise, for mean analyses $n \geq 1$.

MAX=25/n   Maximum number of partitions. $1 \leq n \leq 89$.

SYMMETRY=0/n   Percentage premium for symmetry option. (Punch decimals e.g., 60.%=.60).

RANK=NORANK/ALL/UP/AT/DOWN

Predictor ranking option
NORANK: no ranking - predictor ranks are ignored
ALL: simple ranking

UP: range ranking with a preference for predictors with high ranks, i.e., towards 1.

AT: range ranking with a preference for predictors with a rank "at" the current rank.

DOWN: range ranking with a preference for low ranked predictors, i.e., towards 9.

RANGE=(nup;ndown;lup;ldown)

for range ranking only

eligible range =   nup: number of ranks "UP" for
[a−NUP,a+NDOWN]   actual splitting
                   ndown: number of ranks "DOWN" for actual splitting

lookahead range =   lup: number of ranks "UP" for
[a−LUP,a+LDOWN]   the lookahead$\geq$nup
                   ldown: number of ranks "DOWN" for the lookahead$\geq$ndown

where a is the current rank at which the algorithm is operating.

TREE=0/n   Number of pre-specified splits to be made (see predefined splits cards, 12. below).

TRACE=ELIG/NOTR/BEST/BSS/MIN/ALL

Print trace option
ELIG: print only eligible splits
NOTR: suppress all printing
BEST: print only the best split for each predictor
BSS: print "ELIG" + splits which do not meet the reducibility criterion, i.e., BSS too small
MIN: print "ELIG" + splits with a resultant group with too few cases
ALL: print the entire trace

COMPUTE/NOCOMP   Command to execute the COMPUTE mode: generate any predefined splits if TREE=n,n>0; execute the splitting algorithm under current parameters, and if RESID is specified, generating residuals for those groups which cannot be split.

OUTPUT/NOOUT   Command to execute the OUTPUT mode: generate residuals for any remaining final groups; write final Tables.

12. Predefined split cards: TREE=n,n>0, must be specified on the control parameter card. The TREE option is turned off after the splits are made. For each split one card:

PARENT=n   Number of the group to be split.

CHILD=n   Number of the first resultant group. (Even number, the second group will be numbered n+1.)

VARIABLE=n   Variable number for the predictor used to
                          make the split.

CLASS=$(c_1,c_2,...)$ List of predictor classes to be put into
                          the first resultant group. Remaining
                          classes go to the second child.

13. If the NOOUTPUT command appears on the control parameter card (11)
     the analysis step is repeated (predictor cards, etc.). Parameters
     default to the previously defined values with the exception of the
     COMPUTE and OUTPUT commands. Predictor cards need only be included
     for those predictors being redefined. New predictors may not be de-
     fined. Also, the maximum class value may not be altered.

     If the OUTPUT command was specified, then the next analysis packet
     is executed (local filter, etc.). Parameters take on the original
     defaults.

H. Generated Variables on 'Formatted' Output Files

Generated variables are added to the input variable list in the following
order.[1]

Variable	Relevant Keyword
1. Dependent variable	YVAR
2. Weight variable	WEIGHT
3. Covariate	XVAR
4. Subset selector variable	SUBSET
5. Identification variable	IDVAR
6. Residual	RESID
7. Predicted value	CALC
8. Group number variable	GROUP
9. Recode variables, in the order in which they appear in AID3 internal RECODE stream	(RECODE)
10. Predictors, in the order they appear	PRED

Note: Only those variable numbers not listed on the input variable list are added, and they follow the input variables. For example if the variables are

Variable	Number
Y	20
predictors	2-5,12
residual	10
other input	1,6-9

[1]This information is necessary when generating a formatted output file so
that the output field descriptors are in the correct order on the FORMAT cards.

and the variable list card is V1-V9* then the output variable list order is V1-V9, V20,V10,V12*.

I.   OSIRIS Residual Files[1]

If OUTFILE=OUT is specified on the I/O parameter card, then an OSIRIS type 3 dictionary is generated with the following specifications:[2]

Variable	Field Width[3]	Number of Decimals	Missing Data	Name
Y,X	7	p	9...9	s
Predictors	2	0	-	p/s
Residual	p	p	9...9	p/'AID3 RESIDUAL'
Predicted Value	p	p	9...9	p/'PREDICTED VALUE'
Group Number	3	-	000	p/'GROUP NUMBER'
Other input variables	s	s	s	s
AID3 Internal Recode generated variables	2	0	-	AID VARIABLE NUMBER x

OSIRIS recode variables (R-type) may not have the same variable number as V-type variables if an OSIRIS residual file is generated. R-type variables become V-type variables on the output data file (i.e., R-type variables are designated by negative numbers, e.g., R10=-10, the absolute value is taken as the variable number for the output dictionary).

---

[1] See the OSIRIS User's Manual for a complete description of dictionary files.

[2] s denotes a specification in the input dictionary, if any; p denotes a parameter specification.

[3] Field widths may be overridden by specifying a variable number v, 9100<v< 9999. The hundredths digit of v is the field width. For example, variable 9476 has a field width of 4.

Appendix IV
Program Documentation

AID3 was written for an IBM 360/40 computer. AID includes 30 FORTRAN IV subprograms, OSIRIS subroutines written in FORTRAN IV and assembly language, and an overlay structure (see Diagram 1). The size of the program after linking with the overlay is 85,000 bytes, and the core requirement is 104K. It uses five scratch files all written without format control. Parameter and variable information are stored in labelled common blocks.

A. Program Structure

The program flow is controlled by the main program (ZAID3). After calling an initialization program to read and check parameter cards, read the dictionary, and initialize the input and output data and scratch files, the main program determines in which mode the program should be operating (input, compute, or output) and calls the appropriate subroutines. The input mode is executed automatically after the initialization stage and again after completion of each output phase. Compute and output commands from the user control the other two modes.

1. Initialization: The input and output units are defined; the input dictionary or format is read; if specified, an output dictionary is generated; all parameter cards are read and checked for errors. Execution is terminated if any errors occur.

2. Input: The input and output parameters are defined; the data set is read, recoded, and stored; non-valid data is eliminated for the current analysis packet and outputted onto the residual file if requested; sample statistics are generated and printed, including the optional 1-way analysis of variance on the predictor configuration.

3. Compute: Computation parameters are defined; any splits defined for the starting tree option are made; the lookahead algorithm is initiated and operates under the given parameters--symmetry takes precedence over

120

ranking which in turn takes precedence over the lookahead; any group which cannot be split is deemed a final group and if specified is outputted onto the residual file. When the splitting process terminates, if the output mode is _not_ specified, the program redefines computation parameters and continues the splitting process from where it stopped under the new parameters.

4. Output: Any remaining unsplit group becomes a final group and, if specified, is outputted onto the residual file; final tables are generated, including the analysis of variance on final groups.

Diagram 2 gives the overall structure of the program.

B. Program Storage

AID3 uses five temporary scratch files. Three are direct access files (ISR01, ISR02, FT05F001), and two are sequential (FT03F001, FT04F001).

1. AUNIT (ISR01): a direct access file (written and read with the OSIRIS subroutine DIRECT) used to store the input data matrix, one observation per record. Two additional records are written, following the data matrix, containing the missing data codes. If NV denotes the total number of variables referenced by the program, then the record length is 4(NV+7) bytes $\leq$ 1228. Chart 1 shows the storage needed.

2. BUNIT (ISR02): a direct access file (written and read with DIRECT) used to store information for each group: a list of the record numbers in AUNIT containing the observations in the group; group totals; and class totals for each predictor. The record length is 896 bytes. Chart 2 shows the storage needed for each group.

3. CUNIT (05): a direct access file (FORTRAN IV DEFINE FILE) used for the lookahead process and final tables. The maximum number of records used is 200, and the maximum record length is 224 words. The file is created with the statement

    DEFINE FILE 5(200,224,U,IC) .

4. NSCR (03): an unformatted sequential file used to store information for each group on which a split attempt has been made. There are up to nine records per group, with a maximum record length of 126 words.

5. NSETUP (04): an unformatted sequential file used to store the input parameters (local filter and label, I/O parameters, internal recode statements, predictor information, and computation parameters).

The input and output units necessary to run AID3 are given below.

Unit	Function
FT01F001	control card input
FT03F001	NSCR
FT04F001	NSETUP
FT05F001	CUNIT

FT06F001	printer	
FT07F001	formatted input data file	omit if using
FT08F001	formatted output data file	OSIRIS data files
ISR01	AUNIT	
ISR02	BUNIT	
DICTIN	input dictionary	
DATAIN	input data file	omit if using
DICTOUT	output dictionary	formatted data files
DATAOUT	output data file	

C. Execution without OSIRIS

The AID3 subprograms are written in FORTRAN IV level G, however they use OSIRIS subroutines[1] some of which are written in IBM assembler, in particular the OSIRIS input and output, filter, and recode routines.

With the exception of the OSIRIS program DIRECT which reads and writes the direct access scratch files ISR01 and ISR02, the code using the OSIRIS options may be deleted from the program and a comparable feature will still be available. For example,

OSIRIS	AID3
OSIRIS data sets	Formatted data sets
Multivariate Recode	Internal Recode
Global/local filter	Subset selector
or missing data	filter

Running the program without OSIRIS will, however, be less efficient.

The subroutine DIRECT can be replaced with FORTRAN IV DEFINE FILES. This is tedious, since DIRECT is used throughout the program, i.e., during all modes, input, compute, and output.

Table A4.1 gives a list of all the AID3, OSIRIS, and IBM programs called by each of the AID3 subroutines. Also included are the labelled common areas used by each AID3 subroutine.

---

[1]See the OSIRIS Subroutine Manual

122

Diagram 1

Overlay Structure

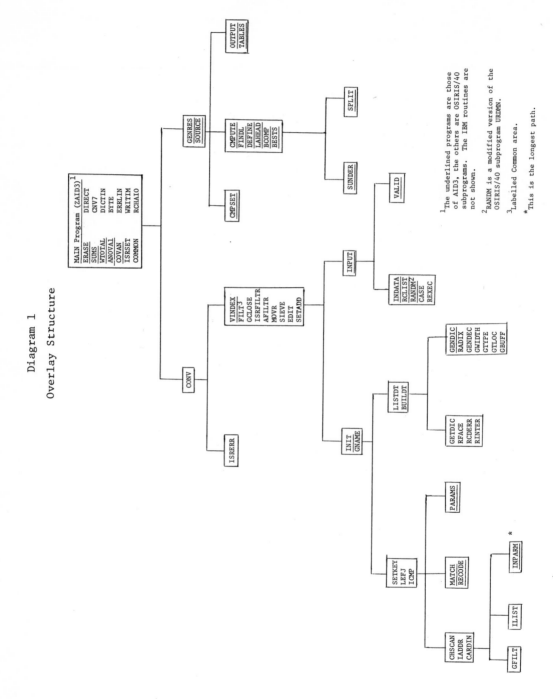

^{1}The underlined programs are those of AID3, the others are OSIRIS/40 subprograms. The IBM routines are not shown.

^{2}RANDM is a modified version of the OSIRIS/40 subprogram URDMN.

^{3}Labelled Common area.

*This is the longest path.

Diagram II

AID3 Program Structure

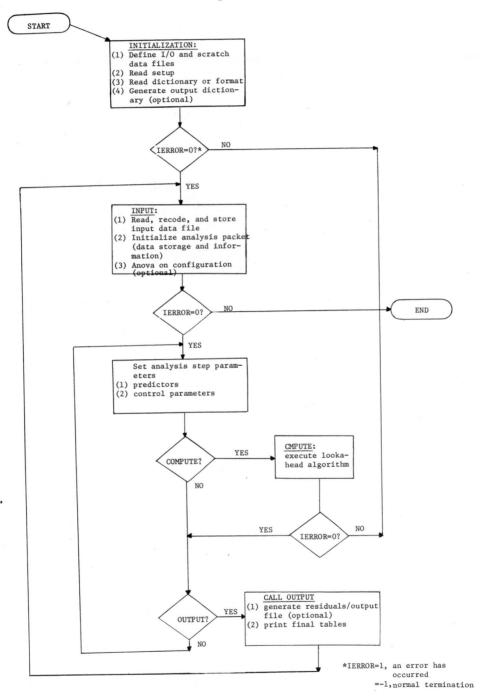

TABLE A4.1 AID3 SUBPROGRAMS REFERENCING TABLE

MAIN (ZAID3)	AID3	OSIRIS	FORTRAN	LABELLED COMMON
MAIN (ZAID3)	INIT, INPUT, CMPSET, CMPUTE, OUTPUT	ISRSET*	DIOCS#, IBCOM#	LABELS, DSTORE, OPTION, PREDS, SPLITC, ELIGC, SYMTRY, RANKC
ERASE	—	—	—	
SUMS	—	—	—	PREDS
WTOTAL	—,	DIRECT*	—	DSTORE, PREDS
ANOVA1	COVAN		IBCOM#	DSTORE, OPTION, PREDS, GROUPS, SPLITC, FACTOR
COVAN	—		IBCOM#	OPTION, FACTOR
VINDEX			—	VLIST
INIT	INPARM, RECODE, PARAMS, GENDIC	GFILT*, ILLIST, SETKEY, GETDIC*	IBCOM#	LABELS, VLIST, DSTORE, OPTION, ELIGC, DEPEND, YREAD, FILT
INPARM	ERASE, VINDEX	LEFJ*, ISRFILTR*, SETKEY, GNAME*	IBCOM#, FRXPI#, FIXPI#, MINO	LABELS, VLIST, DSTORE, OPTION, PREDS, SPLITC, ELIGC, SYMTRY, RANKC, DEPEND, YREAD, FILT
RECODE	VINDEX, MATCH		IBCOM#	OPTION, RECORD
MATCH				
PARAMS	VINDEX	SETKEY, GNAME*	IBCOM#	LABELS, VLIST, DSTORE, OPTION, PREDS, SPLITC, ELIGC, SYMTRY, RANKC, DEPEND, YREAD
GENDIC		GNAME*, GWIDTH*, GNDEC*, RCHAIO*, RADIX*, CNV7*, LISTDT, MOVE*	IBCOM#, FIXPI#, ALOG10	LABELS, VLIST, OPTION, PREDS, DEPEND, YREAD, FILT
INPUT	ERASE, ANOVA1, INDATA, VALID	SETADD*	IBCOM#	LABELS, VLIST, DSTORE, OPTION, PREDS, GROUPS, SPLITC, SYMTRY, RANKC, DEPEND, YREAD, FILT, FACTOR
INDATA	ERASE, RCLIST	DIRECT*, CASE*, GCLOSE*	IBCOM#, SQRT	LABELS, VLIST, DSTORE, OPTION, PREDS, GROUPS, SPLITC, DEPEND, YREAD
RCLIST	VINDEX, RANDM		ALOG, ALOG10, ARSIN IBCOM#, FRXPI#, SQRT	VLIST, OPTION, RECORD
VALID	ERASE, SUMS, WTOTAL	DIRECT*, SIEVE*, CNV7*, RCHAIO*	IBCOM#	VLIST, DSTORE, OPTION, PREDS, GROUPS, SPLITC, DEPEND, YREAD, FILT, FACTOR
GENRES		DIRECT*, RCHAIO*, CNV7*	IBCOM#	VLIST, DSTORE, OPTION, PREDS, GROUPS, SPLITC, DEPEND, YREAD
SOURCE				GROUPS, SPLITC, FACTOR
CMPSET	ERASE			VLIST, OPTION, PREDS, SPLITC, ELIGC, SYMTRY, RANKC, DEPEND, FACTOR
CMPUTE	SOURCE, GENRES, FINDL, DEFINE, LAHEAD		IBCOM#	LABELS, VLIST, DSTORE, OPTION, PREDS, GROUPS, SPLITC, ELIGC, SYMTRY, RANK, DEPEND, FACTOR, BESTS
FINDL				GROUPS
DEFINE	GENRES, FINDL, SUNDER		IBCOM#	VLIST, DSTORE, OPTION, PREDS, GROUPS, SPLITC, SYMTRY, RANKC, DEPEND, FACTOR, BESTS
SUNDER	ERASE, SUMS, WTOTAL	DIRECT*	IBCOM#	VLIST, DSTORE, OPTION, PREDS, GROUPS, SPLITC, RANKC, DEPEND, FACTOR
LAHEAD	ERASE, FINDL, SUNDER, SPLIT, BCOMP	DIRECT*	IBCOM#, SORT, MINO, MAXO	VLIST, DSTORE, OPTION, PREDS, GROUPS, SPLITC, ELIGC, SYMTRX, RANKC, BESTS
SPLIT	ERASE		IBCOM#, SORT, MINO, MAXO	VLIST, OPTION, PREDS, GROUPS, SPLITC, ELIGC, DEPEND
BCOMP			MINO, MAXO	PREDS, ELIGC, RANKC, BESTS
OUTPUT	SOURCE, GENRES, ANOVA1, TABLES	DIRECT*, RCHAIO*	IBCOM#	VLIST, DSTORE, OPTION, GROUPS, SPLITC, DEPEND, YREAD, FACTOR
TABLES	ERASE, COVAN	DIRECT*	IBCOM#, SORT, MINO, AMAXI	VLIST, DSTORE, OPTION, PREDS, GROUPS, SPLITC, ELIGC, DEPEND, FACTOR

* denotes a 360 assembly language routine

125

Chart 1 - STORAGE AREA "AUNIT"[1]

NA Records of Length = NELEM + NV $\leq$ 307 words

NV $\leq$ 300, the total number of variables accessed (input + generated)

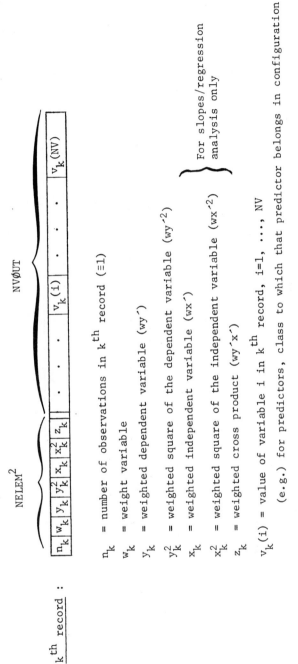

k^{th} record :

NELEM[2]						NVØUT				
n_k	w_k	y_k	y_k^2	x_k	x_k^2	z_k	$\cdot$	$\cdot$	$v_k(i)$	$\cdot\ \cdot\ \cdot$	$v_k(NV)$

n_k = number of observations in k^{th} record ($\equiv 1$)

w_k = weight variable

y_k = weighted dependent variable (wy´)

y_k^2 = weighted square of the dependent variable (wy´²)

x_k = weighted independent variable (wx´)

x_k^2 = weighted square of the independent variable (wx´²)

z_k = weighted cross product (wy´x´)

$v_k(i)$ = value of variable i in k^{th} record, i=1, ..., NV

(e.g.) for predictors, class to which that predictor belongs in configuration

For slopes/regression analysis only

[1]The file contains 1 record per observation plus 2 final records containing the missing data 1 and missing data 2 codes respectively (NA + 2 records total).

[2]Space for all 7 elements must be allotted regardless of the analysis type.

Chart 2 - STORAGE AREA "BUNIT"

For each Group L: NRECB$_L$ + NP + 1 RECORDS (NP = number of predictors)

k_α = Record number in "AUNIT" of αth observation in Group L.

α = 1,2,..., N$_L$; N$_L$ = number of cases in Group L

(k_{N_L+1} = NA + 1 ≡ EØF)

| k_1 | $\cdot$ | $\cdot$ | $\cdot$ | k_{224} |

k_{N_L+1}

NRECB$_L$ Records of Length 224 Words [1]

Group Totals [2]   e.g. YSQ$_L$ = $\sum_{\alpha=1}^{N_L} w_\alpha y_\alpha^{-2}$

| N$_L$ | W$_L$ | Y$_L$ | YSQ$_L$ | X$_L$ | XSQ$_L$ | Z$_L$ |

| n$_{1,1}$ | w$_{1,1}$ | y$_{1,1}$ | y$_{1,1}^2$ | x$_{1,1}$ | x$_{1,1}^2$ | z$_{1,1}$ | $\cdot$ | $\cdot$ | n$_{1,NC}$ | w$_{1,NC}$ | y$_{1,NC}$ | y$_{1,NC}^2$ | x$_{1,NC}$ | x$_{1,NC}^2$ | z$_{1,NC}$ |

Class totals for First Predictor (Classes 1,...,NC)

NP Records

| n$_{NP,1}$ | w$_{NP,1}$ | y$_{NP,1}$ | y$_{NP,1}^2$ | x$_{NP,1}$ | x$_{NP,1}^2$ | z$_{NP,1}$ |

Class Totals for NPth Predictor

[1] NRECB$_L$ = (N$_L$ + 1)/224

[2] x, x^2 and z elements are generated for slopes or regression analyses only; however, the space must be allocated regardless.

Appendix V
Examples of Output

It is difficult to demonstrate all the options available with this program. An example of a pre-set tree was given earlier in chapter II. We present here three runs, the first two done as a pair.

The first run is an analysis of house values for a national sample of home-owners, with extensive recoding, a one-step lookahead, a premium for symmetry, and one variable ranked 0 so that its splits are suppressed.

The second run is an analysis of the residuals from the first run, without lookahead or symmetry premiums, but with three ranks of predictors.

The third run deals with the dominance of income in explaining house value by searching for different regressions (of house value on income), rather than merely different mean house values. It is, of course, still dominated by differences in level, not slope (income elasticity), and the overall regression (income effect) accounts for more of the variance than the subgroup differences in regression.

The three figures which follow summarize the main results, derivable from the three Group Summary Tables in the output. The data are weighted to offset oversampling among low income families and minority group members. Comments have been added on the computer print-out, but a few overall notes may be appropriate here. Neither the lookahead nor the symmetry premium made any substantial difference. Splits on groups 2, 4 and 7 of the first housevalue analysis were altered, but subsequent splits were made in each case on the predictor that would have been used earlier without the lookahead. Since the symmetry premium only operates when it is the second of a pair that is being split and looks only at the identical split (predictor and subclass division), it is understandable that it would require substantial losses in explanatory power to achieve symmetry.

The ranking in the second run also made little difference. Group 5 was split on race, reducing the error variance by less than commuting time would have, but a later split was made of the white group using commuting time. Since commuting time is highly correlated with more basic things like age (retired) and city size and distance from center, it was purposely kept out of the analysis until the very end by the ranking.

The third--regression--run selects groups with different regression (levels or slopes), but the print-out also gives the subgroup regressions for each subclass of each predictor for each subgroup developed. Table A5-1 gives examples for three predictors.

These runs took extensive computer time both because of the elaborate recode even of data filtered out and not used, and because of the lookahead and the printing of a lot of detailed output, and because of the large sample.

For further details, see the comments added to the computer print-out which follows.

Figure A5-1

House Value (1970) by Family and Location Factors*

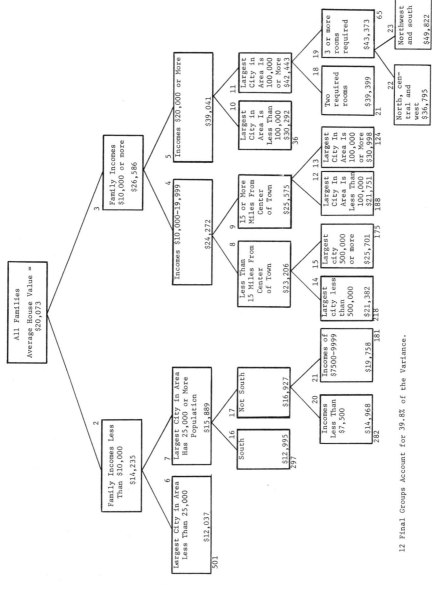

12 Final Groups Account for 39.8% of the Variance.

*Excludes trailers; all house values less than $5,000 increased to $5,000; and those over $75,000 reduced to $75,000.

46807 MTR 45

130

Figure A5-2

Residuals of House Value Related to Factors Affecting Price or Demand or Inertia

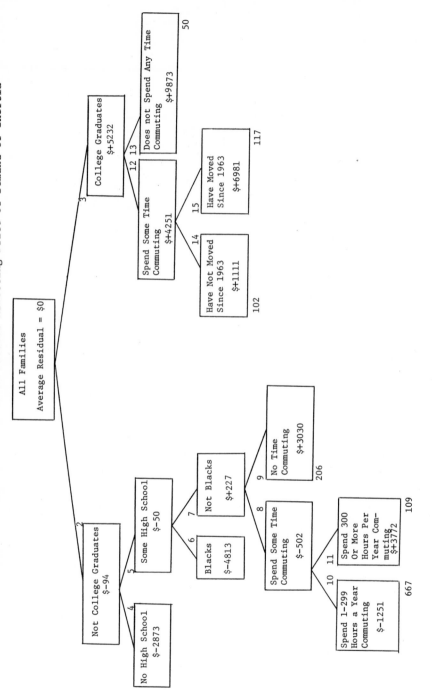

8 Final groups account for 11.6% of the residual variance or an additional 7.0% of the original variance

46807 MTR 45

131

Figure A5-3

Regressions of House Value on Income* for Home Owners

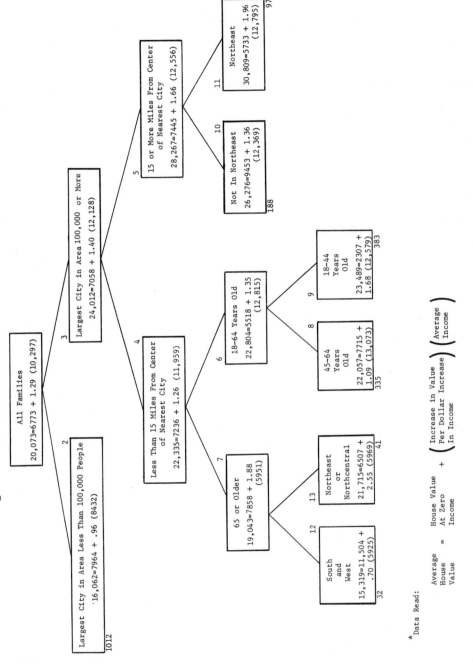

*Data Read:

$$\begin{matrix} \text{Average} \\ \text{House} \\ \text{Value} \end{matrix} = \begin{matrix} \text{House Value} \\ \text{At Zero} \\ \text{Income} \end{matrix} + \left(\begin{matrix} \text{Increase in Value} \\ \text{Per Dollar Increase} \\ \text{In Income} \end{matrix} \right) \left(\begin{matrix} \text{Average} \\ \text{Income} \end{matrix} \right)$$

46807 MTR 46

Table A5-1

REGRESSIONS OF HOUSE VALUE ON INCOME FOR SUBCLASSES OF THREE PREDICTORS
(for all home owners)

	Average House Value	Marginal Increment (Slope of Regression Line on Income)	Average Income	Number of Cases
"Required" Number of Rooms (family/size and structure)				
2	$17,620	1.07	$ 7,956	661
3	21,220	1.46	10,900	557
4	22,560	1.50	12,390	486
5	19,990	1.59	11,560	225
6 or more	19,980	1.38	12,280	159
Race				
White	20,690	1.24	10,560	1626
Black	11,780	0.89	8,872	406
Other	19,870	1.25	9,594	56
Size of Largest City in Area				
SMSA's				
500,000 or more	25,830	1.46	12,630	633
100,000-499,999	21,540	1.24	11,450	443
50,000-99,999	18,550	.93	10,280	222
Not SMSA's				
25,000-49,999	18,460	.87	9,486	144
10,000-24,999	15,780	1.08	8,460	200
Less than 10,000	13,940	.86	7,004	446

46807 MTR 46

JOB 12

Only the cards (lines) beginning with
a slash (/) are actually prepared and
constitute the job control language (JCL).

Name and number of the dictionary file

```
//M02695Q  JOB  (,                                                          00000070
//  48362,AID3,,60,10),BAKER,MSGLEVEL=(1,1)                                 00000080
//  EXEC  ISRSYS                                                            00000090
XXQSIRIS  PROC LIB=DSIRPGM,LIB1=SRCLIB,LIB2=CPSLIB,LIB3=ISPLIB,             00000100
XX           DI=*.FT4F001,VOL=REF=*.FT48F001,                              00000110
XX           DA=*.FT47F001,VOL=REF=*.FT47F001,,
XX           P=ISRSYS,SP1=1000,SP2=600
XXGO   EXEC   PGM=&P
IEF653I SUBSTITUTION JCL - PGM=ISRSYS                                       00000120
XXSTFPLIB  DD  DSN=&LIB,DISP=SHR
IEF653I SUBSTITUTION JCL - DSN=X468361Z,DISP=SHR                            00000130
XX         DD DSN=&LIB1,DISP=SHR
IEF653I SUBSTITUTION JCL - DSN=DSIRPGM,DISP=SHR
XX         DD DSN=&LIB2,DISP=SHR                                           00000140
IEF653I SUBSTITUTION JCL - DSN=CPSLIB,DISP=SHR
XX         DD DSN=&LIB3,DISP=SHR                                           00000150
IEF653I SUBSTITUTION JCL - DSN=ISRLIB,DISP=SHR
XXSYSPUNCH DD  SYSOUT=B                                                     00000160
XXSYSPRINT DD  SYSOUT=A                                                     00000170
XXSYSOUT   DD  SYSOUT=A                                                     00000180
XXFT02F001 DD  SYSOUT=R                                                     00000190
XXFT03F001 DD  UNIT=SYSDA,SPACE=(TRK,(100,50)),                            00000200
XX         DCB=(RECFM=VBS,LRECL=204,BLKSIZE=204,BUFNO=1)                    00000210
XXFT04F001 DD UNIT=SYSDA,SPACE=(TRK,(200,50)),                             00000220
XX         DCB=(RECFM=VBS,LRECL=204,BLKSIZE=204,BUFNO=1)                    00000230
XXFT05F001 DD UNIT=SYSDA,SPACE=(TRK,(50,50)),                              00000240
XX         DCB=(RECFM=VBS,LRECL=204,BLKSIZE=204,BUFNO=1)                    00000250
XXFT06F001 DD  SYSOUT=A                                                     00000260
XXFT07F001 DD  UNIT=SYSDA,SPACE=(TRK,(50,50)),                             00000270
XX         DCB=(RECFM=VBS,LRECL=200,BLKSIZE=204,BUFNO=1)                    00000280
XXFT08F001 DD  UNIT=SYSDA,SPACE=(TRK,(50,10)),                             00000290
XX         DCB=(RECFM=FB,LRECL=80,BLKSIZE=80)                               00000300
XXFT46F001 DD UNIT=SYSDA,SPACE=(TRK,(5,5)),                                C0000310
XX         DCB=(RECFM=FB,LRECL=80,BLKSIZE=800)                             00000320
XXFT47F001 DD UNIT=SYSDA,SPACE=(TRK,(100,20)),                             00000330
XX         DCB=(RECFM=FR,LRECL=80,BLKSIZE=3520)                            00000340
XXFT48F001 DD UNIT=SYSDA,SPACE=(TRK,(100,20)),                             00000350
XX         DCB=(RECFM=FB,LRECL=80,BLKSIZE=3520)                            00000360
XXFT49F001 DD  UNIT=SYSDA,SPACE=(TRK,(200,50)),                            00000370
XX         DCB=(RECFM=FR,LRECL=80,BLKSIZE=3520)                            00000380
XXFT50F001 DD  DSN=ISRNEWS,DISP=SHR,LABEL=(,,,IN)                          00000390
XXFT09F001 DD  VOL=REF=*.FT47F001,DSN=*.FT47F001,DISP=(OLD,DELETE)         00000400
IEF653I SUBSTITUTION JCL - UNIT=SYSDA,SPACE=(TRK,(1000),,CONTIG)            00000410
XXISR01    DD  UNIT=SYSDA,SPACE=(TRK,(ESP1),,CONTIG)
IEF653I SUBSTITUTION JCL - UNIT=SYSDA,SPACE=(TRK,(ESP2),,CONTIG)            00000420
XXISR02    DD UNIT=SYSDA,SPACE=(TRK,(ESP2),,CONTIG)
IEF653I SUBSTITUTION JCL - UNIT=SYSDA,SPACE=(TRK,(600),,CONTIG)            00000430
XXISR03    DD UNIT=SYSDA,SPACE=(TRK,(50),,CONTIG)                          00000440
XXISR09    DD UNIT=SYSDA,SPACE=(TRK,(200),,CONTIG)                         00000450
XXISR10    DD UNIT=SYSDA,SPACE=(TRK,(200),,CONTIG)                         00000460
XXUCLOAD   DD  DSN=*.FT07F001,VOL=REF=*.FT07F001,DISP=(OLD,DELETE)         00000470
XXSORTWK01 DD  DSN=*.ISR01,DISP=(OLD,DELETE),VOL=REF=*.ISR01               00000480
XXSORTWK02 DD  DSN=*.ISR02,DISP=(OLD,DELETE),VOL=REF=*.ISR02               00000490
XXSORTWK03 DD DSN=*.ISR09,DISP=(OLD,DELETE),VOL=REF=*.ISR09                00000500
XXSORTWK04 DD  DSN=*.ISR10,DISP=(OLD,DELETE),VOL=REF=*.ISR10               00000510
XXSORTLIB  DD  DSN=SYS1.SORTLIB,DISP=SHR                                    J0000520
XXSORTIN   DD  VOL=REF=*.FT47F001,DSN=*.FT47F001,DISP=(OLD,PASS)           00000530
XXSORTOUT  DD  VOL=REF=*.FT47F001,DSN=*.FT47F001,DISP=(OLD,PASS),          00000540
XX         DCB=(RECFM=FB,LRECL=80,BLKSIZE=800)
//DICTIN DD DSN=D1B9QXM5,UNIT=TAPE,VOL=SER=12988,DISP=OLD,LABEL=1
X/DICTIN DD  DSN=&DICTIN,DISP=(OLD,PASS),                                  00000550
IEF653I SUBSTITUTION JCL - DSN=*.FT48F001,VOL=REF=*.FT48F001,DISP=(OLD,PASS),
```

Name and number of the data file

```
XX   DCB=BUFNO=1                                                         00000560
//DATAIN DD DSN=DAB90XM3,UNIT=TAPE,VOL=SER=2988,DISP=OLD,LABEL=2         00000570
X/DATAIN  DD  DSN=&DA,DISP=(OLD,PASS),
IEF653I SUBSTITUTION JCL - DSN=*.FT47F001,VOL=REF=*.FT47F001,DISP=(OLD,PASS),
XX   DCB=BUFNO=1                                                         00000580
XXDICTOUT DD  VOL=REF=*.FT48F001,DSN=*.FT48F001,DISP=(OLD,PASS),         00000590
XX   DCB=BUFNO=1                                                         00000600
XXDATAOUT  DD  VOL=REF=*.FT47F001,DSN=*.FT47F001,DISP=(OLD,PASS),        00000610
XX   DCB=BUFNO=1                                                         00000620
XXFT01F001 DD UNIT=SYSDA,SPACE=(TRK,(50,10)),DCB=(RECFM=F,BLKSIZE=80)    00000630
XXSYSIN DD DSN=*.FT01F001,DISP=(OLD,DELETE),VOL=REF=*.FT01F001           00000640
//SYSUDUMP DD SYSOUT=A
//SETUP DD *
//
IEF236I ALLOC. FOR M026959 GO
IEF237I 132 ALLOCATED TO STEPLIB
IEF237I 133 ALLOCATED TO
IEF237I 132 ALLOCATED TO
IEF237I 132 ALLOCATED TO
IEF237I 080 ALLOCATED TO SYSPUNCH
IEF237I 0E0 ALLOCATED TO SYSPRINT
IEF237I 0E1 ALLOCATED TO SYSOUT
IEF237I 081 ALLOCATED TO FT02F001
IEF237I 130 ALLOCATED TO FT03F001
IEF237I 131 ALLOCATED TO FT04F001
IEF237I 132 ALLOCATED TO FT05F001
IEF237I 0E2 ALLOCATED TO FT06F001
IEF237I 130 ALLOCATED TO FT07F001
IEF237I 131 ALLOCATED TO FT08F001
IEF237I 131 ALLOCATED TO FT46F001
IEF237I 132 ALLOCATED TO FT47F001
IEF237I 130 ALLOCATED TO FT48F001
IEF237I 132 ALLOCATED TO FT49F001
IEF237I 132 ALLOCATED TO FT50F001
IEF237I 130 ALLOCATED TO FT09F001
IEF237I 130 ALLOCATED TO ISR01
IEF237I 131 ALLOCATED TO ISR02
IEF237I 132 ALLOCATED TO ISR03
IEF237I 131 ALLOCATED TO ISR09
IEF237I 130 ALLOCATED TO ISR10
IEF237I 130 ALLOCATED TO UCLOAD
IEF237I 130 ALLOCATED TO SORTWK01
IEF237I 131 ALLOCATED TO SORTWK02
IEF237I 130 ALLOCATED TO SORTWK03
IEF237I 130 ALLOCATED TO SORTWK04
IEF237I 133 ALLOCATED TO SORTLIB
IEF237I 130 ALLOCATED TO SORTIN
IEF237I 130 ALLOCATED TO SORTOUT
IEF237I 281 ALLOCATED TO DICTIN
IEF237I 281 ALLOCATED TO DATAIN
IEF237I 131 ALLOCATED TO DICTOUT
IEF237I 130 ALLOCATED TO DATAOUT
IEF237I 132 ALLOCATED TO FT01F001
IEF237I 132 ALLOCATED TO SYSIN
IEF237I 0E3 ALLOCATED TO SYSUDUMP
IEF237I 0A0 ALLOCATED TO SETUP
IEC209I M026959 2988 281 TR=C00,TW=000,FG=000,CL=000,N=000,SID=00046
IEC209I M026959 2988 281 TP=000,TW=000,EG=000,CL=000,N=000,SID=04660
IEF285I   X468361Z                      KEPT
IEF285I   VOL SER NOS= ISRA             KEPT
IEF285I   QSIRPGM   ISRA   .
```

```
IEF285I   CPSLIB                                                  KEPT
IEF285I   VOL SER NOS= MFT1  .
IEF285I   ISRLIB                                                  KEPT
IEF285I   VOL SER NOS= ISRA  .
IEF285I   SYS73160.T091518.RF000.M026959.R0000253                DELETED
IEF285I   VOL SER NOS= PJK001.
IEF285I   SYS73160.T091518.RF000.M026959.R0000254                DELETED
IEF285I   VOL SER NOS= ISRB  .
IEF285I   SYS73160.T091518.RF000.M026959.R0000255                DELETED
IEF285I   VOL SER NOS=
IEF285I   SYS73160.T091518.RF000.M026959.R0000256                DELETED
IEF285I   VOL SER NOS= PJK001.
IEF285I   SYS73160.T091518.RF000.M026959.R0000257                DELETED
IEF285I   VOL SER NOS= PJK001.
IEF285I   SYS73160.T091518.RF000.M026959.R0000258                DELETED
IEF285I   VOL SER NOS= ISRB  .
IEF285I   SYS73160.T091518.RF000.M026959.R0000259                DELETED
IEF285I   VOL SER NOS= ISRA  .
IEF285I   SYS73160.T091518.RF000.M026959.R0000260                DELETED
IEF285I   VOL SER NOS= PJK001.
IEF285I   SYS73160.T091518.RF000.M026959.R0000261                DELETED
IEF285I   VOL SER NOS= ISRB  .
IEF285I   SYS73160.T091518.RF000.M026959.R0000262                DELETED
IEF285I   VOL SER NOS= ISRA  .
IEF285I   ISRNEWS                                                 KEPT
IEF285I   VOL SER NOS= ISRA  .
IEF283I   SYS73160.T091518.RF000.M026959.R0000260                NOT DELETED 8
IEF285I   VOL SER NOS= PJK001 1.
IEF285I   SYS73160.T091518.RF000.M026959.R0000263                DELETED
IEF285I   VOL SER NOS= PJK001.
IEF285I   SYS73160.T091518.RF000.M026959.R0000264                DELETED
IEF285I   VOL SER NOS= ISRB  .
IEF285I   SYS73160.T091518.RF000.M026959.R0000265                DELETED
IEF285I   VOL SER NOS= ISRA  .
IEF285I   SYS73160.T091518.RF000.M026959.R0000266                DELETED
IEF285I   VOL SER NOS= PJK001.
IEF285I   SYS73160.T091518.RF000.M026959.R0000267                DELETED
IEF285I   VOL SER NOS= PJK001.
IEF283I   SYS73160.T091518.RF000.M026959.R0000257                NOT DELETED 8
IEF285I   VOL SER NOS= PJK001 1.
IEF283I   SYS73160.T091518.RF000.M026959.R0000263                NOT DELETED 8
IEF285I   VOL SER NOS= PJK001 1.
IEF283I   SYS73160.T091518.RF000.M026959.R0000264                NOT DELETED 8
IEF285I   VOL SER NOS= ISRB  1.
IEF283I   SYS73160.T091518.RF000.M026959.R0000266                NOT DELETED 8
IEF285I   VOL SER NOS= PJK001 1.
IEF283I   SYS73160.T091518.RF000.M026959.R0000267                NOT DELETED 8
IEF285I   VOL SER NOS= PJK001 1.
IEF285I   SYS1.SORTLIB                                            KEPT
IEF285I   VOL SER NOS= MFT1  .
IEF285I   SYS73160.T091518.RF000.M026959.R0000260                PASSED
IEF285I   VOL SER NOS= PJK001.
IEF285I   SYS73160.T091518.RF000.M026959.R0000260                PASSED
IEF285I   VOL SER NOS= PJK001.
IEF285I   DI890XMS                                                KEPT
IEF285I   VOL SER NOS= 2988  .
IEF285I   DA890XMS                                                KEPT
IEF285I   VOL SER NOS= 2988  .
IEF285I   SYS73160.T091518.RF000.M026959.R0000261                PASSED
IEF285I   VOL SER NOS= ISRB  .
```

136

```
IEF285I   SYS73160.T091518.RF000.M026959.R0000260              PASSED
IEF285I   VOL SER NOS= PJK001.
IEF285I   SYS73160.T091518.RF000.M026959.R0000268              DELETED
IEF285I   VOL SER NOS= ISRA .
IEF283I   SYS73160.T091518.RF000.M026959.R0000268              NOT DELETED 8
IEF283I   VOL SER NOS= ISRA 1.
IEF285I   SYS73160.T091518.RF000.M026959.R0000270              DELETED
IEF285I   VOL SER NOS=
ISR011I   STEP GO      EXECUTION TIME = 2049.72 SEC.
ISR013I   PARTITION  2: SIZE= 104, LWM=F0F000, HWM=F0F030 , CORE ALLOCATED= 104, CORE USED= 96
IEF285I   SYS73160.T091518.RF000.M026959.R0000260              KEPT
IEF285I   VOL SER NOS= PJK001.
IEF285I   SYS73160.T091518.RF000.M026959.R0000260              KEPT
IEF285I   VOL SER NOS= PJK001.
IEF285I   SYS73160.T091518.RF000.M026959.R0000261              KEPT
IEF285I   VOL SER NOS= ISRR .
IEF285I   SYS73160.T091518.RF000.M026959.R0000260              KEPT
IEF285I   VOL SER NOS= PJK001.
ISR012I   TOT. M026959 EXECUTION TIME =  2049.72 SEC.
ISR016I   TIME OF DAY = 13.59.00, DATE = 73.160
```

```
*****
*****   INSTITUTE FOR SOCIAL RESEARCH MONITOR SYSTEM    02/05/73
*****   FASTER VERSIONS OF TABLES, MDC, AND REGRESSN NOW AVAILABLE BY SPECIFYING
*****
*****         //     EXEC OSIRIS,LIB=X485321X,LIB1=OSIRPGM

        SAVINGS ARE 10-45% FOR TABLES, 45% FOR MDC AND 20% FOR REGRESSN

*****TIME IS 12:37: 0

*****LISTING OF SET-UP FOLLOWS:
```

```
CARD
NO.    12345678901234567890123456789012345678901234567890123456789012345678901234567890
                1         2         3         4         5         6         7         8
  1   $RUN AID3
  2   INCLUDE V1264=1 AND V1109=0-1 AND V542=0-1 AND V1499=1-9*
  3   MTR 45, PROJECT 468070,AID3
  4   *
  5   V101,V542,V603,V1009,V1109,V1122,V1146,V1168,V1240,V1250,V1274,V1276,V1365,
  6   V1370,V1490,V1498,V1499,V1506,V1572,V1609,V1719,V1720,V1264,V1485*
  7   807MTR45 MORGAN
  8   YVAR=1122 WEIG=1609 RECODE MDOP=NONE TABL=(BSS,ELIG,PRED,MEAN)
  9   RESI=(2005,0,8) RESN='HOUSE VALUE RESIDUALS'**
 10   2  IFV1719  LT  3000              V2001  =    1
 11      OR       IN  3000   4999                    2
 12                   5000   7499                    3
 13                   7500   9999                    4
 14                  10000  14999                    5
 15                  15000  19999                    6
 16                  20000                           7
 17   3  IFV1365  GE  1                 V2002  =    1    MARRIED
 18                             GOTO           4
 19   4  IFV1240  EQ  1                 V2002  =    2    SNGL MAN
 20      ALT                            V2002  =    3    SNGL SMN
 21      T
 22               V1720  MPY  100V1720
 23               V1719       DIVV1720
 24      IFV2003  LT  -5               V2003  =    1    BRACKET
 25      OR       IN  -4     4                        2    PERCENT
 26                   5     9                         3    CHANGE
 27                  10    19                         4    IN
 28                  20                               5    INCOME
 29   5  IFV1274  GE  1                 V2004  =    1    HOW
 30      IFV 603  EQ  1                 V2004  = GOTO     LONG
 31      IFV 101  IN  7               8V2004  = GOTO     LIVED
 32                             GOTO                      HERE
 33      IFV 101  IN  7               8V2004  = GOTO
 34      IFV 101  IN  4               6V2004  =    4
 35      ALT                           V2004  =    5
 36   6  IFV1168  IN   7              9V1168  =    6    TRUNCATE
 37   7  IFV1009  EQ   1               V1009  =    2    NINE
 38   8  IFV1009  GT   6               V1009  =    6    CODES
 39   9  IFV1370  NE   1               V1370  =    0
 40  10  IFV1490  OUT  1              2V1490  =    3
 41  11  IFV1250  OUT  1              3V1250  =    5
CARD
NO.    12345678901234567890123456789012345678901234567890123456789012345678901234567890
                1         2         3         4         5         6         7         8
```

Right-margin annotations (handwritten, pointing to card groups):

- *This listing of the 70 cards is produced by the OSIRIS monitor.*
- *This variable list gives all the variables to be read off the input data file.* (cards 5–6)
- *Means analysis, weighted dependent variable, residuals but no output file, print all tables.* (cards 8–9)
- *Create a 7-category code from a 5-digit income field.* (cards 10–16)
- *Creates one classification from two others.* (cards 17–21)
- *Integer arithmetic requires multiplying by 100 before dividing and bracketing.* (cards 22–28)
- *Creates one classification from three using "GOTO" to avoid recoding a case twice.* (cards 29–35)
- *Truncating predictor classifications.* (cards 36–41)

138

```
CARD
NO.        1         2         3         4         5         6         7         8
     1234567890123456789012345678901234567890123456789012345678901234567890
42    12  IFV1122 GT  75000              V1122  =  75000        1       BRACKET
43        ORV1122 LT   5000              V1122  =   5000        2        ANNUAL
44    13  IFV1719 GT  25000              V1719  =  25000        3        HOURS
45    14  IFV1276 GT      5              V1276  =               4      COMMUTNG
46    15  IFV1146 IN      1            99V1146  =               5
47        OR             100                149
48                       150                199
49                       200                299
50                 GE    300
51          END
52  PRED=2001 MAXC=7       PREN='3-YR AVE $ INC'*
53  PRED=(1168,1009) MAXC=6*
54  PRED=2002 MAXC=3 PREN='SEX & MAR STATUS'*
55  PRED=1506*
56  PRED=1498 MAXC=5*
57  PRED=1572 MAXC=4 F*
58  PRED=1490 MAXC=3 F RANK=0 END*
59  LOOK=(1,1) REDU=(.6,.12) MIN=3 RANK=ALL TRACE=BEST SYMM=30.
60  SECOND STAGE OF 807NTR45 MORGAN
61  YVAR=2005 WEIG=1609 TABL=(ELIG,MEAN)*
62  PRED=1276 MAXC=5 RANK=2*
63  PRED=2004 PREN='HOW LONG LIVD HERE' MAXC=5 RANK=2*
64  PRED=1485*
65  PRED=1490 F MAXC=3*
66  PRED=1250 MAXC=5*
67  PRED=2003 PREN='% CHANGE IN INCOME' MAXC=5*
68  PRED=1370 MAXC=1*
69  PRED=1146 MAXC=6 RANK=3 END*
70  REDU=.6 MIN=3 RANK=UP RANGE=(2,2,2)*
```

First analysis strategy specified : predictors: whether maintained subclass order and rank.

* 1-step lookahead, simple ranking, 30% premium for symmetry, print best split in trace, minimum group size=3.

Range ranking with preference UP, no lookahead

A card with /* after this indicates the end of the setup.

Execution of the program begins with a listing and interpretation of the setup.

AIDS: OSIRIS SEARCHING FOR STRUCTURE - JULY 1973

THE FILTER IS:

INCLUDE V1264=1 AND V1109=0-1 AND V542=0-1 AND V1499=1-9*

MTR 45, PROJECT 468070, AIDS

*

THE VARIABLE LIST IS:

V101,V542,V603,V1009,V1109,V1122,V1146,V1168,V1240,V1250,V1274,V1276,V1365,
V1370,V1490,V1498,V1499,V1506,V1572,V1609,V1719,V1720,V1264,V1485*

Using the input variable list the dictionary file is read for a description of each variable.

	VAR.	TYPE	VARIABLE NAME	TLOC	WIDTH	NODEC	RESP.	MDCODE1	MDCODE2	REFNO	ID	TSEQNO
T	101	0	WHEN MOVED IN 5:36	270	1	0	1		0000009			00000
T	542	0	CHANGE IN FU COMP 15:25	1070	1	0	1					00000
T	603	0	MOVED SINCE SPRNG6816-38	1149	1	0	1		0000009			00000
T	1009	0	BKT AGE HEAD 9V1009	1831	1	0	1					00000
T	1109	0	CHANGE IN FU COMP 21:18	2021	1	0	1					00000
T	1122	0	HOUSE VALUE 21:38-42	2041	1	0	1					00000
T	1146	0	HRS HEAD TRVL WK22:30-37	2103	5	0	1					00000
T	1168	0	# REQUIRED ROOMS 23:12	2154	3	0	1					00000
T	1240	0	SEX OF HEAD 26:40	2351	1	0	1					00000
T	1250	0	PUB TRANSP GOOD 26:52	2363	1	0	1		0000009			00000
T	1264	0	OWN OR RENT? 26:67	2378	1	0	1					00000
T	1274	0	MOVED SINCE SPRING 26:77	2388	1	0	1		0000009			00000
T	1276	0	MIGHT MOVE 26:79	2390	1	0	1		0000009			00000
T	1365	0	MARITAL STATUS 29:10	2514	1	0	1					00000
T	1370	0	EXPECT CHILDREN ? 29:18	2521	1	0	1		0000009			00000
T	1485	0	EDUCATION OF HEAD 31:43	2657	1	0	1		0000009			00000
T	1490	0	RACE 31:48	2662	1	0	1		0000009			00000
T	1498	0	DIST TO CNTR SMSA 31:58	2672	1	0	1		0000009			00000
T	1499	0	TYPE OF STRUCTURE 31:59	2673	1	0	1		0000009			00000
T	1506	0	LRGST PLAC/SMSA PSU31:66	2680	1	0	1					00000
T	1572	0	CURRENT REGION 0V472	2838	1	0	1	0000009				00000
T	1609	0	WEIGHT 0V509	2892	2	0	1				COR	00000
T	1719	0	MEAN MONEY INCOME	3179	5	0	1				COR	00000
T	1720	0	SLOPE MONEY INCOME	3184	6	0	1				COR	00000

HOUSE VALUE TRUNCATED TO 5000-75000 BY SQUEEZING EXTREME CASES   807MTR45 MORGAN

YVAR=1122 WEIG=1609 RECODE MOOP=NONE TABLE=(BSS,ELIG,PRED,MEAN)

RESI=(2305,0.8) RESN='HOUSE VALUE RESIDUALS'**

NO	LOG TEST		REL	A OPERAND	P OPERAND	RES		OP	C OPERAND	D OPERAND	TEXT
?	IFV1719		LT	3000		0V2001		=	1	0	

```
0  OR      IN                              MARRIED
0                  3000    4999    0    0
0                  5000    7499    0    0
0                  7500    9999    0    0
0                  10000   14999   0    0
3  IFV1365         20000   0       1    0V2002 = GOTO  2
0  IFV1240 EQ      0       0       0V2002 = GOTO  3   SNGL MAN
4  ALT T           0       0       0V1720 = MPY   100V    SNGL SMN
0                                  0V2003 = DIVV  1720V
0  IFV2003 LT      -5      4       0V2003 =       1   1720   BRACKET
0  OR      IN      -4      9       0V2003        1719   PERCENT
0                  5       19      0    2             CHANGE
0                  10      0       0    3             IN
0                  20      0       0    4             INCOME
5  IFV1274 GE      0       0       0V2004 = GOTO  1   HOW
0                  1       0       0V2004 = GOTO  6
0  IFV 603 EQ      1       0       0V2004 = GOTO  2   LONG
0  IFV 101 IN      0       0       8V2004 = GOTO  6   LIVED
0  IFV 101 IN      7       0       6V2004 = GOTO  3   HERE
0                  0       4       0V2004        6
0  ALT            0       5       9V1168        4
6  IFV1168 IN      7       7       0V1009        5   TRUNCATE
7  IFV1009 EQ                      0V1009        2   NINE
8  IFV1009 GT      6       0       0V1370        6   CODES
9  IFV1370 NE      1                2V1490       3
10 IFV1490 OUT     1                3V1250       5
11 IFV1250 GT      75000   75000    0V1122       75000
12 IFV1122 LT      5000    5000     0V1122       5000
13 ORV1122 GT      25000   25000    0V1719       25000
14 IFV1276 GT      5                0V1276       5
15 IFV1146 IN      1                99V1146      1
0  OR              100     149      0    1             BRACKET
0                  150     199      0    2             ANNUAL
0                  200     299      0    3             HOURS
0                  300     0        0    4             COMMUTNG
0  END            0       0        0    5
```

PRED=2001 MAXC=7   PREN='3-YR AVE $ INC'*

PRED=(1168,1009) MAXC=6*

PRED=2002 MAXC=3 PREN='SEX & MAR STATUS'*

PRED=1506*

PRED=1498 MAXC=5*

PRED=1572 MAXC=4 F*

PRED=1490 MAXC=3 F RANK=0 END*

LOOK=(1,1) REDU=(.6,.12) MIN=3 RANK=ALL TRACE=BEST SYMM=30.   *

COMPUTE   SPECIFIED

OUTPUT   SPECIFIED

SECOND STAGE OF 8Q7NTR45 MORGAN

YVAR=2005 WEIG=1609 TABL=(ELIG,MEAN)*

PRED=1276 MAXC=5 RANK=2*

PRED=2004 PREN='HOW LONG LIVD HERE' MAXC=5 RANK=2*

PRED=1485*

PRED=1490 F MAXC=3*

PRED=1250 MAXC=5*

PRED=2003 PREN='% CHANGE IN INCOME' MAXC=5*

PRED=1370 MAXC=1*

PRED=1146 MAXC=6 RANK=3 END*

REDU=.6 MIN=3 RANK=UP RANGE=(2,2,7,2)*

COMPUTE   SPECIFIED

OUTPUT   SPECIFIED

THE COMPLETE VARIABLE LIST IS:

```
101   542   603  1009  1109  1127  1146  1168  1240  1250  1274  1276  1365  1370  1490  1498  1499  1506  1572  1609
1710  1720  1264  1485  2005  2001  2002  2003  2004
```

These variables, appended to the input variable list, are variables generated using the residual and recode options.

HOUSE VALUE TRUNCATED TO 5000-75000 BY SQUEEZING EXTREME CASES   807MTR45 MORGAN

2088 OBSERVATIONS READ AFTER GLOBAL FILTER

Y AVERAGE =   2.007342E 04
STANDARD DEVIATION = 1.278252E 04
BOUNDARIES = -4.383923E 04   8.398600E 04

2088 CASES INCLUDED IN THE ANALYSIS
    0 FILTERED (LOCAL/SUBSET SELECTOR)
    0 MISSING DATA CASES
    0 OUTLIERS INCLUDED
    0 INVALID PREDICTOR VALUES

2088 SAMPLE OBSERVATIONS - WITH TOTALS
    WEIGHTS =   8.157500E 04
    DEPENDENT VARIABLE (Y) = 1.637489D 09   AVERAGE =   2.007342E 04
    Y-SQUARED =   4.615239D 13   VARIANCE = 1.633931E 08

STAGE 1 OF THE ANALYSIS
BEST SPLIT BASED ON MEANS
1-STEP LOOKAHEAD WITH 1 FORCED SPLITS

SPLITTING CRITERIA -
    MAXIMUM NUMBER OF SPLITS = 25
    MINIMUM # OBSERVATIONS IN A GROUP = 3
    %AGE OF TOTAL SS N SPLITS MUST EXPLAIN = 0.6(N=1), 0.1(N=2),
    PREMIUM FOR SYMMETRY = 30.0
    PRINT CASES OUTSIDE 5.0 STANDARD DEVIATIONS OF PARENT GROUP MEAN

    8 RANKED PREDICTORS SPECIFIED
PREDICTOR RANK PREFERENCE   AT
SPLIT ATTEMPT RANGE -   0 RANKS UP,   0 RANKS DOWN
ELIGIBILITY RANGE -   0 RANKS UP,   0 RANKS DOWN

	PREDICTOR	VARIABLE NUMBER	TYPE	MAX CLASS	RANK
1	3-YR AVE $ INC.	V2001	M	7	1
2	# REQUIRED ROOMS 23:12	V1168	M	6	1
3	BKT AGE HEAD $V1009	V1009	M	6	1
4	SEX & MAR STATUS	V2002	M	3	1
5	LRGST PLAC/SMSA PSU31:66	V1506	M	9	1
6	DIST TO CNTR SMSA 31:58	V1469	M	5	1
7	CURRENT REGION 0V472	V1572	F	4	1
8	RACE 31:48	V1490	F	3	0

WEIGHTED Y VARIABLE 1122 HOUSE VALUE   21:38-42 SCALED BY 1.0E 00
RESIDUAL-HOUSE VALUE RESIDUALS V2005- SCALE FACTOR 1.0E 00
    GROUP NO V   0, PREDICTED VALUE V 0- SCALE FACTOR 2.5E 08

    1 CANDIDATES -   GROUP   SS
                         1   1.332240E 13

ATTEMPT SPLIT ON GROUP   1 WITH SS = 1.332240E 13

LOOKAHEAD TENTATIVE PARTITION

```
SPLIT ATTEMPT ON GROUP  1 WITH N =    2088, SS =   1.33224OE 13
    BEST SPLIT ON PREDICTOR 2001 = 3.102057E 12 AFTER CLASS  4
    BEST SPLIT ON PREDICTOR 1168 = 2.726633E 11 AFTER CLASS  4
    BEST SPLIT ON PREDICTOR 1009 = 4.380196E 11 AFTER CLASS  5
    BEST SPLIT ON PREDICTOR 2002 = 3.803388E 11 AFTER CLASS  1
    BEST SPLIT ON PREDICTOR 1506 = 1.288775E 12 AFTER CLASS  1
    BEST SPLIT ON PREDICTOR 1498 = 6.637311E 11 AFTER CLASS  3
    BEST SPLIT ON PREDICTOR 1572 = 5.695026E 11 AFTER CLASS  3
    BEST SPLIT ON PREDICTOR 1490 = 4.048007E 11 AFTER CLASS  3
TENTATIVE SPLIT 1. SPLIT GROUP  1 ON PREDICTOR 2001 WITH BSS = 3.102057E 12
    GROUP  2 WITH 1261 OBSERVATIONS FROM  4 CLASSES =  1  2  3  4
           W= 4.30130E 04  Y= 6.12273D 08  YSQ= 1.17260D 13  X=
    GROUP  3 WITH  827 OBSERVATIONS FROM  3 CLASSES =  5  6  7
           W= 3.85620E 04  Y= 1.02522D 09  YSQ= 3.44664D 13  X=

SPLIT ATTEMPT ON GROUP  3 WITH N =     827, SS =   7.209825E 12
    BEST SPLIT ON PREDICTOR 2001 = 1.111591E 12 AFTER CLASS  6
    BEST SPLIT ON PREDICTOR 1168 = 1.474717E 10 AFTER CLASS  2
    BEST SPLIT ON PREDICTOR 1009 = 2.999766E 10 AFTER CLASS  2
    BEST SPLIT ON PREDICTOR 2002 = 3.170894E 09 AFTER CLASS  1
    BEST SPLIT ON PREDICTOR 1506 = 4.843247E 10 AFTER CLASS  1
    BEST SPLIT ON PREDICTOR 1498 = 6.205892E 10 AFTER CLASS  1
    BEST SPLIT ON PREDICTOR 1572 = 3.152271E 11 AFTER CLASS  4

1-STEP LOOKAHEAD TO SPLIT GROUP  1, TOTAL BSS =   4.213648E 12
    1. SPLIT GROUP  1 ON PREDICTOR 2001, BSS =  3.102057E 12
    2. SPLIT GROUP  3 ON PREDICTOR 2001, BSS =  1.111591E 12
TENTATIVE SPLIT 1. SPLIT GROUP  1 ON PREDICTOR 1168 WITH BSS = 2.726633E 11
    GROUP  2 WITH  661 OBSERVATIONS FROM  1 CLASSES =  2
           W= 2.91370E 04  Y= 5.13416D 08  YSQ= 1.29566D 13  X=
    GROUP  3 WITH 1427 OBSERVATIONS FROM  4 CLASSES =  3  4  5  6
           W= 5.24380E 04  Y= 1.12407D 09  YSQ= 3.32358D 13  X=

SPLIT ATTEMPT ON GROUP  3 WITH N =    1427, SS =   9.139882E 12
    BEST SPLIT ON PREDICTOR 2001 = 2.232880E 12 AFTER CLASS  5
    BEST SPLIT ON PREDICTOR 1168 = 2.751463E 10 AFTER CLASS  2
    BEST SPLIT ON PREDICTOR 1009 = 1.484448E 11 AFTER CLASS  5
    BEST SPLIT ON PREDICTOR 2002 = 1.507097E 11 AFTER CLASS  1
    BEST SPLIT ON PREDICTOR 1506 = 8.852666E 11 AFTER CLASS  1
    BEST SPLIT ON PREDICTOR 1498 = 3.935432E 11 AFTER CLASS  3
    BEST SPLIT ON PREDICTOR 1572 = 4.414253E 11 AFTER CLASS  4

1-STEP LOOKAHEAD TO SPLIT GROUP  1, TOTAL BSS =   2.505543E 12
    1. SPLIT GROUP  1 ON PREDICTOR 1168, BSS =  2.726633E 11
    2. SPLIT GROUP  3 ON PREDICTOR 2001, BSS =  2.232880E 12
TENTATIVE SPLIT 1. SPLIT GROUP  1 ON PREDICTOR 1009 WITH BSS = 4.380196E 11
    GROUP  2 WITH 1759 OBSERVATIONS FROM  4 CLASSES =  2  3  4  5
           W= 6.60020E 04  Y= 1.39918D 09  YSQ= 4.07739D 13  X=
    GROUP  3 WITH  329 OBSERVATIONS FROM  1 CLASSES =  6
           W= 1.55730E 04  Y= 2.38312D 08  YSQ= 5.41854D 12  X=

SPLIT ATTEMPT ON GROUP  2 WITH N =    1759, SS =   1.111268E 13
    BEST SPLIT ON PREDICTOR 2001 = 2.477005E 12 AFTER CLASS  5
    BEST SPLIT ON PREDICTOR 1168 = 8.328210E 10 AFTER CLASS  4
    BEST SPLIT ON PREDICTOR 1009 = 8.709053E 10 AFTER CLASS  4
    BEST SPLIT ON PREDICTOR 2002 = 1.683258E 11 AFTER CLASS  1
    BEST SPLIT ON PREDICTOR 1506 = 9.942010E 11 AFTER CLASS  2
```

Group 1 (the whole selected data set) is searched for the best split on each predictor in turn.

Partition group 1 on the first predictor (V2001) and try for the best second split on the child with the largest remaining variance.

The best total BSS for the two splits, the first on V2001.

Repeat the process making the first split on the second predictor (V1/68).

BEST SPLIT ON PREDICTOR 1498 =   4.563906E 11 AFTER CLASS   3
BEST SPLIT ON PREDICTOR 1572 =   4.739396E 11 AFTER CLASS   3

1-STEP LOOKAHEAD TO SPLIT GROUP   1, TOTAL BSS =   2.915025E 12
    1. SPLIT GROUP   1 ON PREDICTOR 1009, BSS =   4.380196E 11
    2. SPLIT GROUP   2 ON PREDICTOR 2001, BSS =   2.477005E 12
TENTATIVE SPLIT 1. SPLIT GROUP   1 ON PREDICTOR 2002 WITH BSS = 3.802388E 11
    GROUP   2 WITH 1660 OBSERVATIONS FROM 1 CLASSES = 1
              W= 6.66840E 04 Y= 1.40661D 09 YSQ= 4.10219D 13 X=
    GROUP   3 WITH   428 OBSERVATIONS FROM 2 CLASSES = 2   3
              W= 1.48910E 04 Y= 2.30879D 08 YSQ= 5.17054D 12 X=

SPLIT ATTEMPT ON GROUP   2 WITH N =   1660, SS =   1.135127E 13
BEST SPLIT ON PREDICTOR 2001 =   2.501147E 12 AFTER CLASS   4
BEST SPLIT ON PREDICTOR 1168 =   1.402407E 11 AFTER CLASS   2
BEST SPLIT ON PREDICTOR 1009 =   2.172649E 11 AFTER CLASS   5

SEX & MAR STATUS   CONSTANT - NO SPLIT
BEST SPLIT ON PREDICTOR 1506 =   1.216348E 12 AFTER CLASS   2
BEST SPLIT ON PREDICTOR 1498 =   5.137016E 11 AFTER CLASS   3
BEST SPLIT ON PREDICTOR 1572 =   5.588994E 11 AFTER CLASS   3

1-STEP LOOKAHEAD TO SPLIT GROUP   1, TOTAL BSS =   2.881386E 12
    1. SPLIT GROUP   1 ON PREDICTOR 2002, BSS =   3.802388E 11
    2. SPLIT GROUP   2 ON PREDICTOR 2001, BSS =   2.501147E 12
TENTATIVE SPLIT 1. SPLIT GROUP   1 ON PREDICTOR 1506 WITH BSS = 1.288775E 12
    GROUP   2 WITH 1076 OBSERVATIONS FROM 2 CLASSES = 1   2
              W= 4.11590E 04 Y= 9.88315D 08 YSQ= 3.15359D 13 X=
    GROUP   3 WITH 1012 OBSERVATIONS FROM 4 CLASSES = 3   4   5   6
              W= 4.04160E 04 Y= 6.49174D 08 YSQ= 1.46565D 13 X=

SPLIT ATTEMPT ON GROUP   2 WITH N =   1076, SS =   7.804341E 12
BEST SPLIT ON PREDICTOR 2001 =   1.737969E 12 AFTER CLASS   5
BEST SPLIT ON PREDICTOR 1168 =   1.188162E 11 AFTER CLASS   2
BEST SPLIT ON PREDICTOR 1009 =   1.722349E 11 AFTER CLASS   4
BEST SPLIT ON PREDICTOR 2002 =   3.119723E 11 AFTER CLASS   1
BEST SPLIT ON PREDICTOR 1506 =   1.848010E 11 AFTER CLASS   1
BEST SPLIT ON PREDICTOR 1498 =   2.937691E 11 AFTER CLASS   2
BEST SPLIT ON PREDICTOR 1572 =   2.787367E 11 AFTER CLASS   2

1-STEP LOOKAHEAD TO SPLIT GROUP   1, TOTAL BSS =   3.026744E 12
    1. SPLIT GROUP   1 ON PREDICTOR 1506, BSS =   1.288775E 12
    2. SPLIT GROUP   2 ON PREDICTOR 2001, BSS =   1.737969E 12
TENTATIVE SPLIT 1. SPLIT GROUP   1 ON PREDICTOR 1498 WITH BSS = 6.633711E 11
    GROUP   2 WITH 1304 OBSERVATIONS FROM 3 CLASSES = 1   2   3
              W= 5.07440E 04 Y= 1.13140D 09 YSQ= 3.39227D 13 X=
    GROUP   3 WITH   784 OBSERVATIONS FROM 2 CLASSES = 4   5
              W= 3.08310E 04 Y= 5.06080D 08 YSQ= 1.26960D 13 X=

SPLIT ATTEMPT ON GROUP   2 WITH N =   1304, SS =   8.696735E 12
BEST SPLIT ON PREDICTOR 2001 =   1.873763E 12 AFTER CLASS   5
BEST SPLIT ON PREDICTOR 1168 =   1.296543E 11 AFTER CLASS   2
BEST SPLIT ON PREDICTOR 1009 =   2.204862E 11 AFTER CLASS   4
BEST SPLIT ON PREDICTOR 2002 =   2.072489E 11 AFTER CLASS   1
BEST SPLIT ON PREDICTOR 1506 =   4.940051E 11 AFTER CLASS   1
BEST SPLIT ON PREDICTOR 1498 =   2.342267E 11 AFTER CLASS   2
BEST SPLIT ON PREDICTOR 1572 =   3.481105E 11 AFTER CLASS   2

```
1-STEP LOOKAHEAD TO SPLIT GROUP   1, TOTAL RSS =  2.537134E 12
     1. SPLIT GROUP   1 ON PREDICTOR 1498, BSS =    6.633711E 11
     2. SPLIT GROUP   2 ON PREDICTOR 2001, RSS =  1.873763E 12
TENTATIVE SPLIT 1. SPLIT GROUP   1 ON PREDICTOR 1572 WITH BSS = 5.695026E 11
   GROUP  2 WITH   790 OBSERVATIONS FROM  1 CLASSES =  3
         W= 2.37430E 04 Y= 3.78693D 08 YSQ=9.16820D 12 X=
   GROUP  3 WITH  1298 OBSERVATIONS FROM  3 CLASSES =  2  4  1
         W= 5.78320E 04 Y= 1.25880D 09 YSQ= 3.70242D 13 X=

SPLIT ATTEMPT ON GROUP   3 WITH N =     1298, SS =  9.624702E 12
   BEST SPLIT ON PREDICTOR 2001 =  2.012377E 12 AFTER CLASS  4
   BEST SPLIT ON PREDICTOR 1168 =  2.224659E 11 AFTER CLASS  2
   BEST SPLIT ON PREDICTOR 1009 =  3.248908E 11 AFTER CLASS  5
   BEST SPLIT ON PREDICTOR 2002 =  3.620859E 11 AFTER CLASS  1
   BEST SPLIT ON PREDICTOR 1506 =  8.785892E 11 AFTER CLASS  2
   BEST SPLIT ON PREDICTOR 1498 =  3.664312E 11 AFTER CLASS  3
   BEST SPLIT ON PREDICTOR 1572 =  2.575974E 11 AFTER CLASS  4

1-STEP LOOKAHEAD TO SPLIT GROUP   1, TOTAL BSS =  2.581879E 12
     1. SPLIT GROUP   1 ON PREDICTOR 1572, BSS =  5.695026E 11
     2. SPLIT GROUP   3 ON PREDICTOR 2001, BSS =  2.012377E 12
```

***** PARTITION OF GROUP 1 *****

FROM ELIGIBLE PREDICTORS AROUND THE CURRENT RANK 1,   0 UP AND 0 DOWN

    MAXIMUM ELIGIBLE BSS AT EACH STEP   MAXIMUM TOTAL BSS (LOOKAHEAD)
    1.SPLIT 1 ON V2001 BSS= 3.10206E 12   SPLIT 1 ON V2001 BSS = 3.10206E 12
    2.SPLIT 3 ON V2001 BSS= 1.11159E 12   SPLIT 3 ON V2001 BSS = 1.11159E 12
    PF(2)= 1.599E 10, TOTAL= 4.21365E 12   TOTAL= 4.21365E 12
        PREDICTOR 2001 HAS RANK 1

SPLIT GROUP   1 ON 3-YR AVF $ INC   V2001
    GROUP   2 WITH 1261 OBSERVATIONS FROM 4 CLASSES = 1 2 3 4
            W= 4.30130E 04 Y= 6.12273D 08 YSQ= 1.17260D 13 X=
    GROUP   3 WITH   827 OBSERVATIONS FROM 3 CLASSES = 5 6 7
            W= 3.85620E 04 Y= 1.02522D 09 YSQ= 3.44664D 13 X=

    2 CANDIDATES -   GROUP   SS
                      2   3.01051 2E 12
                      3   7.209825E 12

        ATTEMPT SPLIT ON GROUP   3 WITH SS = 7.209825E 12

LOOKAHEAD TENTATIVE PARTITION

```
SPLIT ATTEMPT ON GROUP   3 WITH N =      827,  SS  =  7.209825E 12
     BEST SPLIT ON PREDICTOR 2001 =  1.111591E 12  AFTER CLASS  6
     BEST SPLIT ON PREDICTOR 1168 =  1.474717E 10  AFTER CLASS  2
     BEST SPLIT ON PREDICTOR 1009 =  2.999766E 10  AFTER CLASS  3
     BEST SPLIT ON PREDICTOR 2002 =  3.170894E 09  AFTER CLASS  3
     BEST SPLIT ON PREDICTOR 1506 =  4.843247E 11  AFTER CLASS  1
     BEST SPLIT ON PREDICTOR 1498 =  6.205802E 10  AFTER CLASS  1
     BEST SPLIT ON PREDICTOR 1572 =  3.152271E 11  AFTER CLASS  4
     BEST SPLIT ON PREDICTOR 1490 =  9.516037E 10  AFTER CLASS  2
TENTATIVE SPLIT 1. SPLIT GROUP  3 ON PREDICTOR 2001 WITH BSS =  1.111591E 12
   GROUP  4 WITH  705 OBSERVATIONS FROM 2 CLASSES =    5   6
       W= 3.25190E 04  Y= 7.89293D 08  YSQ= 2.32347D 13  X=
   GROUP  5 WITH  122 OBSERVATIONS FROM 1 CLASSES =    7
       W= 6.04300E 03  Y= 2.35924D 08  YSQ= 1.12317D 13  X=

SPLIT ATTEMPT ON GROUP   4 WITH N =      705,  SS  =  4.077182E 12
     BEST SPLIT ON PREDICTOR 2001 =  2.028198E 11  AFTER CLASS  5
     BEST SPLIT ON PREDICTOR 1168 =  1.491495E 10  AFTER CLASS  4
     BEST SPLIT ON PREDICTOR 1009 =  1.466528E 10  AFTER CLASS  3
     BEST SPLIT ON PREDICTOR 2002 =  1.929234E 09  AFTER CLASS  1
     BEST SPLIT ON PREDICTOR 1506 =  2.657847E 11  AFTER CLASS  1
     BEST SPLIT ON PREDICTOR 1498 =  4.518104E 10  AFTER CLASS  2
     BEST SPLIT ON PREDICTOR 1572 =  1.709934E 11  AFTER CLASS  4

1-STEP LOOKAHEAD TO SPLIT GROUP  3, TOTAL BSS =  1.377376E 12
    1. SPLIT GROUP  3 ON PREDICTOR 2001, BSS =  1.111591E 12
    2. SPLIT GROUP  4 ON PREDICTOR 1506, BSS =  2.657847E 11
TENTATIVE SPLIT 1. SPLIT GROUP  3 ON PREDICTOR 1168 WITH BSS =  1.474717E 10
   GROUP  4 WITH  186 OBSERVATIONS FROM 1 CLASSES =    2
       W= 8.93300E 03  Y= 2.28740D 08  YSQ= 7.32278D 12  X=
   GROUP  5 WITH  641 OBSERVATIONS FROM 4 CLASSES =    3   4   5   6
       W= 2.95790E 04  Y= 7.96477D 08  YSQ= 2.71336D 13  X=

SPLIT ATTEMPT ON GROUP   5 WITH N =      641,  SS  =  5.636833E 12
     BEST SPLIT ON PREDICTOR 2001 =  9.491542E 11  AFTER CLASS  6
     BEST SPLIT ON PREDICTOR 1168 =  1.956223E 10  AFTER CLASS  4
     BEST SPLIT ON PREDICTOR 1009 =  2.937691E 10  AFTER CLASS  3
     BEST SPLIT ON PREDICTOR 2002 =  9.730785E 08  AFTER CLASS  1
     BEST SPLIT ON PREDICTOR 1506 =  3.869833E 11  AFTER CLASS  1
     BEST SPLIT ON PREDICTOR 1498 =  5.837933E 10  AFTER CLASS  1
     BEST SPLIT ON PREDICTOR 1572 =  3.034998E 11  AFTER CLASS  4

1-STEP LOOKAHEAD TO SPLIT GROUP  3, TOTAL BSS =  0.639014E 11
    1. SPLIT GROUP  3 ON PREDICTOR 1168, BSS =  1.474717E 10
    2. SPLIT GROUP  5 ON PREDICTOR 2001, BSS =  9.491542E 11
TENTATIVE SPLIT 1. SPLIT GROUP  3 ON PREDICTOR 1009 WITH BSS =  2.999766E 10
   GROUP  4 WITH  428 OBSERVATIONS FROM 2 CLASSES =    2   3
       W= 1.95570E 04  Y= 5.36948D 08  YSQ= 1.85477D 13  X=
   GROUP  5 WITH  399 OBSERVATIONS FROM 3 CLASSES =    4   5   6
       W= 1.90050E 04  Y= 4.88260D 08  YSQ= 1.59187D 13  X=

SPLIT ATTEMPT ON GROUP   4 WITH N =      428,  SS  =  3.805554E 12
     BEST SPLIT ON PREDICTOR 2001 =  8.456975E 11  AFTER CLASS  6
     BEST SPLIT ON PREDICTOR 1168 =  3.4750R6F 10  AFTER CLASS  5
     BEST SPLIT ON PREDICTOR 1009 =  3.297352E 10  AFTER CLASS  4
     BEST SPLIT ON PREDICTOR 2002 =  6.239027F 08  AFTER CLASS  2
     BEST SPLIT ON PREDICTOR 1506 =  4.029384E 11  AFTER CLASS  1
```

```
BEST SPLIT ON PREDICTOR 1498 =    2.723362E 10  AFTER CLASS   1
REST SPLIT ON PREDICTOR 1572 =    3.254444E 11  AFTER CLASS   2

1-STEP LOOKAHEAD TO SPLIT GROUP   3, TOTAL BSS =  8.756952E 11
    1. SPLIT GROUP   3 ON PREDICTOR 1009, BSS =  2.999766E 10
    2. SPLIT GROUP   4 ON PREDICTOR 2001, BSS =  8.456975E 11
TENTATIVE SPLIT 1. SPLIT GROUP   3 ON PREDICTOR 2002 WITH BSS = 3.1708946 09
   GROUP   4 WITH    782 OBSERVATIONS FROM 1 CLASSES = 1
           W= 3.65570E 04 Y= 9.74368D 08  YSQ= 3.27634D 13  X=
   GROUP   5 WITH     45 OBSERVATIONS FROM 2 CLASSES =   2   3
           W= 2.00500E 03 Y= 5.08483D 07  YSQ= 1.70305D 12  X=

SPLIT ATTEMPT ON GROUP   4 WITH N =       782, SS =  6.793158E 12
BEST SPLIT ON PREDICTOR 2001 =    1.033711E 12  AFTER CLASS   6
BEST SPLIT ON PREDICTOR 1168 =    1.726376E 10  AFTER CLASS   4
BEST SPLIT ON PREDICTOR 1009 =    2.568592E 10  AFTER CLASS   3

SEX & MAR STATUS       CONSTANT  - NO SPLIT
BEST SPLIT ON PREDICTOR 1506 =    4.706512E 11  AFTER CLASS   1
BEST SPLIT ON PREDICTOR 1498 =    4.860359F 10  AFTER CLASS   1
BEST SPLIT ON PREDICTOR 1572 =    3.118717E 11  AFTER CLASS   4

1-STEP LOOKAHEAD TO SPLIT GROUP   3, TOTAL BSS =  1.036882E 12
    1. SPLIT GROUP   3 ON PREDICTOR 2002, BSS =  3.1708946 09
    2. SPLIT GROUP   4 ON PREDICTOR 2001, BSS =  1.033711E 12
TENTATIVE SPLIT 1. SPLIT GROUP   3 ON PREDICTOR 1506 WITH BSS = 4.843247E 11
   GROUP   4 WITH    326 OBSERVATIONS FROM 1 CLASSES = 1
           W= 1.51140E 04 Y= 4.68540D 08  YSQ= 1.77001D 13  X=
   GROUP   5 WITH    501 OBSERVATIONS FROM 5 CLASSES =   2   3   4   5   6
           W= 2.34480E 04 Y= 5.56676D 08  YSQ= 1.67663D 13  X=

SPLIT ATTEMPT ON GROUP   5 WITH N =       501, SS =  3.550351E 12
BEST SPLIT ON PREDICTOR 2001 =    4.462341E 11  AFTER CLASS   6
REST SPLIT ON PREDICTOR 1168 =    7.574913E 09  AFTER CLASS   3
REST SPLIT ON PREDICTOR 1009 =    1.474403E 10  AFTER CLASS   4
REST SPLIT ON PREDICTOR 2002 =    1.212888E 10  AFTER CLASS   2
REST SPLIT ON PREDICTOR 1506 =    4.996884E 10  AFTER CLASS   2
REST SPLIT ON PREDICTOR 1498 =    1.218131E 10  AFTER CLASS   1
REST SPLIT ON PREDICTOR 1572 =    1.539995E 10  AFTER CLASS   4

1-STEP LOOKAHEAD TO SPLIT GROUP   3, TOTAL BSS =  9.305588E 11
    1. SPLIT GROUP   3 ON PREDICTOR 1506, BSS =  4.843247E 11
    2. SPLIT GROUP   5 ON PREDICTOR 2001, BSS =  4.462341E 11
TENTATIVE SPLIT 1. SPLIT GROUP   3 ON PREDICTOR 1498 WITH BSS = 6.205892E 10
   GROUP   4 WITH    155 OBSERVATIONS FROM 1 CLASSES = 1
           W= 7.03500E 03 Y= 1.68139D 08  YSQ= 4.91865D 12  X=
   GROUP   5 WITH    672 OBSERVATIONS FROM 4 CLASSES =   2   3   4   5
           W= 3.15270E 04 Y= 8.57077D 08  YSQ= 2.95478D 13  X=

SPLIT ATTEMPT ON GROUP   5 WITH N =       672, SS =  6.247688F 12
BEST SPLIT ON PREDICTOR 2001 =    9.680789E 11  AFTER CLASS   6
REST SPLIT ON PREDICTOR 1168 =    1.565314E 10  AFTER CLASS   3
REST SPLIT ON PREDICTOR 1009 =    2.117285E 10  AFTER CLASS   3
REST SPLIT ON PREDICTOR 2002 =    3.523215E 08  AFTER CLASS   2
REST SPLIT ON PREDICTOR 1506 =    4.780164E 11  AFTER CLASS   1
REST SPLIT ON PREDICTOR 1498 =    7.677254E 10  AFTER CLASS   1
REST SPLIT ON PREDICTOR 1572 =    2.813204E 11  AFTER CLASS   4
```

```
1-STEP LOOKAHEAD TO SPLIT GROUP   3. TOTAL BSS =  1.030138E 12
    1. SPLIT GROUP  2 ON PREDICTOR 1498, BSS =  6.205892E 10
    2. SPLIT GROUP  5 ON PREDICTOR 2001, BSS =  9.680789E 11
TENTATIVE SPLIT 1. SPLIT GROUP  3 ON PREDICTOR 1572 WITH BSS = 3.152271E 11
  GROUP   4 WITH    631 OBSERVATIONS FROM  3 CLASSES =   3   2   4
          W= 2.82770E 04 Y= 7.03020D 08 YSQ= 2.18480D 13 X=
  GROUP   5 WITH    196 OBSERVATIONS FROM  1 CLASSES =   1
          W= 1.02850E 04 Y= 3.22196D 08 YSQ= 1.26184D 13 X=

SPLIT ATTEMPT ON GROUP   4 WITH N =     631,  SS =  4.369614E 12
BEST SPLIT ON PREDICTOR 2001 =  6.060654E 11 AFTER CLASS 12
BEST SPLIT ON PREDICTOR 1168 =  6.520046E 09 AFTER CLASS  6
BEST SPLIT ON PREDICTOR 1009 =  2.945135E 10 AFTER CLASS  3
BEST SPLIT ON PREDICTOR 2002 =  1.551892E 08 AFTER CLASS  2
BEST SPLIT ON PREDICTOR 1506 =  1.326627E 11 AFTER CLASS  2
BEST SPLIT ON PREDICTOR 1468 =  2.222981E 10 AFTER CLASS  1
BEST SPLIT ON PREDICTOR 1572 =  1.726376E 10 AFTER CLASS  3

1-STEP LOOKAHEAD TO SPLIT GROUP   3. TOTAL BSS =  9.212925E 11
    1. SPLIT GROUP  3 ON PREDICTOR 1572, BSS =  3.152271E 11
    2. SPLIT GROUP  4 ON PREDICTOR 2001, BSS =  6.060654E 11
```

FROM ELIGIBLE PREDICTORS AROUND THE CURRENT RANK 1,   0 UP AND 0 DOWN

***** PARTITION OF GROUP 3 *****

MAXIMUM ELIGIBLE BSS AT EACH STEP   MAXIMUM TOTAL BSS (LOOKAHEAD)
1. SPLIT   3 ON V2001 BSS= 1.11159E 12   SPLIT   3 ON V2001 BSS = 1.11159E 12
2. SPLIT   4 ON V1506 BSS= 2.65785E 11   SPLIT   4 ON V1506 BSS = 2.65785E 11
PE(2)= 1.599E 10, TOTAL= 1.37738E 12   TOTAL= 1.37738E 12
     PREDICTOR 2001 HAS RANK 1

SPLIT GROUP 3 ON 3-YR AVE $ INC.   V2001
GROUP   4 WITH 705 OBSERVATIONS FROM   2 CLASSES = 5 6
        W= 3.25190E 04 Y= 7.89293D 08 YSQ= 2.32347D 13 X=
GROUP   5 WITH 122 OBSERVATIONS FROM   1 CLASSES = 7
        W= 6.04300E 03 Y= 2.35924D 08 YSQ= 1.12317D 13 X=

     3 CANDIDATES -   GROUP   SS
                          2   3.010512E 12
                          4   4.077182E 12
                          5   2.021067E 12

          ATTEMPT SPLIT ON GROUP   2 WITH SS = 3.010512E 12

```
                          LOOKAHEAD TENTATIVE PARTITION

SPLIT ATTEMPT ON GROUP    2 WITH N =      1261, SS  = 3.010512E 12
   REST SPLIT ON PREDICTOR 2001 =  1.887342E 11 AFTER CLASS   3

SYMMETRIC SPLIT INELIGIBLE - RESULTANT GROUP TOO SMALL
   BEST SPLIT ON PREDICTOR 1168 =  1.054448E 10 AFTER CLASS   4
   REST SPLIT ON PREDICTOR 1009 =  2.628780E 09 AFTER CLASS   5
   REST SPLIT ON PREDICTOR 2002 =  1.279263E 09 AFTER CLASS   1
   REST SPLIT ON PREDICTOR 1506 =  1.563909E 11 AFTER CLASS   4
   BEST SPLIT ON PREDICTOR 1498 =  8.093644E 10 AFTER CLASS   3
   REST SPLIT ON PREDICTOR 1572 =  1.372607E 11 AFTER CLASS   3
   BEST SPLIT ON PREDICTOR 1490 =  9.628654E 10 AFTER CLASS   2
TENTATIVE SPLIT 1. SPLIT GROUP   2 ON PREDICTOR 2001 WITH BSS =  1.887342E 11

EXTREME CASES LYING OUTSIDE THE INTERVAL (-2.761231E 04,  5.608148E 04)
      Y         W          WY           V1122
    60000     53.0     3.18000E 06      60000
    60000     48.0     2.88000E 06      60000
    60000     53.0     3.18000E 06      60000
    75000     24.0     1.80300E 06      75000
    GROUP   6 WITH    899 OBSERVATIONS FROM  3 CLASSES =  1   2   3
           W= 2.89780E 04 Y= 3.70246D 08 YSQ= 6.46847D 12 X=
    GROUP   7 WITH    362 OBSERVATIONS FROM  1 CLASSES =  4
           W= 1.40350E 04 Y= 2.42026D 08 YSQ= 5.25749D 12 X=

SPLIT ATTEMPT ON GROUP    6 WITH N =       899, SS  = 1.737908E 12
   BEST SPLIT ON PREDICTOR 2001 =  6.386772E 10 AFTER CLASS   1
   BEST SPLIT ON PREDICTOR 1168 =  5.869928E 09 AFTER CLASS   3
   BEST SPLIT ON PREDICTOR 1009 =  3.208643E 09 AFTER CLASS   2
   BEST SPLIT ON PREDICTOR 2002 =  1.898237E 10 AFTER CLASS   2
   BEST SPLIT ON PREDICTOR 1506 =  6.039798E 10 AFTER CLASS   4
   BEST SPLIT ON PREDICTOR 1498 =  4.410311E 10 AFTER CLASS   3
   BEST SPLIT ON PREDICTOR 1572 =  6.607497E 10 AFTER CLASS   2

1-STEP LOOKAHEAD TO SPLIT GROUP   2, TOTAL BSS =  2.548092E 11
   1. SPLIT GROUP   2 ON PREDICTOR 2001, BSS =  1.887342E 11
   2. SPLIT GROUP   6 ON PREDICTOR 1572, BSS =  6.607497E 10
TENTATIVE SPLIT 1. SPLIT GROUP   2 ON PREDICTOR 1168 WITH BSS =  1.054448E 10

EXTREME CASES LYING OUTSIDE THE INTERVAL (-2.761231E 04,  5.608148E 04)
      Y         W          WY           V1122
    60000     53.0     3.18000E 06      60000
    60000     48.0     2.88000E 06      60000
    60000     53.0     3.18000E 06      60000
    75000     24.0     1.80000E 06      75000
    GROUP   6 WITH   1028 OBSERVATIIONS FROM  3 CLASSES =  2   3   4
           W= 3.85740E 04 Y= 5.55564D 08 YSQ= 1.06816D 13 X=
    GROUP   7 WITH    233 OBSERVATIONS FROM  2 CLASSES =  5   6
           W= 4.43900E 03 Y= 5.67081D 07 YSQ= 1.04432D 12 X=

SPLIT ATTEMPT ON GROUP    6 WITH N =      1028, SS  = 2.680100E 12
   BEST SPLIT ON PREDICTOR 2001 =  1.853190E 11 AFTER CLASS   3
   BEST SPLIT ON PREDICTOR 1168 =  3.248488E 09 AFTER CLASS   5
   BEST SPLIT ON PREDICTOR 1009 =  4.081058E 09 AFTER CLASS   1
   BEST SPLIT ON PREDICTOR 2002 =  3.002073E 09 AFTER CLASS   1
   BEST SPLIT ON PREDICTOR 1506 =  1.318050E 11 AFTER CLASS   4
   BEST SPLIT ON PREDICTOR 1498 =  6.848250E 10 AFTER CLASS   4
   BEST SPLIT ON PREDICTOR 1572 =  1.070942E 11 AFTER CLASS   2
```

```
1-STEP LOOKAHEAD TO SPLIT GROUP   2, TOTAL BSS =  1.958635E 11
     1. SPLIT GROUP   2 ON PREDICTOR 1168, BSS =  1.054448E 10
     2. SPLIT GROUP   6 ON PREDICTOR 2001, BSS =  1.853190E 11
TENTATIVE SPLIT 1. SPLIT GROUP   2 ON PREDICTOR 1009 WITH BSS = 2.628780E 09

EXTREME CASES LYING OUTSIDE THE INTERVAL (-2.761231E 04, 5.608148E 04)
    Y        W          WY          V1122
60000     53.0     3.1800E 06      60000
60000     48.0     2.8800E 06      60000
60000     53.0     3.1800E 06      60000
75000     24.0     1.8000E 06      75000
GROUP   6 WITH   965 OBSERVATIONS FROM   4 CLASSES =  2   3   4   5
         W= 2.90270E 04 Y= 4.18168D 08 YSQ=7.92797D 12 X=
GROUP   7 WITH   296 OBSERVATIONS FROM  1 CLASSES =  6
         W= 1.33860E 04 Y= 1.94104D 08 YSQ= 3.79799D 12 X=

SPLIT ATTEMPT ON GROUP   6 WITH N =       965,  SS  =  1.903773E 12
BEST SPLIT ON PREDICTOR 2001 BSS =  1.086272E 11 AFTER CLASS  3
BEST SPLIT ON PREDICTOR 1168 BSS =  1.004641E 10 AFTER CLASS  4
BEST SPLIT ON PREDICTOR 1009 BSS =  1.277882E 09 AFTER CLASS  2
BEST SPLIT ON PREDICTOR 2002 BSS =  7.344226E 09 AFTER CLASS  2
BEST SPLIT ON PREDICTOR 1506 BSS =  9.267105E 10 AFTER CLASS  4
BEST SPLIT ON PREDICTOR 1498 BSS =  4.313632E 10 AFTER CLASS  4
BEST SPLIT ON PREDICTOR 1572 BSS =  9.653715E 10 AFTER CLASS  3


1-STEP LOOKAHEAD TO SPLIT GROUP   2, TOTAL BSS =  1.112560E 11
     1. SPLIT GROUP   2 ON PREDICTOR 1009, BSS =  2.628780E 09
     2. SPLIT GROUP   6 ON PREDICTOR 2001, BSS =  1.086272E 11
TENTATIVE SPLIT 1. SPLIT GROUP   2 ON PREDICTOR 2002 WITH BSS = 1.279263E 09

EXTREME CASES LYING OUTSIDE THE INTERVAL (-2.761231E 04, 5.608148E 04)
    Y        W          WY          V1122
60000     53.0     3.1800E 06      60000
60000     48.0     2.8800E 06      60000
60000     53.0     3.1800E 06      60000
75000     24.0     1.8000E 06      75000
GROUP   6 WITH   878 OBSERVATIONS FROM  1 CLASSES =  1
         W= 3.01270E 04 Y= 4.32242D 08 YSQ=8.25847D 12 X=
GROUP   7 WITH   383 OBSERVATIONS FROM   2 CLASSES =  2   3
         W= 1.28860E 04 Y= 1.80030D 08 YSQ= 3.46749D 12 X=

SPLIT ATTEMPT ON GROUP   6 WITH N =       878,  SS  =  2.056949E 12
BEST SPLIT ON PREDICTOR 2001 BSS =  1.656110E 11 AFTER CLASS  3
BEST SPLIT ON PREDICTOR 1168 BSS =  1.324876E 10 AFTER CLASS  4
BEST SPLIT ON PREDICTOR 1009 BSS =  2.674917E 09 AFTER CLASS  3

SFX & MAR STATUS         CONSTANT - NO SPLIT
BEST SPLIT ON PREDICTOR 1506 BSS =  1.138795E 11 AFTER CLASS  4
BEST SPLIT ON PREDICTOR 1498 BSS =  6.668734E 10 AFTER CLASS  4
BEST SPLIT ON PREDICTOR 1572 BSS =  1.174730E 11 AFTER CLASS  3


1-STEP LOOKAHEAD TO SPLIT GROUP   2, TOTAL BSS =  1.668903E 11
     1. SPLIT GROUP   2 ON PREDICTOR 2002, BSS =  1.279263E 09
     2. SPLIT GROUP   6 ON PREDICTOR 2001, BSS =  1.656110E 11
TENTATIVE SPLIT 1. SPLIT GROUP   2 ON PREDICTOR 1506 WITH BSS = 1.563909E 11

EXTREME CASES LYING OUTSIDE THE INTERVAL (-2.761231E 04, 5.608148E 04)
             WY                      V1122
```

154

with the 15.64x10^10 from the first split on city size and 11.08x10^10 from a second split on income, the total power is greater than any pair of splits, therefore group 2 will be split on city size (V1506).

```
60000    53.0    3.1800E 06    60000
60000    49.0    2.8800E 06    60000
60000    53.0    3.1800E 06    60000
75000    24.0    1.8000E 06    75000
GROUP  6 WITH  760 OBSERVATIONS FROM  4 CLASSES =  1  2  3  4
       W= 2.45430E 04  Y= 3.89580 08  YSQ= 7.98458D 12  X=
GROUP  7 WITH  501 OBSERVATIONS FROM  2 CLASSES =  5  6
       W= 1.84700E 04  Y= 2.22315D 08  YSQ= 3.74138D 12  X=

SPLIT ATTEMPT ON GROUP  6 WITH N =     760,  SS =  1.78864 3E 12
  BEST SPLIT ON PREDICTOR 2001 =  1.10838 7E 11  AFTER CLASS  3
  BEST SPLIT ON PREDICTOR 1168 =  7.76470 5E 09  AFTER CLASS  5
  BEST SPLIT ON PREDICTOR 1000 =  3.64799 6E 09  AFTER CLASS  2
  BEST SPLIT ON PREDICTOR 2002 =  2.09924 9E 09  AFTER CLASS  1
  BEST SPLIT ON PREDICTOR 1506 =  1.67111 6E 10  AFTER CLASS  2
  BEST SPLIT ON PREDICTOR 1498 =  1.74378 2E 10  AFTER CLASS  1
  BEST SPLIT ON PREDICTOR 1572 =  7.37390 1E 10  AFTER CLASS  3

1-STEP LOOKAHEAD TO SPLIT GROUP  2, TOTAL BSS =  2.67229 6E 11
   1. SPLIT GROUP    2 ON PREDICTOR 1506, BSS =  1.56390 9E 11
   2. SPLIT GROUP    6 ON PREDICTOR 2001, BSS =  1.10838 7E 11
TENTATIVE SPLIT 1. SPLIT GROUP  2 ON PREDICTOR 1498 WITH RSS =  8.09364 4E 10

EXTREME CASES LYING OUTSIDE THE INTERVAL (-2.76123 1E 04,  5.60814 8E 04)
  Y          W         V1122
60000    53.0    3.1800E 06    60000
60000    48.0    2.8800E 06    60000
60000    53.0    3.1800E 06    60000
75000    24.0    1.8000E 06    75000
GROUP  6 WITH  673 OBSERVATIONS FROM  3 CLASSES =  1  2  3
       W= 2.13770E 04  Y= 3.33794D 08  YSQ= 6.71694D 12  X=
GROUP  7 WITH  588 OBSERVATIONS FROM  2 CLASSES =  4  5
       W= 2.16360E 04  Y= 2.78479D 08  YSQ= 5.09002D 12  X=

SPLIT ATTEMPT ON GROUP  6 WITH N =     673,  SS =  1.50488 2E 12
  BEST SPLIT ON PREDICTOR 2001 =  7.17173 6E 10  AFTER CLASS  3
  BEST SPLIT ON PREDICTOR 1168 =  2.38236 5E 10  AFTER CLASS  4
  BEST SPLIT ON PREDICTOR 1009 =  4.61058 9E 09  AFTER CLASS  2
  BEST SPLIT ON PREDICTOR 2002 =  2.70742 3E 09  AFTER CLASS  2
  BEST SPLIT ON PREDICTOR 1506 =  7.17760 8E 10  AFTER CLASS  3
  BEST SPLIT ON PREDICTOR 1498 =  3.28277 7E 10  AFTER CLASS  1
  BEST SPLIT ON PREDICTOR 1572 =  7.08124 3E 10  AFTER CLASS  2

1-STEP LOOKAHEAD TO SPLIT GROUP  2, TOTAL BSS =  1.52712 5E 11
   1. SPLIT GROUP    2 ON PREDICTOR 1498, BSS =  8.09364 4E 10
   2. SPLIT GROUP    6 ON PREDICTOR 1506, BSS =  7.17608 F 10
TENTATIVE SPLIT 1. SPLIT GROUP  2 ON PREDICTOR 1572 WITH BSS =  1.37260 7E 11

EXTREME CASES LYING OUTSIDE THE INTERVAL (-2.76123 1E 04,  5.60814 8E 04)
  Y          W         V1122
60000    53.0    3.1800E 06    60000
60000    48.0    2.8800E 06    60000
60000    53.0    3.1800E 06    60000
75000    24.0    1.8000E 06    75000
GROUP  6 WITH  597 OBSERVATIONS FROM  1 CLASSES =  3
       W= 1.54950E 04  Y= 1.83677D 08  YSQ= 2.98483D 12  X=
GROUP  7 WITH  664 OBSERVATIONS FROM  3 CLASSES =  2  1  4
       W= 2.75180E 04  Y= 4.28950D 08  YSQ= 8.74114D 12  X=
```

```
SPLIT ATTEMPT ON GROUP   7 WITH N =      664,  SS =   2.065736E 12
  BEST SPLIT ON PREDICTOR 2001 = 1.186411E 11 AFTER CLASS  3
  BEST SPLIT ON PREDICTOR 1168 = 2.715812E 09 AFTER CLASS  5
  BEST SPLIT ON PREDICTOR 1009 = 2.517631E 09 AFTER CLASS  5
  BEST SPLIT ON PREDICTOR 2002 = 5.719982E 09 AFTER CLASS  1
  BEST SPLIT ON PREDICTOR 1506 = 9.607997E 10 AFTER CLASS  4
  BEST SPLIT ON PREDICTOR 1498 = 6.120853E 10 AFTER CLASS  4
  BEST SPLIT ON PREDICTOR 1572 = 2.891553E 10 AFTER CLASS  2

1-STEP LOOKAHEAD TO SPLIT GROUP   2,  TOTAL RSS =  2.559018E 11
  1. SPLIT GROUP   2 ON PREDICTOR 1572, RSS = 1.372607E 11
  2. SPLIT GROUP   7 ON PREDICTOR 2001, RSS = 1.186411E 11
```

FROM ELIGIBLE ***** PARTITION OF GROUP 2 *****
PREDICTORS AROUND THE CURRENT RANK 1,   0 UP AND 0 DOWN

```
    MAXIMUM ELIGIBLE RSS AT EACH STEP          MAXIMUM TOTAL RSS (LOOKAHEAD)
1.SPLIT   2 ON V2001 RSS= 1.8R734E 11    SPLIT  2 ON V1506 RSS = 1.56391E 11
2.SPLIT   6 ON V1572 PSS= 6.60750F 10    SPLIT  6 ON V2001 RSS = 1.10839F 11
PF(2)= 1.599F 10, TOTAL= 2.54809E 11                 TOTAL= 2.67230E 11
        PREDICTOR 1506 HAS RANK 1
```

SYMMETRY SPLIT ON V2001 = 0.0
    SYMMETRIC / MAX SPLIT = 0.0 PERCENT

SPLIT GROUP   2 ON LRGST PLAC/SMSA PSU31:66 V1506

EXTREME CASES LYING OUTSIDE THE INTERVAL (-2.761231E 04, 5.608148E 04)
```
   Y         W          WY         V1122
60000     53.0    3.18000E 06     60000
60000     48.0    2.88000E 06     60000
60000     53.0    3.18000F 06     60000
75000     24.0    1.80000F 06     75000
GROUP   6 WITH   501 OBSERVATIONS FROM  2 CLASSES =  5   6
        W= 1.84700E 04 Y= 2.22315D 08 YSQ= 3.74138D 12 X=
GROUP   7 WITH   760 OBSERVATIONS FROM  4 CLASSES =  1   2   3   4
        W= 2.45430F 04 Y= 3.89570 OR Y= 7.98458D 12 X=
```

```
   4 CANDIDATES -      GROUP       SS.
                         6     1.065477E 12
                         4     4.077182E 12
                         5     7.021067E 12
                         7     1.788649E 12
```

        ATTEMPT SPLIT ON GROUP   4 WITH SS = 4.077182E 12

Omit the rest of the splitting process.

```
***** PARTITION OF GROUP 22 *****
FROM ELIGIBLE PREDICTORS AROUND THE CURRENT RANK 1.    0 UP AND  0 DOWN

      MAXIMUM ELIGIBLE RSS AT EACH STEP     MAXIMUM TOTAL RSS (LOOKAHEAD)

GROUP 22 COULD NOT BE SPLIT

END OF STAGE 1 OF THE ANALYSIS.  12 FINAL GROUPS.  12 INELIGIBLE FOR SPLITTING.

      VARIATION EXPLAINED (BSS(IO)/TSS) =  39.8%

      1-WAY ANALYSIS OF VARIANCE ON FINAL GROUPS

      SOURCE       SUM OF SQUARES      DF        MEAN SQUARE

      BETWEEN      5.307254E 12        12.       4.422711E 11
      ERROR        8.015149E 12        81524.    9.831658E 07
      TOTAL        1.332240E 13        81536.    1.633931E 08
```

A summary of the variance within (error) and between the final groups. Note that with weighted data one cannot use the degrees of freedom, or calculate F-Tests.

This is the main result – the split record from which the branching diagram can be made.

GROUP SUMMARY TABLE
23 GROUPS OF WHICH 12 ARE FINAL

GROUP   1 , N =   2388, SUM W = 8.157600E 04
Y MEAN= 2.007342E 04, VARIANCE=1.633931E 08, SS(L)/TSS= 1.000, BSS/TSS= 0.233
SPLIT ON 3-YR AVE $ INC   , BSS(L) = 3.102057E 12 INTO
    2 WITH CLASSES   1   2   3   4
    3 WITH CLASSES   5   6   7

GROUP   3 , N =   827, SUM W = 3.856200E 04
Y MEAN= 2.658618E 04, VARIANCE= 1.371938E 08, SS(L)/TSS= 0.541, BSS/TSS= 0.083
SPLIT ON 3-YR AVE $ INC   , BSS(L) = 1.111591E 12 INTO
    4 WITH CLASSES   5   6
    5 WITH CLASSES   7

GROUP   2 , N =   1261, SUM W = 4.301300E 04
Y MEAN= 1.423459E 04, VARIANCE= 7.004651E 07, SS(L)/TSS= 0.226, BSS/TSS= 0.012
SPLIT ON LRGST PLAC/SMSA PSU31:66, BSS(L) = 1.563909E 11 INTO
    6 WITH CLASSES   5   6
    7 WITH CLASSES   1   2   3   4

GROUP   4 , N =   705, SUM W = 3.251900E 04
Y MEAN= 2.427173E 04, VARIANCE= 1.255571E 08, SS(L)/TSS= 0.306, BSS/TSS= 0.003
SPLIT ON DIST TO CNTR SMSA   31:58, BSS(L) = 4.518104E 10 INTO
    8 WITH CLASSES   1   2
    9 WITH CLASSES   3   4   5

GROUP   5 , N =   122, SUM W = 6.043000E 03
Y MEAN= 3.904086E 04, VARIANCE= 3.372119E 08, SS(L)/TSS= 0.152, BSS/TSS= 0.014
SPLIT ON LRGST PLAC/SMSA PSU31:66, BSS(L) = 1.798738E 11 INTO
   10 WITH CLASSES   3   4   5   6
   11 WITH CLASSES   1   2

GROUP   9 , N =   312, SUM W = 1.462700E 04
Y MEAN= 2.557518E 04, VARIANCE= 1.651233E 08, SS(L)/TSS= 0.181, BSS/TSS= 0.023
SPLIT ON LRGST PLAC/SMSA PSU31:66, BSS(L) = 3.032692E 11 INTO
   12 WITH CLASSES   3   4   5   6
   13 WITH CLASSES   1   2

GROUP   8 , N =   393, SUM W = 1.789200E 04
Y MEAN= 2.320613E 04, VARIANCE= 9.102715E 07, SS(L)/TSS= 0.122, BSS/TSS= 0.006
SPLIT ON LRGST PLAC/SMSA PSU31:66, BSS(L) = 8.140305E 10 INTO
   14 WITH CLASSES   2   3   5   6
   15 WITH CLASSES   1

GROUP   7 , N =   760, SUM W = 2.454300E 04
Y MEAN= 1.588874E 04, VARIANCE= 7.297443E 07, SS(L)/TSS= 0.134, BSS/TSS= 0.006
SPLIT ON CURRENT REGION OV472   , BSS(L) = 7.373901E 10 INTO
   16 WITH CLASSES   3
   17 WITH CLASSES   1   2   4

GROUP   6*, N =   501, SUM W = 1.847000E 04
Y MEAN= 1.203654E 04, VARIANCE= 5.780226E 07, SS(L)/TSS= 0.080, BSS/TSS= 0.0

GROUP 11 , N =   86, SUM W = 4.351000E 03
Y MEAN= 4.244310E 04, VARIANCE= 3.295334E 08, SS(L)/TSS= 0.106, BSS/TSS= 0.001
SPLIT ON # REQUIRED ROOMS 23:12 , BSS(L) = 1.231448E 10 INTO
   18 WITH CLASSES   2
   19 WITH CLASSES   3   4   5   6

GROUP 10*, N =   36, SUM W = 1.692000E 03

Y MEAN= 3.029196E 04, VARIANCE= 2.577897E 08,   SS(L)/TSS= 0.032, BSS/TSS= 0.0

GROUP 17 , N =   463, SUM W = 1.806100E 04
   Y MEAN= 1.692718E 04, VARIANCE= 7.825883E 07,   SS(L)/TSS= 0.106, BSS/TSS= 0.008
   SPLIT ON 3-YR AVE $ INC   , BSS(L) = 1.001768E 11 INTO
       20 WITH CLASSES   1   2   3
       21 WITH CLASSES   4

GROUP 16*, N =   297, SUM W = 6.482000E 03
   Y MEAN= 1.299527E 04, VARIANCE= 4.714030E 07,   SS(L)/TSS= 0.023, BSS/TSS= 0.0

GROUP 19 , N =   65, SUM W = 3.333000E 03
   Y MEAN= 4.337286E 04, VARIANCE= 3.608515E 08,   SS(L)/TSS= 0.089, BSS/TSS= 0.011
   SPLIT ON CURRENT REGION OV472   , PSS(L) = 1.413889E 11 INTO
       22 WITH CLASSES   2   4
       23 WITH CLASSES   3   1

GROUP 18*, N =   21, SUM W = 1.018000E 03
   Y MEAN= 3.939901E 04, VARIANCE= 2.275338E 08,   SS(L)/TSS= 0.017, BSS/TSS= 0.0

GROUP 12*, N =   188, SUM W = 8.578000E 03
   Y MEAN= 2.175148E 04, VARIANCE= 1.386882E 08,   SS(L)/TSS= 0.089, BSS/TSS= 0.0

GROUP 15*, N =   175, SUM W = 7.556000E 03
   Y MEAN= 2.570084E 04, VARIANCE= 1.244561E 08,   SS(L)/TSS= 0.070, BSS/TSS= 0.0

GROUP 13*, N =   124, SUM W = 6.049000E 03
   Y MEAN= 3.099752E 04, VARIANCE= 1.534795E 08,   SS(L)/TSS= 0.069, BSS/TSS= 0.0

GROUP 21*, N =   181, SUM W = 7.389000E 03
   Y MEAN= 1.975753E 04, VARIANCE= 9.629286E 07,   SS(L)/TSS= 0.053, BSS/TSS= 0.0

GROUP 14*, N =   218, SUM W = 1.033600E 04
   Y MEAN= 2.138240E 04, VARIANCE= 5.91037AE 07,   SS(L)/TSS= 0.046, BSS/TSS= 0.0

GROUP 20*, N =   282, SUM W = 1.067200E 04
   Y MEAN= 1.496752E 04, VARIANCE= 5.666890E 07,   SS(L)/TSS= 0.045, BSS/TSS= 0.0

GROUP 23*, N =   31, SUM W = 1.683000E 03
   Y MEAN= 4.982159E 04, VARIANCE= 3.220828E 08,   SS(L)/TSS= 0.039, BSS/TSS= 0.0

GROUP 22*, N =   34, SUM W = 1.650000E 03
   Y MEAN= 3.679515E 04, VARIANCE= 3.236129E 08,   SS(L)/TSS= 0.039, BSS/TSS= 0.0

100*PSS/TSS TABLE FOR 1-STEP LOOK-AHEAD
23 GROUPS, 8 PREDICTORS
< INDICATES LESS THAN 2 SPLITS WERE MADE

GROUP NUMBER (* INDICATES THE GROUP IS FINAL)

PREDICTOR	1	3	2	4	5	9	8	7	6*	11	10*	17	16*	19	18*	12*	15*	13*	21*	14*
2001	31.6	10.3	1.5	2.2	*****<	2.0	1.1	1.2	0.3<	*****<	*******<	1.3	0.3<	******<	*******<	0.0<	0.4<	0.5<	*****<	0.2<
1168	18.8	7.2	1.5	1.7	1.4	2.3	0.8	1.0	0.1<	1.2	0.1<	0.9	0.0<	1.2	******<	0.2<	0.1<	0.2<	0.2<	0.0<
1009	21.9	6.6	0.8	1.6	1.6	2.2	0.8	0.8	0.0<	0.9	0.2<	0.8	0.0<	1.1	0.3<	0.1<	0.0<	0.2<	0.5<	0.1<
2002	21.6	7.8	1.3	1.9	1.4	2.2	0.8	0.7	0.0<	1.0	0.2<	0.7	0.0<	0.0<	0.0<	0.1<	0.0<	0.0<	0.1<	0.1<
1506	22.7	7.0	2.0	2.3	2.1	2.5	1.2	0.6	0.0<	1.0	0.3<	0.7	0.0<	0.9	0.3<	0.1<*****<	0.1<	0.1<	0.1<	0.0<
1498	19.0	7.7	1.1	2.6	1.9	1.4	0.5	1.1	0.1<	0.8	0.0<	0.9	0.0<	1.0	0.1<	0.0<	0.6<	0.3<	0.2<	0.1<
1572	19.4	6.9	1.9	2.2	1.7	1.7	1.1	1.3	0.1<	1.0	0.0<	0.9	******<	1.4	0.1<	0.0<	0.6<	0.4<	0.0<	0.0<
1490	3.0<	0.7<	0.7<	0.5<	0.2<	0.0<	0.4<	0.6<	0.3<	0.3<	0.0<	0.2<	0.2<	0.0<	0.0<	0.0<	0.5<	0.0<	0.1<	0.1<

GROUP NUMBER (* INDICATES THE GROUP IS FINAL)

PREDICTOR	20*	23*	22*
2001	0.1<	*****<******<	
1168	0.0<	0.2<	0.2<
1009	0.1<	0.1<	0.2<
2002	0.1<	0.0<******<	
1506	0.1<	0.0<	0.0<
1498	0.1<	0.3<	0.3<
1572	0.2<	0.0<	0.0<
1490	0.1<*****<		0.0<

Comparison of this table with the next one shows where the lookahead reveals more two-split power in selecting an inferior predictor for the first split -
See groups 2, 4, 7 for example.

100*RSS/TSS TABLE FOR 0-STEP LOOK-AHEAD
23 GROUPS, 8 PREDICTORS

GROUP NUMBER (* INDICATES THE GROUP IS FINAL)

PREDICTOR	1	3	2	4	5	9	8	7	6*	11	10*	17	16*	19	18*	12*	15*	13*	21*	14*
2001	23.3	8.3	1.4	1.5*******	*******	1.0	0.7	0.8	0.3*******	*******	*******	0.8	0.3********	********	*******	0.0	0.4	0.5*******	*******	0.2
1168	2.0	0.1	0.1	0.1	0.2	0.4	0.1	0.1	0.1	0.1	0.1	0.1	0.0	0.3*******	0.3	0.2	0.1	0.2	0.2	0.0
1009	3.3	0.2	0.0	0.1	1.0	0.0	0.1	0.0	0.0	0.6	0.2	0.0	0.0	0.3	0.3	0.1	0.0	0.2	0.5	0.1
2002	2.9	0.0	0.0	0.0	0.1	0.0	0.0	0.0	0.0	0.0	0.0	0.0	0.0	0.0	0.0	0.0	0.0	0.0	0.0	0.1
1506	9.7	3.6	1.2	2.0	1.4	2.3	0.6	0.1	0.1	0.0	0.3	0.1	0.0	0.0	0.3	0.1*******	*******	0.1	0.1	0.0
1498	5.0	0.5	0.6	0.3	0.6	0.5	0.1	0.1	0.1	0.4	0.0	0.1	0.0	0.5	0.1	0.0	0.0	0.3	0.2	0.0
1572	4.3	2.4	1.0	1.3	1.2	0.7	0.5	0.6	0.1	0.7	0.0	0.2*******	*******	1.1	0.1	0.0	0.6	0.4	0.0	0.0
1490	3.0	0.7	0.7	0.5	0.2	0.2	0.4	0.6	0.3	0.3	0.0	0.2	0.2	0.0	0.0	0.0	0.5	0.0	0.1	0.1

GROUP NUMBER (* INDICATES THE GROUP IS FINAL)

PREDICTOR	20*	23*	22*
2001	70*	0.1*******	
1168	0.0	0.2	0.2
1009	0.1	0.1	0.2
2002	0.1	0.0*******	
1506	0.1	0.0	0.0
1498	0.1	0.3	0.3
1572	0.1	0.0	0.0
1490	0.2	0.1*******	0.0

100*RSS/TSS TABLE FOR 0-STEP LOOK-AHEAD
23 GROUPS, 8 PREDICTORS

MAXIMUM RSS REGARDLESS OF ELIGIBILITY

GROUP NUMBER (* INDICATES THE GROUP IS FINAL)

PREDICTOR	1	3	2	4	5	9	8	7	6*	11	10*	17	16*	19	18*	12*	15*	13*	21*	14*
2001	23.3	8.3	1.4	1.5*******		1.0	0.7	0.8	0.3**************		0.3**************	0.8	0.3**************	0.3**************	0.3**************	0.0	0.4	0.5	0.5*******	0.2
1168	2.0	0.1	0.1	0.1	0.2	0.4	0.1	0.1	0.1	0.1	0.1	0.1	0.0	0.3	0.3	0.2	0.1	0.2	0.2	0.0
1000	3.3	0.2	0.0	0.1	1.0	0.0	0.1	0.0	0.0	0.6	0.2	0.0	0.0	0.4	0.3	0.1	0.0	0.0	0.5	0.1
2002	2.9	0.0	0.0	0.0	0.2	0.0	0.0	0.1	0.0	0.2	0.0	0.0	0.0	0.1	0.1	0.1*******	0.0*******	0.1	0.0	0.0
1506	9.7	3.6	1.2	2.0	1.4	2.3	0.6	0.1	0.0	0.0	0.3	0.1	0.0	0.1	0.3	0.0	0.0	0.1	0.1	0.0
1498	5.0	0.5	0.6	0.3	0.6	0.5	0.1	0.1	0.1	0.4	0.4	0.1	0.0	0.5	0.1	0.0	0.6	0.3	0.2	0.0
1572	4.3	2.4	1.0	1.3	1.2	0.7	0.5	0.6	0.1	0.7	0.7	0.2*******	0.2*******	1.1	0.1	0.0	0.6	0.4	0.0	0.1
1490	3.0	0.7	0.7	0.5	0.2	0.2	0.4	0.6	0.3	0.3	0.3	0.2	0.2	0.1	0.2	0.0	0.5	0.3	0.1	0.1

GROUP NUMBER (* INDICATES THE GROUP IS FINAL)

PREDICTOR	20*	23*	22*
2001	0.1**************	0.1**************	
1168	0.0	0.2	0.2
1000	0.1	0.1	0.5
2002	0.1	0.0************	
1506	0.1	0.0	0.0
1498	0.1	0.3	0.3
1572	0.2	0.0	0.0
1490	0.1*******	0.0	0.0

PROFILE OF CLASS MEANS AND SLOPES

3-YR AVE $ INC , ETA = 0.351 — GROUP

CLASS		1	2	3	4	5	6*	7	8	9	10*	11
1	N	256	256	0	0	0	141	115	0	0	0	0
1	YMEAN	1.053E 04	1.053E 04	0.0	0.0	0.0	9.661E 03	1.174E 04	0.0	0.0	0.0	0.0
2	N	257	257	0	0	0	114	143	0	0	0	0
2	YMEAN	1.323E 04	1.323E 04	0.0	0.0	0.0	1.164E 04	1.475E 04	0.0	0.0	0.0	0.0
3	N	386	386	0	0	0	141	245	0	0	0	0
3	YMEAN	1.408E 04	1.408E 04	0.0	0.0	0.0	1.265E 04	1.510E 04	0.0	0.0	0.0	0.0
4	N	362	362	0	0	0	105	257	0	0	0	0
4	YMEAN	1.724E 04	1.724E 04	0.0	0.0	0.0	1.442E 04	1.853E 04	0.0	0.0	0.0	0.0
5	N	497	0	497	497	0	0	0	266	231	0	0
5	YMEAN	2.259E 04	0.0	2.259E 04	2.259E 04	0.0	0.0	0.0	2.157E 04	2.372E 04	0.0	0.0
6	N	208	0	208	208	0	0	0	127	81	0	0
6	YMEAN	2.799E 04	0.0	2.799E 04	2.799E 04	0.0	0.0	0.0	2.636E 04	3.047E 04	0.0	0.0
7	N	122	0	122	0	122	0	0	0	0	36	86
7	YMEAN	3.904E 04	0.0	3.904E 04	0.0	3.904E 04	0.0	0.0	0.0	0.0	3.029E 04	4.244E 04

3-YR AVE $ INC , ETA = 0.351 — GROUP

CLASS		10*	17	16*	19	18*	12*	15*	13*	21*	14*
1	N	0	54	61	0	0	0	0	0	0	0
1	YMEAN	0.0	1.296E 04	9.710E 03	0.0	0.0	0.0	0.0	0.0	0.0	0.0
2	N	0	83	60	0	0	0	0	0	0	0
2	YMEAN	0.0	1.636E 04	9.727E 03	0.0	0.0	0.0	0.0	0.0	0.0	0.0
3	N	0	145	100	0	0	0	0	0	0	0
3	YMEAN	0.0	1.505E 04	1.526E 04	0.0	0.0	0.0	0.0	0.0	0.0	0.0
4	N	0	181	76	0	0	0	0	0	181	0
4	YMEAN	0.0	1.576E 04	1.450E 04	0.0	0.0	0.0	0.0	0.0	1.976E 04	0.0
5	N	0	0	0	0	0	153	112	78	0	154
5	YMEAN	0.0	0.0	0.0	0.0	0.0	2.135E 04	2.346E 04	2.822E 04	0.0	2.038E 04
6	N	0	0	0	0	0	35	63	46	0	64
6	YMEAN	0.0	0.0	0.0	0.0	0.0	2.347E 04	2.910E 04	3.528E 04	0.0	2.371E 04
7	N	36	0	0	65	21	0	0	0	0	0
7	YMEAN	3.029E 04	0.0	0.0	4.337E 04	3.940E 04	0.0	0.0	0.0	0.0	0.0

3-YR AVE $ INC , ETA = 0.351 — GROUP

CLASS		20*	23*	22*
1	N	54	0	0
1	YMEAN	1.296E 04	0.0	0.0
2	N	83	0	0
2	YMEAN	1.636E 04	0.0	0.0
3	N	145	0	0
3	YMEAN	1.505E 04	0.0	0.0
4	N	181	0	0
4	YMEAN	1.505E 04	0.0	0.0
7	N	31	34	0
7	YMEAN	4.982E 04	3.680E 04	0.0

REQUIRED ROOMS 23:12 , ETA = 0.024 — GROUP

CLASS		1	2	3	4	5	6*	7	8	9	11
2	N	661	475	186	155	31	219	256	82	73	21
2	YMEAN	1.762E 04	1.413E 04	2.546E 04	2.347E 04	3.546E 04	1.236E 04	1.561E 04	2.182E 04	2.540E 04	3.940E 04
3	N	557	295	262	232	30	115	180	130	102	23
3	YMEAN	2.122E 04	1.481E 04	2.676E 04	2.457E 04	4.352E 04	1.230E 04	1.655E 04	2.353E 04	2.591E 04	4.793E 04

(continuation — CLASS 4–6)

CLASS	stat									
4	N	486	728	258	187	88	99	165	93	28
	YMEAN	2.256E 04	2.803E 04	1.456E 04	2.549E 04	2.767E 04	2.357E 04	1.626E 04	1.203E 04	4.156E 04
5	N	225	84	141	72	34	38	96	45	5
	YMEAN	1.999E 04	2.590E 04	1.308E 04	2.316E 04	2.231E 04	2.403E 04	1.570E 04	9.273E 03	3.937E 04
6	N	159	67	92	59	15	44	63	29	
	YMEAN	1.998E 04	2.442E 04	1.207E 04	2.197E 04	1.807E 04	2.367E 04	1.297E 04	1.029E 04	4.004E 04

REQUIRED ROOMS 23:12 , ETA = 0.024

GROUP

CLASS	stat	10*	17	20*	23*	22*	16*	18*	19	12*	15*	13*	21*	14*
2	N	10	177	139	0	0	79	21	0	51	32	22	38	50
	YMEAN	2.707E 04	1.671E 04	1.491E 04	0.0	0.0	1.236E 04	3.940E 04	0.0	2.310E 04	2.309E 04	3.024E 04	2.294E 04	2.100E 04
3	N	7	107	59	12	11	73	0	23	65	52	37	48	78
	YMEAN	2.755E 04	1.756E 04	1.511E 04	5.154E 04	4.324E 04	1.403E 04	0.0	4.793E 04	2.132E 04	2.555E 04	3.283E 04	2.002E 04	2.200E 04
4	N	13	93	42	16	16	72	0	28	43	43	45	51	56
	YMEAN	3.080E 04	1.739E 04	1.519E 04	5.059E 04	3.366E 04	1.326E 04	0.0	4.156E 04	2.349E 04	2.656E 04	3.138E 04	1.364E 04	2.118E 04
5	N	3	55	26	4	5	41	0	9	20	20	12	29	18
	YMEAN	4.125E 04	1.698E 04	1.598E 04	5.015E 04	3.091E 04	1.112E 04	0.0	3.937E 04	1.901E 04	2.714E 04	2.882E 04	1.760E 04	2.132E 04
6	N	16	31	16	3	2	32	0	5	8	28	8	15	16
	YMEAN	3.430E 04	1.252E 04	1.232E 04	3.651E 04	4.497E 04	1.398E 04	0.0	4.004E 04	1.431E 04	2.709E 04	2.229E 04	1.269E 04	2.011E 04

REQUIRED ROOMS 23:12 , ETA = 0.024

GROUP

BKT AGE HEAD 9V1009 , ETA = 0.049

GROUP

CLASS	stat	1	2	3	4	5	6*	7	8	9
2	N	372	152	220	140	12	75	145	87	53
	YMEAN	1.987E 04	2.574E 04	1.404E 04	2.379E 04	4.556E 04	1.235E 04	1.507E 04	2.207E 04	2.641E 04
3	N	530	276	254	238	38	79	124	111	114
	YMEAN	2.370E 04	2.844E 04	1.502E 04	2.561E 04	4.415E 04	1.181E 04	1.678E 04	2.513E 04	2.609E 04
4	N	479	243	236	200	43	87	149	89	89
	YMEAN	2.134E 04	2.511E 04	1.413E 04	2.315E 04	3.384E 04	1.127E 04	1.621E 04	2.234E 04	2.417E 04
5	N	378	123	255	97	26	113	142	56	41
	YMEAN	1.908E 04	2.625E 04	1.442E 04	2.347E 04	3.639E 04	1.303E 04	1.559E 04	2.183E 04	2.581E 04
6	N	329	33	296	30	3	147	8	15	15
	YMEAN	1.530E 04	2.786E 04	1.388E 04	2.647E 04	4.252E 04	1.167E 04	1.590E 04	2.651E 04	2.643E 04

BKT AGE HEAD 9V1009 , ETA = 0.049

GROUP

CLASS	stat	10*	16*	18*	19	12*	15*	13*	21*	14*
2	N	3	61	1	8	34	35	19	49	52
	YMEAN	3.191E 04	1.271E 04	3.000E 04	5.154E 04	2.220E 04	2.385E 04	3.321E 04	1.772E 04	2.105E 04
3	N	9	62	4	25	60	64	54	59	60
	YMEAN	3.628E 04	1.322E 04	5.657E 04	4.485E 04	2.037E 04	2.756E 04	3.233E 04	1.927E 04	2.287E 04
4	N	13	77	5	25	55	45	34	32	66

```
        YMEAN  2.625E 04  1.756E 04  1.313E 04  3.654E 04  3.861E 04  2.117E 04  2.592E 04  2.853E 04  2.018E 04  1.997E 04
  5  N           9         85         57          6         11         25         25         16         29         31
        YMEAN  3.067E 04  1.644E 04  1.356E 04  4.805E 04  3.425E 04  2.285E 04  2.323E 04  2.999E 04  1.869E 04  2.073E 04
  6  N           2        109         40          1                    14          6          1         12          9
        YMEAN  2.500E 04  1.705E 04  1.258E 04  7.500E 04  0.0        2.683E 04  2.687E 04  2.100E 04  3.046E 04  2.626E 04


                      BKT AGE HEAD 9V1009      , ETA = 0.049
                                                 GROUP

  CLASS       20*        23*        22*
    2  N       35          6          2
        YMEAN 1.243E 04  5.388E 04  4.300E 04
    3  N       54         13         12
        YMEAN 1.545E 04  4.755E 04  4.170E 04
    4  N       40          9         16
        YMEAN 1.462E 04  4.759E 04  2.942E 04
    5  N       56          3          3
        YMEAN 1.500E 04  5.767E 04  3.838E 04
    6  N       97          1          1
        YMEAN 1.542E 04  0.0        7.500E 04


                      SEX & MAR STATUS      , ETA = 0.029
                                              GROUP

  CLASS        1          2          3          4          5          6*         7          8          9         11
    1  N      1660        878        782        664        118        377        501        367        297         84
        YMEAN 2.109E 04  1.435E 04  2.665E 04  2.433E 04  3.883E 04  1.218E 04  1.609E 04  2.321E 04  2.569E 04  4.209E 04
    2  N       82         65         17         14          3         24         41          7          7          1
        YMEAN 1.443E 04  1.171E 04  2.296E 04  1.916E 04  4.032E 04  1.184E 04  1.161E 04  2.052E 04  1.759E 04  5.500E 04
    3  N      346        318         28         27          1        100        218         19          8          1
        YMEAN 1.580E 04  1.450E 04  2.686E 04  2.546E 04  6.000E 04  1.162E 04  1.630E 04  2.522E 04  2.596E 04  6.000E 04


                      SEX & MAR STATUS      , ETA = 0.029
                                              GROUP

  CLASS       10*        16*        17         19         18*        21*        13*        15*        12*        14*
    1  N       34        205        296         64         20        157        118        167        179        200
        YMEAN 3.016E 04  1.309E 04  1.727E 04  4.312E 04  3.863E 04  1.978E 04  3.100E 04  2.583E 04  2.194E 04  2.119E 04
    2  N        2         18         23          0          1          3          2          0          5          7
        YMEAN 3.258E 04  8.208E 03  1.309E 04  0.0        5.500E 04  1.814E 04  3.263E 04  0.0        1.582E 04  1.759E 04
    3  N        0         74        144          1          0         21          4          8          4         11
        YMEAN 0.0        1.418E 04  1.686E 04  6.000E 04  0.0        1.984E 04  3.026E 04  2.187E 04  2.107E 04  2.677E 04


                      SEX & MAR STATUS      , ETA = 0.029
                                              GROUP

  CLASS       20*        23*        22*
    1  N      139         30         34
        YMEAN 1.428E 04  4.551E 04  3.680E 04
    2  N       20          0          0
        YMEAN 1.223E 04  0.0        0.0
    3  N      123          1          0
        YMEAN 1.636E 04  6.000E 04  0.0


                      LRGST PLAC/SMSA PSU31:66, ETA = 0.123
                                                 GROUP

  CLASS        1          3          7          4          5          8          9          6*        11
    1  N      633        326        307        266         60        175         91          0         60
        YMEAN 2.583E 04  3.100E 04  1.673E 04  2.800E 04  4.276E 04  2.570E 04  3.187E 04  0.0        4.276E 04
    2  N      443        212        231        186         26        153         33          0         26
```

(Continued from preceding page — classes 3–6 and mean)

CLASS	stat	10*	17	16*	18*	19	12*
3	YMEAN	2.154E 04	2.542E 04	1.622E 04	4.169E 04	2.306E 04	2.849E 04
3	N	222	90	132	12	78	18
4	YMEAN	1.855E 04	2.305E 04	1.463E 04	3.195E 04	2.164E 04	2.590E 04
4	N	144	54	90	11	43	43
5	YMEAN	1.846E 04	2.369E 04	1.495E 04	3.082E 04	2.182E 04	2.182E 04
5	N	200	60	140	8	52	51
6	YMEAN	1.578E 04	2.248E 04	1.245E 04	3.462E 04	2.068E 04	2.069E 04
6	N	446	85	361	5	80	76
	YMEAN	1.394E 04	2.101E 04	1.185E 04	1.809E 04	2.120E 04	2.141E 04

LRGST PLAC/SMSA PSU31:66, ETA = 0.123
GROUP

CLASS	stat	10*	17	16*	18*	19	12*	15*	13*	21*	14*
1	N	0	217	90	12	48	0	175	91	78	0
1	YMEAN	0.0	1.760E 04	1.198E 04	4.498E 04	4.224E 04	0.0	2.570E 04	3.187E 04	1.980E 04	0.0
2	N	0	121	110	9	17	0	57	33	57	153
2	YMEAN	0.0	1.742E 04	1.389E 04	3.192E 04	4.673E 04	0.0	0.0	2.849E 04	2.120E 04	2.189E 04
3	N	12	63	69	0	0	18	0	0	27	60
3	YMEAN	3.195E 04	1.585E 04	1.261E 04	0.0	0.0	2.590E 04	0.0	0.0	1.728E 04	2.035E 04
4	N	11	62	28	0	0	43	0	0	19	0
4	YMEAN	3.082E 04	1.556E 04	1.276E 04	0.0	0.0	2.182E 04	0.0	0.0	1.954E 04	0.0
5	N	8	0	0	0	0	51	0	0	0	1
5	YMEAN	3.462E 04	0.0	0.0	0.0	0.0	2.069E 04	0.0	0.0	0.0	2.000E 04
6	N	5	0	0	0	0	76	0	0	0	4
6	YMEAN	1.809E 04	0.0	0.0	0.0	0.0	2.141E 04	0.0	0.0	0.0	1.768E 04

LRGST PLAC/SMSA PSU31:66, ETA = 0.123
GROUP

CLASS	stat	20*	23*	22*
1	N	139	21	27
1	YMEAN	1.611E 04	4.899E 04	3.619E 04
2	N	64	10	7
2	YMEAN	1.407E 04	5.176E 04	3.914E 04
3	N	36	0	0
3	YMEAN	1.480E 04	0.0	0.0
4	N	43	0	0
4	YMEAN	1.379E 04	0.0	0.0

DIST TO CNTR SMSA 31:58, ETA = 0.072
GROUP

CLASS	stat	1	2	3	4	5	6*	13*
1	N	386	231	155	136	19	17	214
1	YMEAN	1.885E 04	1.386E 04	2.390E 04	2.218E 04	3.492E 04	8.984E 03	1.446E 04
2	N	582	276	306	257	49	5	271
2	YMEAN	2.280E 04	1.670E 04	2.656E 04	2.373E 04	4.035E 04	9.170E 03	1.681E 04
3	N	336	166	170	144	26	39	127
3	YMEAN	2.504E 04	1.617E 04	3.104E 04	2.797E 04	4.669E 04	1.247E 04	1.764E 04
4	N	245	176	69	62	7	93	83
4	YMEAN	1.739E 04	1.392E 04	2.404E 04	2.293E 04	3.361E 04	1.296E 04	1.481E 04
5	N	539	412	127	106	21	347	65
5	YMEAN	1.597E 04	1.243E 04	2.516E 04	2.387E 04	3.146E 04	1.198E 04	1.494E 04

DIST TO CNTR SMSA 31:58, ETA = 0.072
GROUP

CLASS	stat	10*	17	16*	19	18*	12*	15*	13*	21*	14*
1	N	4	115	99	12	3	0	57	0	37	79
1	YMEAN	2.566E 04	1.533E 04	1.289E 04	3.422E 04	4.983E 04	0.0	2.522E 04	0.0	1.616E 04	2.023E 04

(Statistical cross-tabulation printout — N and YMEAN by CLASS × GROUP)

(continuation from preceding page — classes 2–5)

	G1	G2	G3	G4	G5	G6	G7	G8	G9	G10
2 N	4	182	89	32	13	0	118	0	84	139
2 YMEAN	3.477E 04	1.766E 04	1.354E 04	4.301E 04	3.544E 04	0.0	2.592E 04	0.0	1.991E 04	2.203E 04
3 N	6	70	57	15	5	42	0	102	27	0
3 YMEAN	3.174E 04	1.953E 04	1.406E 04	5.281E 04	4.348E 04	2.133E 04	0.0	3.054E 04	2.262E 04	0.0
4 N	4	52	31	3	0	47	0	15	22	0
4 YMEAN	3.072E 04	1.622E 04	1.106E 04	3.702E 04	0.0	2.058E 04	0.0	2.935E 04	2.157E 04	0.0
5 N	18	44	21	3	0	99	0	7	11	0
5 YMEAN	2.973E 04	1.531E 04	1.116E 04	4.000E 04	0.0	2.250E 04	0.0	4.071E 04	1.820E 04	0.0

DIST TO CNTR SMSA 31:58, ETA = 0.072
GROUP

CLASS	20* N	20* YMEAN	23* N	23* YMEAN	22* N	22* YMEAN
1	78	1.494E 04	4	4.722E 04	8	2.804E 04
2	98	1.546E 04	15	4.535E 04	17	4.067E 04
3	43	1.731E 04	8	6.213E 04	7	4.055E 04
4	30	1.187E 04	1	5.000E 04	2	7.850E 04
5	33	1.432E 04	3	4.000E 04	0	0.0

CURRENT REGION OV472 , ETA = 0.063
GROUP

GROUP	Class 1 N	Class 1 YMEAN	Class 2 N	Class 2 YMEAN	Class 3 N	Class 3 YMEAN	Class 4 N	Class 4 YMEAN
1	364	2.494E 04	617	1.988E 04	790	1.595E 04	317	2.133E 04
2	168	1.611E 04	329	1.453E 04	597	1.185E 04	167	1.710E 04
3	196	3.133E 04	288	2.526E 04	193	2.364E 04	150	2.557E 04
4	164	2.812E 04	242	2.319E 04	168	2.137E 04	131	2.422E 04
5	32	4.694E 04	46	3.558E 04	25	3.714E 04	19	3.457E 04
6*	16	1.495E 04	144	1.271E 04	300	1.103E 04	41	1.319E 04
7	152	1.624E 04	185	1.629E 04	297	1.300E 04	126	1.890E 04
8	85	2.669E 04	137	2.223E 04	80	1.982E 04	91	2.381E 04
9	79	2.963E 04	105	2.443E 04	88	2.281E 04	40	2.503E 04
11	28	4.862E 04	33	3.799E 04	12	4.297E 04	13	3.755E 04

CURRENT REGION OV472 , ETA = 0.063
GROUP

GROUP	Class 1 N	Class 1 YMEAN	Class 2 N	Class 2 YMEAN	Class 3 N	Class 3 YMEAN	Class 4 N	Class 4 YMEAN
10*	4	3.225E 04	13	2.907E 04	13	3.158E 04	6	2.896E 04
12*	36	2.274E 04	68	2.221E 04	64	2.052E 04	20	2.190E 04
13*	43	3.452E 04	37	2.851E 04	24	2.892E 04	20	2.860E 04
14	37	2.258E 04	79	2.080E 04	55	2.084E 04	47	2.197E 04
15*	48	2.986E 04	58	2.435E 04	25	1.684E 04	44	2.618E 04
16*	0	0.0	0	0.0	297	1.300E 04	0	0.0
17	152	1.624E 04	185	1.629E 04	0	0.0	126	1.890E 04
18*	4	3.982E 04	9	4.278E 04	5	3.502E 04	3	3.504E 04
19	24	5.013E 04	24	3.627E 04	5	4.862E 04	10	3.819E 04
21*	55	1.992E 04	77	1.905E 04	55	0.0	49	2.078E 04

CURRENT REGION OV472 , ETA = 0.063
GROUP

GROUP	Class 1 N	Class 1 YMEAN	Class 2 N	Class 2 YMEAN	Class 3 N	Class 3 YMEAN	Class 4 N
20*	97	1.390E 04	108	1.403E 04	0	0.0	77
23*	24	5.013E 04	0	0.0	7	4.862E 04	0
22*	0	0.0	24	3.627E 04	0	0.0	10

YMEAN 1.776E 04   C.0   3.819E 04

31:48, ETA = 0.030 GROUP

RACE

	1	2	3	4	5	9	8	7	6*	11
CLASS										
1 N	1626	872	754	636	118	301	335	470	402	83
YMEAN	2.069E 04	1.470E 04	2.685E 04	2.446E 04	3.945E 04	2.549E 04	2.357E 04	1.652E 04	1.246E 04	4.302E 04
2 N	406	349	57	54	3	9	45	256	93	3
YMEAN	1.179E 04	9.653E 03	1.833E 04	1.707E 04	2.758E 04	2.301E 04	1.551E 04	1.080E 04	7.418E 03	2.758E 04
3 N	56	40	16	15	1	2	13	34	6	0
YMEAN	1.987E 04	1.533E 04	2.894E 04	2.912E 04	2.700E 04	4.095E 04	2.582E 04	1.660E 04	8.772E 03	0.0

31:48, ETA = 0.030 GROUP

RACE

	10*	17	16*	19	18*	12*	15*	13*	21*	14*
CLASS										
1 N	35	346	124	63	20	183	139	118	143	196
YMEAN	2.038E 04	1.727E 04	1.396E 04	4.377E 04	4.050E 04	2.171E 04	2.645E 04	3.082E 04	2.016E 04	2.146E 04
2 N	0	91	165	2	1	4	31	5	28	14
YMEAN	0.0	1.231E 04	9.653E 03	3.186E 04	1.800E 04	2.123E 04	1.391E 04	2.651E 04	1.220E 04	1.690E 04
3 N	1	26	8	0	0	1	5	1	10	8
YMEAN	2.700E 04	1.686E 04	1.581E 04	0.0	0.0	2.800E 04	2.509E 04	5.500E 04	1.777E 04	2.609E 04

31:48, ETA = 0.030 GROUP

RACE

	20*	23*	22*
CLASS			
1 N	203	31	32
YMEAN	1.515E 04	4.982E 04	3.715E 04
2 N	62	0	2
YMEAN	1.235E 04	0.0	3.186E 04
3 N	16	0	0
YMEAN	1.635E 04	0.0	0.0

169

This table gives much the same as the previous table but in a different more cumbersome format. We omit 21 pages of it.

PREDICTOR SUMMARY TABLE.   23 GROUPS

3-YR AVE $ INC   , ETA =

GROUP 1

CLASS	N	W	PCT GROUP TOTAL	SUM	PCT GROUP	PCT TOTAL	MEAN	VARIANCE	SLOPE
1 Y	256	8805.0	10.8	9.271272E 07	5.7	5.7	1.052955E 04	4.233778E 07	
2 Y	257	7736.0	9.5	1.023791E 08	6.3	6.3	1.323411E 04	7.076661E 07	
3 Y	386	12437.0	15.2	1.751543E 08	10.7	10.7	1.408332E 04	6.077859E 07	
4 Y	362	14035.0	17.2	2.420264E 08	14.8	14.8	1.724449E 04	7.744030E 07	
5 Y	497	22398.0	27.5	5.060375E 08	30.9	30.9	2.259298E 04	1.189778E 08	
6 Y	208	10121.0	12.4	2.832548E 08	17.3	17.3	2.798684E 04	1.206158E 08	
7 Y	122	6043.0	7.4	2.359240E 08	14.4	14.4	3.904088E 04	3.372114E 08	

ETA = 0.351, ETA(NSTEP) = 0.316, ETA(0) = 0.233

GROUP 3

CLASS	N	W	PCT GROUP TOTAL	SUM	PCT GROUP	PCT TOTAL	MEAN	VARIANCE	SLOPE
5 Y	497	22398.0	58.1	5.060375E 08	49.4	30.9	2.259298E 04	1.189778E 08	
6 Y	208	10121.0	26.2	2.832548E 08	27.6	17.3	2.798684E 04	1.206158E 08	
7 Y	122	6043.0	15.7	2.359240E 08	23.0	14.4	3.904088E 04	3.372114E 08	

ETA = 0.182, ETA(NSTEP) = 0.191, ETA(0) = 0.154

GROUP 2

CLASS	N	W	PCT GROUP TOTAL	SUM	PCT GROUP	PCT TOTAL	MEAN	VARIANCE	SLOPE
1 Y	256	8805.0	20.5	9.271272E 07	15.1	5.7	1.052955E 04	4.233778E 07	
2 Y	257	7736.0	18.0	1.023791E 08	16.7	6.3	1.323411E 04	7.076661E 07	
3 Y	386	12437.0	28.9	1.751543E 08	28.6	10.7	1.408332E 04	6.077859E 07	
4 Y	362	14035.0	32.6	2.420264E 08	39.5	14.8	1.724449E 04	7.744030E 07	

ETA = 0.085, ETA(NSTEP) = 0.085, ETA(0) = 0.063

GROUP 4

CLASS	N	W	PCT GROUP TOTAL	SUM	PCT GROUP	PCT TOTAL	MEAN	VARIANCE	SLOPE
5 Y	497	22398.0	68.9	5.060375E 08	64.1	30.9	2.259298E 04	1.189778E 08	
6 Y	208	10121.0	31.1	2.832548E 08	35.9	17.3	2.798684E 04	1.206158E 08	

ETA = 0.050, ETA(NSTEP) = 0.073, ETA(0) = 0.050

GROUP 5

CLASS	N	W	PCT GROUP TOTAL	SUM	PCT GROUP	PCT TOTAL	MEAN	VARIANCE	SLOPE
7 Y	122	6043.0	100.0	2.359240E 08	100.0	14.4	3.904088E 04	3.372114E 08	

GROUP 9

CLASS	N	W	PCT GROUP TOTAL	SUM	PCT GROUP	PCT TOTAL	MEAN	VARIANCE	SLOPE
5 Y	731	10615.0	72.6	2.518379E 08	67.3	15.4	2.372472E 04	1.590032E 08	
6 Y	81	4012.0	27.4	1.222502E 08	32.7	7.5	3.047113E 04	1.500305E 08	

ETA = 0.055, ETA(NSTEP) = 0.110, FTA(0) = 0.055

GROUP 8

CLASS	N	W	PCT GROUP TOTAL	SUM	PCT GROUP	PCT TOTAL	MEAN	VARIANCE	SLOPE
5 Y	266	11783.0	65.9	2.541996E 08	61.2	15.5	2.157342E 04	8.119678E 07	
6 Y	127	6109.0	34.1	1.610046E 08	38.8	9.8	2.635531E 04	9.559144E 07	

ETA = 0.057, ETA(NSTEP) = 0.089, ETA(0) = 0.057

GROUP 7

CLASS	N	W	PCT GROUP TOTAL	SUM	PCT GROUP	PCT TOTAL	MEAN	VARIANCE	SLOPE
1 Y	115	3681.0	15.0	4.321102E 07	11.1	2.6	1.173893E 04	4.820251E 07	
2 Y	143	3964.0	16.2	5.848483E 07	15.0	4.9	1.475399E 04	6.323427E 07	
3 Y	245	7259.0	29.6	1.096388E 08	28.1	6.7	1.510385E 04	5.778098E 07	
4 Y	257	9639.0	39.3	1.786229E 08	45.8	10.9	1.853127E 04	8.332960E 07	

ETA = 0.078, ETA(NSTEP) = 0.087, FTA(0) = 0.062

GROUP 6*

CLASS	N	W	PCT GROUP	PCT TOTAL	SUM	PCT GROUP	PCT TOTAL	MEAN	VARIANCE	SLOPE
1 Y	141	5124.0	27.7	6.3	4.950168E 07	22.3	3.0	9.660746E 03	3.659565E 07	
2 Y	114	3772.0	20.4	4.6	4.389426E 07	19.7	2.7	1.163686E 04	7.425475E 07	
3 Y	141	5178.0	28.0	6.3	6.551544E 07	29.5	4.0	1.265265E 04	6.186522E 07	
4 Y	105	4396.0	23.8	5.4	6.340354E 07	28.5	3.9	1.442300E 04	5.214976E 07	

ETA = 0.053, ETA(NSTEP) = 0.038, ETA(0) = 0.038

GROUP 11

CLASS	N	W	PCT GROUP	PCT TOTAL	SUM	PCT GROUP	PCT TOTAL	MEAN	VARIANCE	SLOPE
7 Y	86	4351.0	100.0	5.3	1.867000E 08	100.0	11.3	4.244312E 04	3.295327E 08	

GROUP 10*

CLASS	N	W	PCT GROUP	PCT TOTAL	SUM	PCT GROUP	PCT TOTAL	MEAN	VARIANCE	SLOPE
7 Y	36	1692.0	100.0	2.1	5.125400E 07	100.0	3.1	3.029196E 04	2.577897E 08	

GROUP 17

CLASS	N	W	PCT GROUP	PCT TOTAL	SUM	PCT GROUP	PCT TOTAL	MEAN	VARIANCE	SLOPE
1 Y	54	2301.0	12.7	2.8	2.981147E 07	9.8	1.8	1.295588E 04	4.735947E 07	
2 Y	83	3003.0	16.6	3.7	4.913746E 07	16.1	3.0	1.636279E 04	6.729133E 07	
3 Y	145	5368.0	29.7	6.6	8.078443E 07	26.4	4.9	1.504926E 04	5.267962E 07	
4 Y	181	7389.0	40.9	9.1	1.459888E 08	47.8	8.9	1.975759E 04	9.629045E 07	

ETA = 0.082, ETA(NSTEP) = 0.123, ETA(0) = 0.071

GROUP 16*

CLASS	N	W	PCT GROUP	PCT TOTAL	SUM	PCT GROUP	PCT TOTAL	MEAN	VARIANCE	SLOPE
1 Y	61	1380.0	21.3	1.7	1.339954E 07	15.9	0.8	9.709813E 03	4.408969E 07	
2 Y	60	961.0	14.8	1.2	9.347370E 06	11.1	0.6	9.726711E 03	1.820810E 07	
3 Y	100	1891.0	29.2	2.3	2.885440E 07	34.3	1.8	1.525880E 04	7.308680E 07	
4 Y	76	2250.0	34.7	2.8	3.263403E 07	38.7	2.0	1.450401E 04	2.282747E 07	

ETA = 0.131, ETA(NSTEP) = 0.129, ETA(0) = 0.129

GROUP 19

CLASS	N	W	PCT GROUP	PCT TOTAL	SUM	PCT GROUP	PCT TOTAL	MEAN	VARIANCE	SLOPE
7 Y	65	3333.0	100.0	4.1	1.445618E 08	100.0	8.8	4.337288E 04	3.608504E 08	

GROUP 18*

CLASS	N	W	PCT GROUP	PCT TOTAL	SUM	PCT GROUP	PCT TOTAL	MEAN	VARIANCE	SLOPE
7 Y	21	1018.0	100.0	1.2	4.010819E 07	100.0	2.4	3.939901E 04	2.275338E 08	

GROUP 12*

CLASS	N	W	PCT GROUP	PCT TOTAL	SUM	PCT GROUP	PCT TOTAL	MEAN	VARIANCE	SLOPE
5 Y	153	6943.0	80.9	8.5	1.482040E 08	79.4	9.1	2.134582E 04	1.530113E 08	
6 Y	35	1635.0	19.1	2.0	3.838011E 07	20.6	2.3	2.347407E 04	7.677040E 07	

ETA(NSTEP) = 0.005, ETA(0) = 0.005

GROUP 15*

CLASS	N	W	PCT GROUP	PCT TOTAL	SUM	PCT GROUP	PCT TOTAL	MEAN	VARIANCE	SLOPE
5 Y	112	4555.0	60.3	5.6	1.068696E 08	55.0	6.5	2.346204E 04	1.156645E 08	
6 Y	63	3000.0	39.7	3.7	8.732608E 07	45.0	5.3	2.909899E 04	1.204336E 08	

ETA = 0.061, ETA(NSTEP) = 0.061, ETA(0) = 0.061

GROUP 13*

CLASS	N	W	PCT GROUP	PCT TOTAL	SUM	PCT GROUP	PCT TOTAL	MEAN	VARIANCE	SLOPE
5 Y	78	3672.0	60.7	4.5	1.036338E 08	55.3	6.3	2.822272E 04	1.411110E 08	
6 Y	46	2377.0	39.3	2.9	8.387005E 07	44.7	5.1	3.528399E 04	1.451202E 08	

ETA = 0.078, ETA(NSTEP) = 0.078, ETA(0) = 0.078

GROUP 21*

CLASS	N	W	PCT GROUP	PCT TOTAL	SUM	PCT GROUP	PCT TOTAL	MEAN	VARIANCE	SLOPE
4 Y	181	7389.0	100.0	9.1	1.459888E 08	100.0	8.9	1.975759E 04	9.629045E 07	

171

GROUP CLASS 14*

CLASS	N	W	PCT GROUP	PCT TOTAL	SUM	PCT GROUP	PCT TOTAL	MEAN	VARIANCE	SLOPE
5 Y	154	7228.0	69.9	8.9	1.473300E 08	66.7	9.0	2.038323E 04	5.639320E 07	
6 Y	64	3108.0	30.1	3.8	7.367850E 07	33.3	4.5	2.370608E 04	5.855110E 07	

ETA = 0.039, ETA(NSTEP) = 0.039, ETA(0) = 0.039

GROUP CLASS 20*

CLASS	N	W	PCT GROUP	PCT TOTAL	SUM	PCT GROUP	PCT TOTAL	MEAN	VARIANCE	SLOPE
1 Y	54	2301.0	21.6	2.8	2.981149E 07	18.7	1.8	1.295588E 04	4.735947E 07	
2 Y	83	3003.0	78.1	3.7	4.913747E 07	30.8	3.0	1.636279E 04	6.729176E 07	
3 Y	145	5368.0	50.3	6.6	8.078445E 07	50.6	4.9	1.504926E 04	5.267962E 07	

ETA = 0.025, ETA(NSTEP) = 0.020, ETA(0) = 0.020

GROUP CLASS 23*

CLASS	N	W	PCT GROUP	PCT TOTAL	SUM	PCT GROUP	PCT TOTAL	MEAN	VARIANCE	SLOPE
7 Y	31	1683.0	100.0	2.1	8.384981E 07	100.0	5.1	4.982163E 04	3.220803E 08	

GROUP CLASS 22*

CLASS	N	W	PCT GROUP	PCT TOTAL	SUM	PCT GROUP	PCT TOTAL	MEAN	VARIANCE	SLOPE
7 Y	34	1650.0	100.0	2.0	6.071200E 07	100.0	3.7	3.679515E 04	3.236129E 08	

The second run on the residuals generated in the first run.

SECOND STAGE OF 807NTR45 MORGAN

  2088 OBSERVATIONS READ AFTER GLOBAL FILTER

Y AVERAGE = -1.306527E-01
STANDARD DEVIATION = 9.914672E 03
BOUNDARIES = -4.957349E 04 4.957323E 04

1. ID =   53249, Y =   5.324900E 04
2. ID =   55242, Y =   5.524200E 04
3. ID =   53249, Y =   5.324900E 04

  2088 CASES INCLUDED IN THE ANALYSIS
        0 FILTERED (LOCAL/SUBSET SELECTOR)
        0 MISSING DATA CASES
        3 OUTLIERS INCLUDED
        0 INVALID PREDICTOR VALUES

  2088 SAMPLE OBSERVATIONS - WITH TOTALS
        WEIGHTS =   8.157500E 04
        DEPENDENT VARIABLE (Y) = -1.065800D 04   AVERAGE = -1.306527E-01
        Y-SQUARED =   8.015038D 12   VARIANCE =   9.830075E 07

                    STAGE 2 OF THE ANALYSIS
                 BEST SPLIT BASED ON MEANS
             0-STEP LOOKAHEAD WITH 1 FORCED SPLITS

SPLITTING CRITERIA -
  MAXIMUM NUMBER OF SPLITS = 25
  MINIMUM # OBSERVATIONS IN A GROUP = 3
  %AGE OF TOTAL SS N SPLITS MUST EXPLAIN = 0.6(N=1).
  PRINT CASES OUTSIDE 5.0 STANDARD DEVIATIONS OF PARENT GROUP MEAN

    8   RANKED PREDICTORS SPECIFIED
PREDICTOR RANK PREFERENCE UP
SPLIT ATTEMPT RANGE - 2 RANKS UP, 2 RANKS DOWN
ELIGIBILITY RANGE -   2 RANKS UP, 2 RANKS DOWN
        PREDICTOR   VARIABLE TYPE MAX CLASS RANK
                              NUMBER
   1   MIGHT MOVE   26:79 V1276   M   2   2
   2   HOW LONG LIVD HERE   V2004   M   5   2
   3   EDUCATION OF HEAD 31:43 V1485   M   9   1
   4   RACE   31:48 V1490   F   3   1
   5   PUB TRANSP GOOD 26:52 V1250   M   5   1
   6   % CHANGE IN INCOME   V2003   M   5   1
   7   EXPECT CHILDREN ? 29:18 V1370   M   1   1
   8   HRS HEAD TRVL WK22:30-32 V1146   M   6   3

Note three rank levels, using the last predictor only as a last resort.

Summary of the residual variables.

Range ranking UP: use low rank numbers first.

WEIGHTED Y VARIABLE 2005 AID3 Y-VARIABLE   SCALED BY 1.0E 00

      1 CANDIDATES -   GROUP   SS
                          1   8.015038E 12

ATTEMPT SPLIT ON GROUP   1 WITH SS = 8.015038E 12

Details of the trace only given for eligible splits.

LOOKAHEAD TENTATIVE PARTITION

SPLIT ATTEMPT ON GROUP   1 WITH N =   2088, SS = 8.015038E 12
SUMS- W = 8.157500E 04, Y =-1.065800E 04, YSQ = 8.015038E 12, X =

PREDICTOR EDUCATION OF HEAD   31:43
10 NON-EMPTY CLASSES   0 1 2 3 4 5 6 7 8 9

PARTITION	N	WEIGHT	Y-MEAN	Y-VARIANCE	X-MEAN	X-VARIANCE	SLOPE	BSS
BETWEEN 1	183	5.33200E 03	-4.20937E 03	3.95312E 07	0.0	0.0	0.0	1.01077E 11
AND 2	1905	7.62430E 04	2.54239E 02	1.01103E 08	0.0	0.0	0.0	
BETWEEN 2	642	2.18100E 04	-2.87333E 03	5.91161E 07	0.0	0.0	0.0	2.45753E 11
AND 3	1446	5.97650E 04	1.04839E 03	1.08533E 08	0.0	0.0	0.0	
BETWEEN 3	1006	3.42940E 04	-2.75760E 03	6.94271E 07	0.0	0.0	0.0	3.01530E 11
AND 4	1082	4.72810E 04	1.63726E 03	1.12939E 08	0.0	0.0	0.0	
BETWEEN 4	1368	4.94910E 04	-1.52803E 03	7.76312E 07	0.0	0.0	0.0	2.93755E 11
AND 5	720	3.20840E 04	2.35673E 03	1.21165E 08	0.0	0.0	0.0	
BETWEEN 5	1577	5.82270E 04	-1.27708E 03	7.95989E 07	0.0	0.0	0.0	3.31725E 11
AND 6	511	2.33480E 04	3.18442E 03	1.30950E 08	0.0	0.0	0.0	
BETWEEN 6	1819	6.91500E 04	-9.40164E 02	8.18338E 07	0.0	0.0	0.0	4.01180E 11
AND 7	269	1.24250E 04	5.23152E 03	1.58187E 08	0.0	0.0	0.0	
BETWEEN 7	1981	7.67610E 04	-3.13565E 02	9.24691E 07	0.0	0.0	0.0	1.27786E 11
AND 8	107	4.81400E 03	-4.99769E 03	1.66243E 08	0.0	0.0	0.0	

REST SPLIT ON PREDICTOR 1485 = 4.01180E 11 AFTER CLASS 6

PREDICTOR RACE   31:48
3 NON-EMPTY CLASSES   2 1 3

PARTITION	N	WEIGHT	Y-MEAN	Y-VARIANCE	X-MEAN	X-VARIANCE	SLOPE	BSS
BETWEEN 2	406	5.49300E 03	-4.67897E 03	4.04610E 07	0.0	0.0	0.0	1.28932E 11
AND 1	1682	7.60820E 04	3.37674E 02	1.00799E 08	0.0	0.0	0.0	

BEST SPLIT ON PREDICTOR 1490 = 1.28932E 11 AFTER CLASS 2

PREDICTOR PUR TRANSP GOOD   26:52
3 NON-EMPTY CLASSES   1 3 5

PARTITION N WEIGHT Y-MEAN Y-VARIANCE X-MEAN X-VARIANCE SLOPE BSS

BEST SPLIT ON PREDICTOR 1250 = 1.29418BE 10 AFTER CLASS 3

PREDICTOR % CHANGE IN INCOME
5 NON-EMPTY CLASSES   1 2 3 4 5

PARTITION N WEIGHT Y-MEAN Y-VARIANCE X-MEAN X-VARIANCE SLOPE BSS

BEST SPLIT ON PREDICTOR 2003 = 2.235174E 09 AFTER CLASS 4

PREDICTOR EXPECT CHILDREN ?   29:18
2 NON-EMPTY CLASSES   0 1

PARTITION N WEIGHT Y-MEAN Y-VARIANCE X-MEAN X-VARIANCE SLOPE BSS

BEST SPLIT ON PREDICTOR 1370 = 8.70179E 08 AFTER CLASS 0

PREDICTOR MIGHT MOVE   26:79
2 NON-EMPTY CLASSES   1 5

PARTITION N WEIGHT Y-MEAN Y-VARIANCE X-MEAN X-VARIANCE SLOPE BSS

BEST SPLIT ON PREDICTOR 1276 = 4.164543E 09 AFTER CLASS 1

PREDICTOR HOW LONG LIVD HERE
5 NON-EMPTY CLASSES   1 2 3 4 5

PARTITION	N	WEIGHT	Y-MEAN	Y-VARIANCE	X-MEAN	X-VARIANCE	SLOPE	BSS
BETWEEN 4	838	3.13780E 04	1.35179E 03	1.07215E 08	0.0	0.0	0.0	9.31974E 10
AND 5	1250	5.01970E 04	-8.45209E 02	9.09477E 07	0.0	0.0	0.0	

BEST SPLIT ON PREDICTOR 2004 = 9.31973E 10 AFTER CLASS 4

PREDICTOR HRS HEAD TRVL WK22:30-32
6 NON-EMPTY CLASSES   0 1 2 3 4 5

PARTITION N WEIGHT Y-MEAN Y-VARIANCE X-MEAN X-VARIANCE SLOPE BSS

174

BETWEEN 4 1939 7.28340E 04 -3.11383E 02 9.23840E 07 0.0 0.0 0.0 6.58498E 10
AND 5 249 8.74100E 03 2.59336E 03 1.40612E 08 0.0 0.0 0.0
BEST SPLIT ON PREDICTOR 1146 AFTER CLASS 4

EDUCATION OF HEAD 31:43 YIELDS MAXIMUM BSS = 6.58498E 10

0-STEP LOOKAHEAD TO SPLIT GROUP 1, TOTAL BSS = 4.011800E 11
1. SPLIT GROUP 1 ON PREDICTOR 1485, BSS = 4.011800E 11

FROM ELIGIBLE PREDICTORS AROUND THE CURRENT RANK 1,   2 UP AND 2 DOWN
***** PARTITION OF GROUP 1 *****

    MAXIMUM ELIGIBLE BSS AT EACH STEP   MAXIMUM TOTAL BSS (LOOKAHEAD)
1.SPLIT   1 ON V1485 BSS= 4.01180E 11   SPLIT 1 ON V1485 BSS = 4.01180E 11
PE(1)= 4.809E 10, TOTAL= 4.01180E 11   TOTAL= 4.01180E 11
    PREDICTOR 1485 HAS RANK 1

SPLIT GROUP 1 ON EDUCATION OF HEAD 31:43 V1485

EXTREME CASES LYING OUTSIDE THE INTERVAL (-4.957349E 04, 4.957323E 04)
    Y   W   WY   V2005
  53249   44.0   2.34256E 06   53249
  55242   74.0   1.32581E 06   55242
  53249   48.0   2.55595E 06   53249
  GROUP   2 WITH 1819 OBSERVATIONS FROM 7 CLASSES = 0 1 2   3 4 5 6
          W= 6.91500E 04 Y=-6.50124D 07 YSQ= 5.71682D 12 X=
  GROUP   3 WITH   269 OBSERVATIONS FROM 3 CLASSES = 7 8 9
          W= 1.24250E 04 Y= 6.50017D 07 YSQ= 2.29822D 12 X=

    2 CANDIDATES -   GROUP   SS
                          2   5.65569 5E 12
                          3   1.95816 1E 12

        ATTEMPT SPLIT ON GROUP   2 WITH SS = 5.655695E'12

Omit the trace of split attempts on the remaining groups.

***** PARTITION OF GROUP 6 *****
FROM ELIGIBLE PREDICTORS AROUND THE CURRENT RANK 1,   2 UP AND 2 DOWN

MAXIMUM ELIGIBLE BSS AT EACH STEP   MAXIMUM TOTAL RSS (LOOKAHEAD)

GROUP 6 COULD NOT BE SPLIT

END OF STAGE 2 OF THE ANALYSIS.   8 FINAL GROUPS.   8 INELIGIBLE FOR SPLITTING.

VARIATION EXPLAINED (BSS(0)/TSS) = 11.6%

1-WAY ANALYSIS OF VARIANCE ON FINAL GROUPS

SOURCE	SUM OF SQUARES	DF	MEAN SQUARE
BETWEEN	9.322081E 11	8.	1.165260E 11
ERROR	7.0R2830E 12	81528.	8.687616E 07
TOTAL	8.015038E 12	81536.	9.830075E 07

Summary of variance explained. Mean squares (and F- or t-tests) are inappropriate here because of weighted data.

$$\frac{1.023693 \times 10^{12}}{8.064064 \times 10^{12}} = 12.7\%$$

```
                          GROUP SUMMARY TABLE
                     15 GROUPS OF WHICH 8 ARE FINAL

GROUP   1 ,  N =   2088,  SUM W =  8.157500E 04
  Y MEAN=-1.306527E-01, VARIANCE= 9.830075E 07,  SS(L)/TSS=  1.300, RSS/TSS= 0.050
  SPLIT ON EDUCATION OF HEAD  31:43, RSS(L) = 4.011800E 11
      2 WITH CLASSES  0 1 2 3 4 5 6
      3 WITH CLASSES  7 8 9

GROUP   2 ,  N =   1819,  SUM W =  6.915000E 04
  Y MEAN=-9.401646E 02, VARIANCE= 8.183382E 07,  SS(L)/TSS=  0.706, RSS/TSS= 0.015
  SPLIT ON EDUCATION OF HEAD  31:43, RSS(L) = 1.190583E 11
      4 WITH CLASSES  0 1 2
      5 WITH CLASSES  3 4 5 6

GROUP   5 ,  N =   1177,  SUM W =  4.734000E 04
  Y MEAN=-4.953375E 01, VARIANCE= 8.983806E 07,  SS(L)/TSS=  0.530, BSS/TSS= 0.008
  SPLIT ON RACE              31:48, RSS(L) = 6.239313E 10
      6 WITH CLASSES  2
      7 WITH CLASSES  1 3

GROUP   7 ,  N =    982,  SUM W =  4.474100E 04
  Y MEAN= 2.271636E 02, VARIANCE= 9.112443E 07,  SS(L)/TSS=  0.508, RSS/TSS= 0.011
  SPLIT ON HRS HEAD TRVL WK22:30-32, RSS(L) = 9.139598E 10
      8 WITH CLASSES  1 2 3 4 5
      9 WITH CLASSES  0

GROUP   8 ,  N =    776,  SUM W =  3.550600E 04
  Y MEAN=-5.017549E 02, VARIANCE= 8.285758E 07,  SS(L)/TSS=  0.367, RSS/TSS= 0.014
  SPLIT ON HRS HEAD TRVL WK22:30-32, BSS(L) = 1.136891E 11
     10 WITH CLASSES  1 2 3 4
     11 WITH CLASSES  5

GROUP  10*,  N =    667,  SUM W =  3.021100E 04
  Y MEAN=-1.250889E 03, VARIANCE= 7.198024E 07,  SS(L)/TSS=  0.271, RSS/TSS= 0.0

GROUP   3 ,  N =    269,  SUM W =  1.242500E 04
  Y MEAN= 5.231527E 03, VARIANCE= 1.581666E 08,  SS(L)/TSS=  0.244, RSS/TSS= 0.007
  SPLIT ON HRS HEAD TRVL WK22:30-32, BSS(L) = 5.655285E 10
     12 WITH CLASSES  1 2 3 4 5
     13 WITH CLASSES  0

GROUP  12 ,  N =    219,  SUM W =  1.025800E 04
  Y MEAN= 4.250957E 03, VARIANCE= 1.395635E 08,  SS(L)/TSS=  0.178, RSS/TSS= 0.011
  SPLIT ON HOW LONG LIVD HERE      , BSS(L) = 8.793706E 10
     14 WITH CLASSES  5
     15 WITH CLASSES  1 2 3 4

GROUP   4*,  N =    642,  SUM W =  2.181000E 04
  Y MEAN=-2.873336E 03, VARIANCE= 5.911613E 07,  SS(L)/TSS=  0.161, BSS/TSS= 0.0

GROUP   9*,  N =    206,  SUM W =  9.235000E 03
  Y MEAN= 3.029653E 03, VARIANCE= 1.135218E 08,  SS(L)/TSS=  0.130, BSS/TSS= 0.0

GROUP  15*,  N =    117,  SUM W =  5.487000E 03
  Y MEAN= 6.981141E 03, VARIANCE= 1.454259E 08,  SS(L)/TSS=  0.099, BSS/TSS= 0.0

GROUP  11*,  N =    109,  SUM W =  5.295000E 03
  Y MEAN= 3.772486E 03, VARIANCE= 1.244924E 08,  SS(L)/TSS=  0.081, RSS/TSS= 0.0

GROUP  14*,  N =    102,  SUM W =  4.771000E 03
```

This summarizes the split record in enough detail for making the diagram preceding the examples.

178

Y MEAN= 1.111043E 03, VARIANCE= 1.155824E 08,   SS(L)/TSS= 0.068, BSS/TSS= 0.0

GROUP 13*, N =   50, SUM W =   2.167000E 03
      Y MEAN= 9.873273E 03, VARIANCE= 2.243776E 08,   SS(L)/TSS= 0.059, BSS/TSS= 0.0

GROUP   6*, N =   195, SUM W =   2.599000E 03
      Y MEAN=-4.812793E 03, VARIANCE= 4.412045E 07,   SS(L)/TSS= 0.014, BSS/TSS= 0.0

100*BSS/TSS TABLE FOR 0-STEP LOOK-AHEAD
15 GROUPS, 8 PREDICTORS
< INDICATES LESS THAN 1 SPLITS WERE MADE

GROUP NUMBER (* INDICATES THE GROUP IS FINAL)

PREDICTOR	1	2	5	7	8	10*	3	12	4*	9*	15*	11*	14*	13*	6*
1485	5.0	1.5	0.3	0.1	0.3	0.3	0.2	0.1	0.2	0.1	0.0	0.1	0.1	0.2	0.1
1490	1.6	1.1	0.8	0.1	0.1	0.0	0.2	0.2	0.2	0.0	0.1	0.3	0.0	0.6	*****
2003	0.2	0.1	0.1	0.0	0.0	0.0	0.3	0.1	0.0	0.0	0.3	0.0	0.1	0.4	0.0
1370	0.0	0.0	0.2	0.2	0.2	0.1	0.5	0.5	0.0	0.1	0.2	0.3	0.4	0.2	0.1
1276	0.1	0.0	0.0	0.0	0.0	0.1	0.1	0.0	0.1	0.0	0.0	0.3	0.2	0.3	0.0
2004	1.2	0.4	0.2	0.4	0.5	0.2	0.5	1.1	0.0	0.1	0.1	0.6	0.0	0.3	0.0
1146	0.8	0.6	1.2	1.1	1.4	0.0	0.7	0.3	0.3	*****	0.5	*****	*****	*****	0.0

○ Split made of this group, see group summary table immediately preceding. Note group 5's splits on an inferior predictor because it had a lower rank number. The rows of this table will be ordered by rank whatever the order of the predictor cards.

▢ No split on this predictor here because of inferior rank.

100*BSS/TSS TABLE FOR 0-STEP LOOK-AHEAD
15 GROUPS, 8 PREDICTORS

MAXIMUM BSS REGARDLESS OF ELIGIBILITY

GROUP NUMBER (* INDICATES THE GROUP IS FINAL)

PREDICTOR	1	2	5	7	8	10*	3	12	4*	9*	15*	11*	14*	13*	6*
1485	5.0	1.5	0.3	0.1	0.3	0.3	0.2	0.1	0.2	0.1	0.0	0.1	0.1	0.2	0.1
1490	1.6	1.1	0.8	0.1	0.1	0.0	0.1	0.0	0.2	0.0	0.1	0.1	0.0	0.6*******	0.1
1250	0.2	0.1	0.1	0.0	0.0	0.0	0.3	0.1	0.2	0.0	0.3	0.3	0.1	0.4	0.6*******
2003	0.0	0.1	0.2	0.2	0.2	0.1	0.5	0.5	0.0	0.1	0.3	0.0	0.4	0.2	0.0
1370	0.1	0.0	0.0	0.0	0.0	0.0	0.1	0.0	0.0	0.0	0.2	0.3	0.2	0.3	0.1
1276		0.0	0.0	0.0	0.0	0.1	0.1	0.0	0.1	0.0	0.0	0.0	0.0	0.0	0.0
2004	1.2	0.4	0.2	0.4	0.5	0.2	0.5	1.1	0.0	0.1	0.0	0.6*******	0.3	0.3	0.0
1146	0.8	0.6	1.2	1.1	1.4	C.0	0.7	0.3	0.3*******	0.3*******	0.5******		0.0*******		0.0

PROFILE OF CLASS MEANS AND SLOPES

EDUCATION OF HEAD 31:43, ETA = 0.072 GROUP

CLASS	stat	1	2	5	10*	8	3	12	4*	9*
0	N	68	68	0	0	0	0	0	68	0
0	YMEAN	-4.732E 03	-4.732E 03	0.0	0.0	0.0	0.0	0.0	-4.732E 03	0.0
1	N	115	115	0	0	0	0	0	115	0
1	YMEAN	-3.888E 03	-3.888E 03	0.0	0.0	0.0	0.0	0.0	-3.888E 03	0.0
2	N	459	459	0	0	0	0	0	459	0
2	YMEAN	-2.441E 03	-2.441E 03	0.0	0.0	0.0	0.0	0.0	-2.441E 03	0.0
3	N	364	364	259	152	177	0	0	0	82
3	YMEAN	-1.182E 03	-1.182E 03	-6.607E 02	-2.804E 03	-2.080E 03	0.0	0.0	0.0	2.501E 03
4	N	362	362	317	226	258	0	0	0	59
4	YMEAN	1.183E 02	1.183E 02	2.269E 02	-9.881E 02	-4.630E 02	0.0	0.0	0.0	3.189E 03
5	N	209	209	184	128	153	0	0	0	31
5	YMEAN	1.446E 02	1.446E 02	2.915E 02	-1.205E 03	-1.548E 02	0.0	0.0	0.0	2.429E 03
6	N	242	242	222	161	188	0	0	0	34
6	YMEAN	8.558E 02	8.558E 02	1.130E 03	-2.957E 02	5.504E 02	0.0	0.0	0.0	4.511E 03
7	N	162	0	0	0	0	162	127	0	0
7	YMEAN	5.379E 03	0.0	0.0	0.0	0.0	5.379E 03	4.619E 03	0.0	0.0
8	N	93	0	0	0	0	93	82	0	0
8	YMEAN	5.582E 03	0.0	0.0	0.0	0.0	5.582E 03	4.224E 03	0.0	0.0
9	N	14	0	0	0	0	14	10	0	0
9	YMEAN	-4.791E 02	0.0	0.0	0.0	0.0	-4.791E 02	-9.809E 02	0.0	0.0

EDUCATION OF HEAD 31:43, ETA = 0.072 GROUP

CLASS	stat	15*	11*	14*	13*	6*
3	N	0	32	0	0	105
3	YMEAN	0.0	1.898E 03	0.0	0.0	-6.246E 03
4	N	0	25	0	0	45
4	YMEAN	0.0	3.098E 03	0.0	0.0	-2.171E 03
5	N	0	27	0	0	25
5	YMEAN	0.0	4.704E 03	0.0	0.0	-3.235E 03
6	N	0	20	0	0	20
6	YMEAN	0.0	5.353E 03	0.0	0.0	-6.704E 03
7	N	71	0	56	35	0
7	YMEAN	7.031E 03	0.0	1.554E 03	8.220E 03	0.0
8	N	47	0	40	11	0
8	YMEAN	6.962E 03	0.0	1.368E 03	1.611E 04	0.0
9	N	4	0	6	4	0
9	YMEAN	6.167E 03	0.0	-5.756E 03	2.775E 03	0.0

RACE 31:48, ETA = 0.017 GROUP

CLASS	stat	15*	11*	14*	13*	6*	7	8	10*	3	12	4*	9*
1	N	1626	1382	957	957	754	957	754	648	244	197	425	203
1	YMEAN	3.016E 02	-6.526E 02	1.821E 02	1.821E 02	-5.664E 02	1.821E 02	-5.664E 02	-1.251E 03	5.418E 03	4.265E 03	-2.614E 03	3.029E 03
2	N	406	392	195	0	0	0	0	195	14	11	20	0
2	YMEAN	-4.679E 03	-4.990E 03	-4.813E 03	0.0	0.0	0.0	0.0	-4.813E 03	2.021E 02	4.160E 03	-5.169E 03	0.0
3	N	56	45	25	25	22	25	22	19	11	11	20	3
3	YMEAN	1.804E 03	1.139E 03	2.580E 03	2.580E 03	2.514E 03	2.580E 03	2.514E 03	-1.267E 03	4.000E 03	4.000E 03	-1.008E 03	3.101E 03

1	N	102	106	95	47
	YMEAN	7.280E 03	3.376E 03	9.627E 02	1.065E 04
2	N	8	0	3	3 / 195
	YMEAN	4.866E 03	0.0	1.780E 03	-1.829E 04 / -4.813E 03
3	N	7	3	4	0
	YMEAN	3.226E 03	1.702E 04	5.494E 03	0.0 / 0.0

PUB TRANSP GOOD 26:52, ETA = 0.002

GROUP

GROUP	N (c1)	YMEAN (c1)	N (c2)	YMEAN (c2)	N (c3)	YMEAN (c3)
1	771	-4.460E 02	128	-6.662E 02	1207	3.878E 02
2	676	-1.322E 02	110	-8.901E 02	1049	-6.392E 02
5	461	-6.223E 02	75	-4.151E 02	651	4.456E 02
14*	39	2.831E 03	7	4.721E 02	54	1.651E 03
11*	45	3.038E 03	1	3.392E 03	59	5.220E 03
15*	37	5.203E 03	8	2.607E 02	72	8.719E 03

PUB TRANSP GOOD 26:52, ETA = 0.002

GROUP

GROUP	N (c1)	YMEAN (c1)	N (c2)	YMEAN (c2)	N (c3)	YMEAN (c3)
7	326	-7.711E 01	66	-4.004E 02	598	5.919E 02
8	272	-5.514E 02	55	-1.209E 03	455	-2.145E 02
10*	227	-1.329E 03	48	-1.905E 03	396	-1.069E 03
3	95	4.290E 03	18	4.630E 02	158	6.289E 03
12	76	4.007E 03	17	3.702E 03	126	4.935E 03
4*	215	-3.107E 03	35	-2.047E 03	398	-2.758E 03
9*	54	2.377E 03	11	3.428E 03	143	3.215E 03
13*	19	5.546E 03	1	2.032E 03	32	1.191E 04
6*	135	-5.146E 03	1	-1.907E 03	53	-4.912E 03

% CHANGE IN INCOME , ETA = 0.001

GROUP

GROUP	N (c1)	YMEAN (c1)	N (c2)	YMEAN (c2)	N (c3)	YMEAN (c3)	N (c4)	YMEAN (c4)	N (c5)	YMEAN (c5)
1	331	-1.208E 01	433	-3.069E 02	321	1.471E 02				
2	304	-6.275E 02	369		272	-1.377E 02				
5	166	7.143E 02	238	6.856E 02	193	-7.113E 02				
7	140	1.103E 03	210	8.229E 02	168	-6.123E 02	261	-1.134E 02	195	-2.577E 02
8	80	8.248E 02	165	1.326E 02	148	-1.117E 03	223	-1.062E 03	154	-9.846E 02

% CHANGE IN INCOME , ETA = 0.001

GROUP

GROUP	N (c1)	YMEAN (c1)	N (c2)	YMEAN (c2)	N (c3)	YMEAN (c3)	N (c4)	YMEAN (c4)	N (c5)	YMEAN (c5)
15*	6	1.417E 04	24	5.284E 03	17	5.175E 03	40	6.595E 03	30	8.567E 03
11*	15	8.812E 03	17	4.279E 03	18	8.076E 02	31	2.070E 02	26	2.648E 03
14*	12	-7.228E 03	24	2.495E 03	26	2.131E 03	26	-2.515E 03	14	8.246E 03
13*	9	1.603E 04	16	4.612E 03	6	6.063E 03	6	1.530E 04	14	1.321E 04
6*	26	-5.125E 03	28	-3.403E 03	25	-3.041E 03	47	-3.549E 03	67	-7.086E 03

EXPECT CHILDREN ? 29:18, ETA = 0.000

GROUP	N (c1)	YMEAN (c1)	N (c2)	YMEAN (c2)	N (c3)	YMEAN (c3)	N (c4)	YMEAN (c4)	N (c5)	YMEAN (c5)
10*	65	-1.307E 03	148	-4.030E 02	130	-1.400E 03	192	-1.588E 03	128	-1.778E 03
3	27	7.483E 03	64	4.068E 03	49	3.497E 03	72	4.027E 03	55	9.327E 03
12	18	3.097E 03	48	3.894E 03	43	3.266E 03	66	2.953E 03	44	8.481E 03
4*	138	-2.989E 03	131	-2.702E 03	79	-2.668E 03	132	-3.555E 03	156	-2.595E 03
9*	60	1.462E 03	45	3.496E 03	20	3.094E 03	38	5.712E 03	41	2.490E 03

GROUP

CLASS		1	2	5	7	8	10*	3	12	4*	9*
0	N	1949	1713	1079	896	697	596	236	191	634	199
	YMEAN	-2.941E 01	-9.532E 02	4.302E 00	2.725E 02	-4.815E 02	-1.160E 03	5.456E 03	4.237E 03	-2.855E 03	2.972E 03
1	N	139	106	98	86	79	71	33	28	8	7
	YMEAN	3.641E 02	-7.540E 02	-5.809E 02	-2.227E 02	-6.746E 02	-1.976E 02	3.647E 03	4.347E 03	-5.111E 03	4.463E 03

EXPECT CHILDREN ?   29:18, ETA = 0.000

GROUP

CLASS		15*	11*	14*	13*	6*
0	N	93	101	98	45	183
	YMEAN	7.170E 03	3.228E 03	1.468E 03	1.102E 04	-4.660E 03
1	N	24	8	4	5	12
	YMEAN	6.271E 03	1.081E 04	-8.035E 03	-7.660E 02	-6.177E 03

MIGHT MOVE   26:79, ETA = 0.001

GROUP

CLASS		1	2	5	7	8	10*	3	12	4*	9*
1	N	291	233	177	158	128	107	58	50	56	30
	YMEAN	5.331E 02	-4.320E 02	-1.662E 02	-1.494E 01	-9.853E 02	-2.182E 03	3.945E 03	3.485E 03	-1.362E 03	4.269E 03
5	N	1797	1586	1000	824	648	560	211	169	586	176
	YMEAN	-9.587E 02	-1.023E 03	-7.747E 01	2.741E 02	-4.050E 02	-1.070E 03	5.595E 03	4.484E 03	-3.039E 03	2.819E 03

MIGHT MOVE   26:79, ETA = 0.001

GROUP

CLASS		15*	11*	14*	13*	6*
1	N	29	21	21	8	19
	YMEAN	4.681E 03	4.822E 03	1.853E 03	7.162E 03	-4.312E 03
5	N	88	88	81	42	176
	YMEAN	7.756E 03	3.525E 03	9.111E 03	1.038E 04	-4.870E 03

HOW LONG LIVD HERE   , ETA = 0.014

GROUP

CLASS		1	2	5	7	8	10*	3	12	4*	9*
1	N	175	146	114	77	68	57	29	26	32	9
	YMEAN	2.661E 03	1.179E 03	1.667E 03	2.106E 03	1.888E 03	1.140E 03	8.120E 03	6.486E 03	-1.881E 03	3.840E 03
2	N	148	124	96	80	69	61	24	21	28	11
	YMEAN	2.635E 02	-1.394E 03	-9.899E 02	-5.996E 02	-8.092E 02	-1.127E 03	7.247E 03	7.546E 03	-3.390E 03	6.921E 02
3	N	186	155	114	91	79	66	31	27	41	12
	YMEAN	9.508E 02	-7.520E 02	-1.193E 02	2.726E 02	9.093E 01	-1.322E 03	7.178E 03	6.789E 03	-3.608E 03	1.571E 03
4	N	329	277	199	171	149	124	52	43	78	22
	YMEAN	1.489E 03	3.345E 02	1.500E 03	2.055E 03	1.136E 03	-5.524E 02	6.355E 03	7.091E 03	-3.251E 03	8.630E 03
5	N	1250	1117	656	563	411	359	133	102	463	152
	YMEAN	-8.452E 02	-1.433E 03	-5.996E 02	-4.496E 02	-1.521E 03	-1.867E 03	3.381E 03	1.111E 03	-2.783E 03	2.505E 03

HOW LONG LIVD HERE   , ETA = 0.014

GROUP

CLASS		15*	11*	14*	13*	6*
1	N	26	11	0	3	37
	YMEAN	6.486E 03	6.048E 03	0.0	2.334E 04	-3.801E 03
2	N	21	8	0	8	16
	YMEAN	7.546E 03	1.477E 03	0.0	5.280E 03	-7.904E 03
3	N	27	13	0	4	23
	YMEAN	6.789E 03	6.941E 03	0.0	1.035E 04	-4.489E 03
4	N	43	25	0	9	28
	YMEAN	7.091E 03	8.417E 03	0.0	2.249E 03	-7.545E 03

```
6
N  YMEAN   0.0   0      6.916E 02   1.111E 03   1.135E 04   -3.632E 03
                   52          102          31          91
```

HRS HEAD TRVL WK22:30-32, ETA = 0.017
GROUP

CLASS	1	2	5	7	8	10*	3	12	4*	9*
O N	577	527	233	206	0	0	50	0	294	206
YMEAN	1.096E 03	2.055E 03	2.714E 03	3.030E 03	0.0	0.0	9.873E 03	0.0	-1.879E 03	3.030E 03
1 N	422	354	265	234	734	234	68	68	89	0
YMEAN	-7.592E 02	-1.771E 03	-1.432E 03	-1.223E 03	-1.223E 03	-1.223E 03	3.678E 03	3.678E 03	-3.041E 03	0.0
2 N	286	245	177	150	150	150	41	41	68	0
YMEAN	-1.567E 03	-2.184E 03	-1.575E 03	-1.489E 03	-1.489E 03	-1.489E 03	1.345E 03	1.345E 03	-4.185E 03	0.0
3 N	240	211	154	126	126	126	29	29	57	0
YMEAN	-9.706E 02	-1.775E 03	-1.053E 03	-7.397E 02	-7.397E 02	-7.397E 02	3.876E 02	3.876E 02	-4.440E 03	0.0
4 N	314	266	204	157	157	157	48	48	62	0
YMEAN	-7.412E 02	-2.187E 03	-1.743E 03	-1.469E 03	-1.469E 03	-1.469E 03	5.320E 03	5.320E 03	-3.978E 03	0.0
5 N	249	216	144	109	109	0	33	33	72	0
YMEAN	2.692E 03	1.442E 03	3.195E 03	3.772E 03	3.772E 03	0.0	7.881E 03	7.881E 03	-5.325E 03	0.0

HRS HEAD TRVL WK22:30-32, ETA = 0.017
GROUP

CLASS	15*	11*	14*	13*	6*
O N	0	0	0	50	27
YMEAN	0.0	0.0	0.0	9.873E 03	-3.645E 03
1 N	29	0	30	0	31
YMEAN	6.172E 03	0.0	1.809E 03	0.0	-5.129E 03
2 N	24	0	17	0	27
YMEAN	2.635E 03	0.0	-5.414E 02	0.0	-3.065E 03
3 N	16	0	13	0	28
YMEAN	5.713E 03	0.0	1.599E 03	0.0	-6.085E 03
4 N	24	0	19	0	47
YMEAN	8.065E 03	0.0	1.274E 03	0.0	-6.781E 03
5 N	19	100	14	0	35
YMEAN	1.291E 04	2.772E 03	5.647E 02	0.0	-4.335E 03

...... END OF ANALYSIS ......

The ETA (really η^2) is the fraction of the variance of group 1 accounted for by all the subclass means of that predictor. (The BSS's are for binary splits only).

```
*****TIME IS  13:58:34
NO MORE RUN CARDS IN SETUP. STEP TERMINATED
```

APPENDIX 5 - Second Example, Run 3

```
      INSTITUTE FOR SOCIAL RESEARCH MONITOR SYSTEM    02/05/73                    *****
      FASTER VERSIONS OF TABLES, MDC, AND REGRESSN NOW AVAILABLE BY SPECIFYING    *****
                 //   EXEC OSIRIS,LIB=X485321X,LIB1=OSIRPGM                        *****
      SAVINGS ARE 10-45% FOR TABLES, 45% FOR MDC AND 20% FOR REGRESSN             *****
```

Most of this is identical to the first run so only alterations are noted.

*****TIME IS 0:32:45

*****LISTING OF SET-UP FOLLOWS:

```
CARD                  1         2         3         4         5         6         7        R
NO.          1234567890123456789012345678901234567890123456789012345678901234567890
 1    $RUN AID3
 2    INCLUDE V1264=1 AND V1109=0-1 AND V542=0-1 AND V1499=1-9*
 3    MTR 46, PROJECT 468070,AID3
 4    *
 5    V101,V542,V603,V1009,V1109,V1122,V1146,V1168,V1240,V1250,V1274,V1276,V1365,
 6    V1370,V1490,V1498,V1499,V1506,V1572,V1609,V1719,V1720,V1264,V1485*
 7    HOUSE VALUE TRUNCATED TO 5000-75000 BY SQUEEZING EXTREME CASES  807MTR45 MORGAN
 8    YVAR=1122, WEIGHT=1609, XVAR=1719, ANAL=REGR, RECODE, MDOP=NONE,
 9    TABLES=(FLIG,MEAN)*
10    1    IFV1264    NE    1
11         ORV1109    GT    1
12         ORV 542    GT    1
13         ORV1499    EQ    0                                           0
14    2    IFV1719    LT    3000          . V1264                       1
15         OR         IN    3000   4999   V2001                         2
16                          5000   7499                                 3
17                          7500   9999                                 4
18                          10000  14999                                5
19                          15000  19999                                6
20                          20000                                       7
21    3    IFV1365    GE    1             V2002    =                     1         MARRIED
22                          EQ                      GOTO                 4
23         IFV1240    EQ    1             V2002    =                     2         SNGL MAN
24    ALT                                 V2002    =                     3         SNGL SMN
25    T                                   V1720    MPY   100V1720
26                                        V2003    DIVV1720   V1719
27         IFV2003    LT    -5            V2003    =                     1         BRACKET
28         OR         IN    -4     4                                     2         PERCENT
29                          5      9                                     3         CHANGE
30                          10     19                                    4         IN
31                          20                                          5         INCOME
32    5    IFV1274    EQ    1             V2004    =                     1         HOW
33                                        V2004    GOTO                  6         LONG
34         IFV 603    EQ    1             V2004    GOTO                  6         LIVED
35         IFV 101    IN    7      8V2004 GOTO                           6         HERE
36                                        V2004    GOTO                  6
37                                        V2004    GOTO                  6
38         IFV 101    IN    4      6V2004 =                              4
39    ALT                                 V2004    =                     5
40    6    IFV1168    IN    7      9V1168 =                              7         TRUNCATE
41    7    IFV1009    EQ    1             V1009    =                     2         NINE
             1         2         3         4         5         6         7        8
    1234567890123456789012345678901234567890123456789012345678901234567890
```

Delete

Specify subgroup regressions (of house value on income) instead of means. The covariate (x) must be specified.

CARD
NO.

```
CARD
NO.      1         2         3         4         5         6         7         8
         12345678901234567890123456789012345678901234567890123456789012345678901234567890
                                                                              CODES
42    8  IFV1009  GT  6            V1009  =  6                6
43    9  IFV1370  NE  1            V1370  =  0                0
44   10  IFV1490  OUT 1           2V1490  =  3                3
45   11  IFV1250  OUT 1           3V1250  =  5                5
46   12  IFV1122  GT  75000        V1122  =  75000        75000
47       NRV1122  LT  5000         V1122  =  5000          5000
48   13  IFV1719  GT  25000        V1719  =  25000        25000
49   14  IFV1276  GT  5            V1276  =  5                1
50   15  IFV1146  IN  1          99V1146  =  1              1          BRACKET
51       OR           100          149                      2          ANNUAL
52                    150          199                      3          HOURS
53                    200          299                      4          COMMUTNG
54                GE  300                                    5

55       END
56       PRED=2001 MAXC=7 RANK=0 PREN='3-YR AVE $ INC.'*
57       PRED=(1168,1009) MAXC=6*
58       PRED=2002 MAXC=3 PREN='SEX & MAR STATUS'*
59       PRED=1506*
60       PRED=1498 MAXC=5*
61       PRED=1572 MAXC=4 F*
62       PRED=1490 MAXC=3 F RANK=0 END*
63       MIN=3 REDU=.5 RANK=ALL TRACE=ALL*  }
```

Omit lookahead and symmetry premiums and use a lower reducibility criterion because the main income effect is already removed.

AID3: OSIRIS SEARCHING FOR STRUCTURE - JULY 1973

THE FILTER IS:

INCLUDE V1264=1 AND V1109=0-1 AND V542=0-1 AND V1409=1-9*

    MTR 46, PROJECT 468070,AID3

*

THE VARIABLE LIST IS:

V101,V542,V603,V1009,V1109,V1122,V1146,V1168,V1240,V1250,V1274,V1276,V1365,
V1370,V1430,V1438,V1469,V1506,V1572,V1602,V1719,V1720,V1264,V1485*

	VAR.	TYPE	VARIABLE NAME	TLOC	WIDTH	NODEC	RESP.	MDCODE1	MDCODE2	REFNO	ID	TSEQNO
T	101	0	WHEN MOVED IN 5:36	770	1	0	1		0000009			00000
T	542	0	CHANGE IN FU COMP 15:25	1070	1	0	1					00000
T	603	0	MOVED SINCE SPRNG6816-38	1149	1	0	1		0000009			00000
T	1009	0	BKT AGE HEAD 9V1009	1831	1	0	1					00000
T	1109	0	CHANGE IN FU COMP 21:18	2021	1	0	1					00000
T	1122	0	HOUSE VALUE 21:38-42	2041	5	0	1					00000
T	1146	0	HRS HEAD TRVL WK22:30-32	2103	3	0	1					00000
T	1168	0	# REQUIRED ROOMS 23:12	2154	1	0	1					00000
T	1240	0	SEX OF HEAD 26:40	2351	1	0	1					00000
T	1250	0	PUB TRANSP GOOD 26:52	2363	1	0	1		0000009			00000
T	1264	0	OWN OR RENT? 26:67	2378	1	0	1					00000
T	1274	0	MOVED SINCE SPRING 26:77	2388	1	0	1		0000009			00000
T	1276	0	MIGHT MOVE 26:79	2390	1	0	1		0000009			00000
T	1365	0	MARITAL STATUS 29:10	2514	1	0	1					00000
T	1370	0	EXPECT CHILDREN ? 29:18	2521	1	0	1		0000009			00000
T	1485	0	EDUCATION OF HEAD 31:43	2657	1	0	1		0000009			00000
T	1490	0	RACE 31:48	2662	1	0	1		0000009			00000
T	1498	0	DIST TO CNTR SMSA 31:58	2672	1	0	1		0000009			00000
T	1499	0	TYPE OF STRUCTURE 31:59	2673	1	0	1		0000009			00000
T	1506	0	LRGST PLAC/SMSA PSU31:66	2680	1	0	1					00000
T	1572	0	CURRENT REGION 0V472	2838	1	0	1	0000009				00000
T	1609	0	WEIGHT 0V509	2892	2	0	1				COR	00000
T	1719	0	MEAN MONEY INCOME	3179	5	0	1				COR	00000
T	1720	0	SLOPE MONEY INCOME	3184	6	0	1				COR	00000

HOUSE VALUE TRUNCATED TO 5000-75000 BY SQUEEZING EXTREME CASES   807MTR45 MORGAN

YVAR=1122, WEIGHT=1609, XVAR=1719, ANAL=REGR,   RECODE, MDOP=NONE,

TABLES=(ELIG,MEAN)*

```
NO  LOG TEST  REL A OPERAND B OPERAND RES      OP C OPERAND D OPERAND  TEXT
 1  IFV1264      NF        1          0   0                 0          0
```

```
0  ORV1109  GT   1      0        =   0   0
0  ORV 542  GT   1      0            0   0
2  ORV1499  EQ   0      OV1264   =   1   0
0  IFV1719  LT   3000   OV2001   =   2   0
0  OR       IN   3000   4999         3   0
0               5000   7499         4   0
0               7500   9999         5   0
0              10000   14999        6   0
3  IFV1365  GE  20000   0            7   0   MARRIED
0               1      OV2002   GOTO 1   0   MARRIED
0  IFV1240  EQ   0      OV2007   =    2   0   SNGL MAN
4  ALT                 OV2002   =    3   0   SNGL SMN
0  T        LT   0      OV1720   MPY  100V 0
0                       OV2003   DIVV 1720V 0   BRACKET
0  IFV2003  LT  -5      OV2003   =    1   1720  PERCENT
0  OR       IN  -4      4             2   1719  CHANGE
0               5      9             3         IN
0              10      19            4         INCOME
5  IFV1274  GE  20      0            5   0
0  IFV 603  EQ   0      OV2004   =    1   0
0               1      OV2004   GOTO 6   0
0  IFV 101  IN   0      OV2004   =    2   0   HOW
0  IFV 101  IN   7      8V2304   GOTO 6   0   LONG
0  ALT            4      6V2004        6   0   LIVED
0                       OV2004        4   0   HERE
6  IFV1168  IN   7      9V1168   =    5   0
7  IFV1009  EQ   1      OV100C   =    6   0   TRUNCATE
8  IFV1009  GT   6      OV1009   =    2   0   NINE
9  IFV1370  NE   1      OV1370   =    6   0   CODES
10 IFV1490  OUT  1      2V1490   =    3   0
11 IFV1250  OUT  1      3V1250   =    5   0
12 IFV1122  GT  75000   OV1122   =    6   75000
0  ORV1122  LT   5000   OV1122   =    2   5000
14 IFV1719  GT  25000   OV1719   =    6   25000   BRACKET
15 IFV1276  GT   1      OV1276   =    3   1       ANNUAL
0  IFV1146  IN          99V1146       5   2       HOURS
0  OR       CF   100    149           1   3       COMMUTNG,
0               150    199           2   4
0               200    299           3   5
0               300    0             4   0
0  END      CF    0      0            5
0                0      0             0
```

PRED=2001 MAXC=7 RANK=0 PREN='3-YR AVE $ INC'*

PRED=(1168,1009) MAXC=6*

PRED=2002 MAXC=3 PREN='SEX & MAR STATUS'*

PRED=1506*

PRED=1498 MAXC=5*

PRFD=1572 MAXC=4 F*

PRFD=1490 MAXC=3 F RANK=0 END*

MIN=3 REDU=.5 RANK=ALL TRACE=ALL*

```
COMPUTE      SPECIFIED
OUTPUT       SPECIFIED

THE COMPLETE VARIABLE LIST IS:

  101  542  603  1009  1109  1122  1146  1168  1240  1250  1274  1276  1365  1370  1490  1498  1499  1506  1572  1609
 1710 1720 1264  1485  2001  2002  2003  2004
```

```
HOUSE VALUE TRUNCATED TO 500C-75C00 BY SQUEEZING EXTREME CASES    807MTR45 MORGAN

      2088 OBSERVATIONS READ AFTER GLOBAL FILTER

Y AVERAGE =        2.0C7342E C4
STANDARD DEVIATION =  1.27825ZE 04
BOUNDARIES =  -4.383920E 04    8.398600E 04

   2088 CASES INCLUDED IN THE ANALYSIS
        0 FILTERED (LOCAL/SUBSET SELECTOR)
        0 MISSING DATA CASES
        0 OUTLIERS INCLUDED
        0 INVALID PREDICTOR VALUES

   2088 SAMPLE OBSERVATIONS - WITH TOTALS
        WEIGHTS =            8.157500E 04
        DEPENDENT VARIABLE (Y) =  1.637489D 09    AVERAGE  =   2.007342E 04
        Y-SQUARED =          4.619239D 13    VARIANCE =   1.633931E 08
        COVARIATE (X) =      8.399546D 08    AVERAGE  =   1.029671E 04
        X-SQUARED =          1.152888D 13    VARIANCE =   3.524958E 07
        CROSS-PRODUCTS (Z) =  2.057341D 13    SLOPE    =   1.291759E 00

                    STAGE 1 OF THE ANALYSIS
               BEST SPLIT BASED ON REGR'N
               0-STEP LOOKAHEAD WITH 1 FORCED SPLITS

SPLITTING CRITERIA -
  MAXIMUM NUMBER OF SPLITS =    25
  MINIMUM # OBSERVATIONS IN A GROUP =   3
  %AGE OF TOTAL SS N SPLITS MUST EXPLAIN =  0.5(N=1),
  PRINT CASES OUTSIDE  5.0 STANDARD DEVIATIONS OF PARENT GROUP MEAN

      8    RANKED PREDICTORS SPECIFIED
PREDICTOR RANK PREFERENCE   AT
  SPLIT ATTEMPT RANGE -    0 RANKS UP,  0 RANKS DOWN
  ELIGIBILITY RANGE -      0 RANKS UP,  0 RANKS DOWN
    PREDICTOR              VARIABLE NUMBER   TYPE    MAX CLASS    RANK
  1  3-YR AVE $ INC.            V2001         M         7         0
  2  # REQUIRED ROOMS 23:12     V1168         M         6         1
  3  BKT AGE HEAD $V10C9        V10C9         M         6         1
  4  SEX & MAR STATUS           V2002         M         3         1
  5  LRGST PLAC/SMSA PSU31:66   V1506         M         9         1
  6  DIST TO CNTR SMSA 31:58    V1498         M         5         1
  7  CURRENT REGION OV472       V1572         F         4         1
  8  RACE          31:48        V1490         F         3         0

WEIGHTED Y VARIABLE 1122  HOUSE VALUE     21:38-42  SCALED BY  1.0E 00
COVARIAT-MEAN MONEY INCOME      V1719-  SCALE FACTCR  1.0E 00

      1 CANDIDATES -     GROUP         SS
                           1     1.33224DE 13

                    ATTEMPT SPLIT ON GROUP   1 WITH SS =  1.33224OE 13
```

LOOKAHEAD TENTATIVE PARTITION

SPLIT ATTEMPT ON GROUP   1 WITH N =   2088   SS = 1.33224E 13
SUMS- W = 8.15750E 04, Y = 1.63748E 09, YSQ = 4.61929E 13, X = 9.39544E 08, XSQ = 1.15228E 13, 7 = 2.06734E 13

PREDICTOR # REQUIRED ROOMS 23:12
5 NON-EMPTY CLASSES   2   3   4   5   6

PARTITION	N	WEIGHT	Y-MEAN	Y-VARIANCE	X-MEAN	X-VARIANCE	SLOPE	BSS
BETWEEN 2	661	2.91370E 04	1.76208E 04	1.34392E 08	7.95602E 03	3.50603E 07	1.06818E 00	
AND 3	1427	5.24330E 04	2.14362E 04	1.74421E 08	1.15973E 04	3.06433E 07	1.47149E 00	1.17609E 11
BETWEEN 3	1218	5.33233E 04	2.09299E 04	1.51947E 08	9.28299E 03	3.40712E 07	1.22265E 00	
AND 4	870	2.85523E 04	2.16159E 04	1.81204E 08	1.21793E 04	3.20263E 07	1.50884E 00	8.63691E 10
BETWEEN 4	1704	7.11340E 04	2.00866E 04	1.60302E 08	1.00739E 04	3.52923E 07	1.27774E 00	
AND 5	384	1.04410E 04	1.99834E 04	1.84950E 08	1.18147E 04	3.24125E 07	1.50635E 00	6.37707E 10
BETWEEN 5	1929	7.78800E 04	2.00779E 04	1.61590E 08	1.02022E 04	3.51569E 07	1.29543E 00	
AND 6	159	3.69500E 03	1.95796E 04	2.02690E 08	1.22818E 04	3.39703E 07	1.37642E 00	2.92361E 10

REST SPLIT ON PREDICTOR 1168 = 1.17608E 11 AFTER CLASS 2

PREDICTOR BKT AGE HEAD QV10C5
5 NON-EMPTY CLASSES   2   3   4   5   6

PARTITION	N	WEIGHT	Y-MEAN	Y-VARIANCE	X-MEAN	X-VARIANCE	SLOPE	BSS
BETWEEN 2	372	1.42350E 04	1.98748E 04	1.44940E 08	1.08257E 04	1.90347E 07	1.77756E 00	
AND 3	1716	6.73400E 04	2.01540E 04	1.67369E 08	1.01849E 04	3.86186E 07	1.24434E 00	8.29969E 10
BETWEEN 3	902	3.34870E 04	2.20743E 04	1.75047E 08	1.18262E 04	2.52645E 07	1.72314E 00	
AND 4	1186	4.9C880E 04	1.86300E 04	1.50677E 08	9.23166E 03	3.94673E 07	1.09833E 00	2.28220E 11
BETWEEN 4	1381	5.10150E 04	2.18217E 04	1.70766E 08	1.21373E 04	2.76472E 07	1.50984E 00	
AND 5	707	3.05600E 04	1.71550E 04	1.37650E 08	7.22423E 03	3.28804E 07	1.14261E 00	1.43227E 11
BETWEEN 5	1759	6.60020E 04	2.11990E 04	1.68465E 08	1.16022E 04	3.10754E 07	1.39050E 00	
AND 6	329	1.55733E 04	1.53029E 04	1.14113E 08	4.76387E 03	1.51379E 07	1.50734E 00	1.39603E 11

REST SPLIT ON PREDICTOR 1009 = 2.28220E 11 AFTER CLASS 3

PREDICTOR SEX & MAR STATUS
3 NON-EMPTY CLASSES   1   2   3

PARTITION	N	WEIGHT	Y-MEAN	Y-VARIANCE	X-MEAN	X-VARIANCE	SLOPE	BSS
BETWEEN 1	1660	6.66840E 04	2.10937E 04	1.70328E 08	1.14257E 04	3.24255E 07	1.36936E 00	
AND 2	428	1.48910E 04	1.55046E 04	1.07083E 08	5.24077E 03	1.66594E 07	1.34439E 00	8.38022E 10
BETWEEN 2	1742	6.98820E 04	2.07886E 04	1.68766E 08	1.11953E 04	3.37723E 07	1.35647E 00	
AND 3	346	1.16930E 04	1.57993E 04	1.10312E 08	4.92633E 03	1.28362E 07	1.58826E 00	1.19689E 11

REST SPLIT ON PREDICTOR 2002 = 1.19688E 11 AFTER CLASS 2

PREDICTOR LRGST PLAC/SMSA PSU31:66
6 NON-EMPTY CLASSES   1   2   3   4   5   6

PARTITION	N	WEIGHT	Y-MEAN	Y-VARIANCE	X-MEAN	X-VARIANCE	SLOPE	BSS
BETWEEN 1	633	2.37010E 04	2.58308E 04	2.11870E 08	1.26270E 04	3.72024E 07	1.45647E 00	
AND 2	1455	5.78740E 04	1.77156E 04	1.24519E 08	9.34238E 03	3.13371E 07	1.09374E 00	3.47037E 11
BETWEEN 2	1076	4.11590E 04	2.40121E 04	1.89791E 08	1.21277E 04	3.44958E 07	1.39794E 00	
AND 3	1012	4.04160E 04	1.60623E 04	1.04747E 08	8.43205E 03	2.91535E 07	9.60458E-01	3.50862E 11
BETWEEN 3	1298	5.03480E 04	2.30145E 04	1.79150E 08	1.17912E 04	3.43781E 07	1.34357E 00	
AND 4	790	3.12270E 04	1.53315E 04	1.01702E 08	7.88714E 03	2.72810E 07	9.52956E-01	2.36592E 11
BETWEEN 4	1442	5.51540E 04	2.25180E 04	1.73924E 08	1.15397E 04	3.50440E 07	1.30062E 00	
AND 5	646	2.50610E 04	1.45608E 04	9.57874E 07	7.49371E 03	2.44100E 07	9.49607E-01	2.01075E 11
BETWEEN 5	1642	6.49450E 04	2.16429E 04	1.69051E 08	1.11399E 04	3.50309E 07	1.30540E 00	
AND 6	446	1.66303E 04	1.39443E 04	9.43410E 07	7.00371E 03	2.53641E 07	8.63730E-01	1.42371E 11

BEST SPLIT ON PREDICTOR 1506 = 3.50861E 11 AFTER CLASS 2

PREDICTOR DIST TO CNTR SMSA 31:58
5 NON-EMPTY CLASSES   1   2   4   5

PARTITION	N	WEIGHT	Y-MEAN	Y-VARIANCE	X-MEAN	X-VARIANCE	SLOPE	BSS
BETWEEN 1	386	1.41750E 04	1.88454E 04	1.11413E 08	1.06581E 04	3.52740E 07	1.04984E 00	
AND 2	1702	6.74000E 04	2.03317E 04	1.74009E 08	1.02207E 04	3.52307E 07	1.34702E 00	8.56980E 10
BETWEEN 2	968	3.71490E 04	2.12913E 04	1.43558E 08	1.15528E 04	3.37033E 07	1.21050E 00	

```
AND      3  1120  4.44260E 04  1.90551E 04  1.77832E 08  9.24638E 03  3.41488E 07  1.38168E 00  3.16754E 10
BETWEEN  3  1304  5.07440E 04  2.22962E 04  1.71517E 08  1.16082E 04  3.41821E 07  1.31504E 00  5.79988E 10
AND      4   784  3.08310E 04  1.64149E 04  1.28679E 08  8.13816E 03  2.95526E 07  1.14509E 00
BETWEEN  4  1549  6.04550E 04  2.15046E 04  1.65281E 08  1.17735E 04  3.43420E 07  1.3144RE 00
AND      5   539  2.10800E 04  1.59661E 04  1.35441E 08  7.78065E 03  2.97706E 07  1.11621E 00  4.09532E 10
BEST SPLIT ON PREDICTOR 1468 = 8.56980E 10 AFTER CLASS 1

PREDICTOR CURRENT REGION OV472
4 NON-EMPTY CLASSES    4 2 3   1
PARTITION   N     WEIGHT       Y-MEAN      Y-VARIANCE    X-MEAN      X-VARIANCE    SLOPE        BSS
BETWEEN 4   317  1.32710E 04  2.13324E 04  1.22307E 08  1.06194E 04  3.13668E 07  9.40384E-01
AND     2  1771  6.83040E 04  1.98288E 04  1.71086E 08  1.02340E 04  3.59993E 07  1.34933E 00  7.05985E 10
BETWEEN 2   934  4.01C80E 04  2.03634E 04  1.31437E 08  1.06382E 04  3.36420E 07  1.08504E 00
AND     3  1154  4.14670E 04  1.57929E 04  1.94232E 08  9.96641E 03  3.66160E 07  1.47810E 00  1.12055E 11
BETWEEN 3  1724  6.38510E 04  1.87222E 04  1.36095E 08  9.86245E 03  3.44896E 07  1.14924E 00
AND     1   364  1.77240E 04  2.49414E 04  2.32022E 08  1.18611E 04  3.49511E 07  1.63622E 00  3.01520E 11
REST SPLIT ON PREDICTOR 1572 = 3.015201E 11 AFTER CLASS 3

PREDICTOR 3-YR AVE & INC
7 NON-EMPTY CLASSES   1 2    3    4    5    6    7
PARTITION   N     WEIGHT       Y-MEAN      Y-VARIANCE    X-MEAN      X-VARIANCE    SLOPE        BSS
BETWEEN 1   256  8.30500E 03  1.05296E 04  4.23378E 07  1.92335E 03  4.23077E 05  1.85793E 00
AND     2  1832  7.27700E 04  2.12282E 04  1.65708E 08  1.13099E 04  2.99512E 07  1.33907E 00  2.20117E 10
BETWEEN 2   513  1.65410E 04  1.17944E 04  5.73436E 07  2.85686E 03  1.36197E 06  1.23784E 00
ANC     3  1575  6.50340E 04  2.21791E 04  1.68534E 08  1.21890E 04  2.62059E 07  1.41314E 00  6.19079E 10
BETWEEN 3   899  2.85780E 04  1.27768E 04  6.00404E 07  4.33335E 03  3.91099E 06  7.05368E-01
AND     4  1189  5.25970E 04  2.40334E 04  1.74034E 08  1.35825E 04  2.21234E 07  1.42557E 00  7.27460E 10
BETWEEN 4  1261  4.30130E 04  1.42346E 04  7.00466E 07  5.79847E 03  7.23497E 06  9.30808E-01
AND     5   827  3.85620E 04  2.65862E 04  1.87193E 08  1.53142E 04  1.87425E 07  1.43132E 00  5.46434E 10
BETWEEN 5  1758  6.54110E 04  1.70967E 04  1.02472E 08  8.02113E 03  1.49982E 07  1.17493E 00
AND     6   330  1.61640E 04  3.21195E 04  2.29491E 08  1.95053E 04  1.14318E 07  1.76156E 00  5.44766E 10
BETWEEN 6  1966  7.53320E 04  1.85559E 04  1.18597E 08  9.24882E 03  2.29945E 07  1.18059E 00
AND     7   122  6.04300E 03  3.90410E 04  3.37204E 08  2.33944E 04  3.09720E 06  2.25368E 00  6.59848E 10
BEST SPLIT ON PREDICTOR 2001 = 7.274601E 10 AFTER CLASS 3

PREDICTOR RACE                31:48
3 NON-EMPTY CLASSES   2 3   1
PARTITION   N     WEIGHT       Y-MEAN      Y-VARIANCE    X-MEAN      X-VARIANCE    SLOPE        BSS
BETWEEN 2   406  5.49300E 03  1.17827E 04  5.52670E 07  6.96276E 03  2.54679E 07  8.87249E-01
AND     3  1682  7.60820E 04  2.06720E 04  1.69903E 08  1.05374E 04  3.51028E 07  1.28359E 00  1.16451E 11
BETWEEN 3   462  7.22200E 03  1.38035E 04  8.43736E 07  7.11994E 03  2.60314E 07  1.07415E 00
AND     1  1626  7.42530E 04  2.06917E 04  1.66961E 08  1.05607E 04  3.53912E 07  1.28445E 00  7.27292E 10
BEST SPLIT ON PREDICTOR 1490 = 1.164507E 11 AFTER CLASS 2

LRGST PLAC/SMSA PSU31:66 YIELDS MAXIMUM BSS = 3.508619E 11

O-STEP LOOKAHEAD TO SPLIT GROUP   1, TOTAL BSS = 3.508619E 11
 1. SPLIT GROUP   1 ON PREDICTOR 1506, BSS = 3.508619E 11
```

```
             ***** PARTITION OF GROUP  1 *****
FROM ELIGIBLE PREDICTORS AROUND THE CURRENT RANK  1,      0 UP AND   0 DOWN

    MAXIMUM ELIGIBLE BSS AT EACH STEP          MAXIMUM TOTAL BSS (LOOKAHEAD)
1.SPLIT   1 ON V1506 BSS= 3.50862E 11      SPLIT   1 ON V1506 BSS = 3.50862E 11
PE(1)= 6.661E 10, TOTAL= 3.50862E 11                   TOTAL= 3.50862E 11
    PREDICTOR 1506 HAS RANK 1


SPLIT GROUP   1 ON LRGST PLAC/SMSA PSU31:66 V1506
 GROUP   2 WITH  1012 OBSERVATIONS FROM  4 CLASSES =  3   4   5   6
       W= 4.04160E 04 Y= 6.49174D 08 YSQ= 1.46565D 13 X= 3.40790D 08
       XSQ=4.05066D 12 7= 6.60444D 12
       3 WITH  1076 OBSERVATIONS FROM  2 CLASSES =  1   2
       W= 4.11590E 04 Y= 9.88315D 08 YSQ= 3.15359D 13 X= 4.99164D 08
       XSQ= 7.47221D 12 7= 1.39690D 13

    2 CANDIDATES -     GROUP        SS
                         2      4.229269E 12
                         3      7.804341E 12

        ATTEMPT SPLIT ON GROUP   3 WITH SS = 7.804341E 12
```

*We omit the next 36 pages
tracing the split attempts.*

```
                ***** PARTITION OF GROUP 12 *****
FROM ELIGIBLE PREDICTORS AROUND THE CURRENT RANK 1,    0 UP AND  0 DOWN

    MAXIMUM ELIGIBLE BSS AT EACH STEP         MAXIMUM TOTAL BSS (LOOKAHEAD)

GROUP 12 COULD NOT BE SPLIT

END OF STAGE 1 OF THE ANALYSIS.    7 FINAL GROUPS.    7 INELIGIBLE FOR SPLITTING.

        VARIATION EXPLAINED (BSS(01)/TSS) = 7.4%

        1-WAY ANALYSIS OF VARIANCE ON FINAL GROUPS
```

SOURCE		SUM OF SQUARES	DF	MEAN SQUARE
TOTAL		1.332240E 13	81536.	1.633931E 08
POOLED REGRESSION ON SAMPLE		4.795855E 12	1.	4.795855E 12
BETWEEN INDIV SLOPES	S(1)	3.569814E 11	6.	5.949690E 10
OBSNS BETWEEN INDIV LINES	S(2)	7.539118E 12	81523.	9.247854E 07
GROUP MEANS REGRESSION LINE	S(3)	5.690066E 11	5.	1.138013E 11
MEAN SLOPE VS MEANS REGR SLOPE	S(4)	6.144236E 10	1.	6.144236E 10

A single regression of house value on income over the whole sample accounts for 36% of the variance:

$$\frac{480 \times 10^{10}}{1332 \times 10^{10}} = 36\%$$

This is the unexplained variance around subgroup regression lines.

Total SS (around mean) =
— Expl. by overall regression

$$
\begin{aligned}
&1332 \times 10^{10} \\
&-480 \times 10^{10} \\
\hline
&852 \times 10^{10}
\end{aligned}
$$

— Residual "error"
= Marginal expl. by subgroup regressions (diff. means and diff. slopes)

$$
\begin{aligned}
&852 \times 10^{10} \\
&-754 \times 10^{10} \\
\hline
&98 \times 10^{10}
\end{aligned}
$$

$$\frac{98 \times 10^{10}}{1332 \times 10^{10}} = 7.4\% \text{ of variance}$$

Around mean, explained by different subgroup regressions.

OR:

$$\frac{98 \times 10^{10}}{852 \times 10^{10}} = 11.5\% \text{ of variance around overall regression, explained.}$$

For decomposition of the 98×10^{10}, see text $(S_1 + S_3 + S_4 = 98 \times 10^{10})$.

$\frac{36}{98}$ of it is differences in regression slopes.

NOTE: Mean squares and F-Tests are inappropriate with weighted data.

GROUP SUMMARY TABLE
13 GROUPS OF WHICH 7 ARE FINAL

GROUP   1 , N =   2088, SUM W = 8.15750OE 04   SS(L)/TSS= 1.000, BSS/TSS= 0.026
Y MEAN= 2.007342E 04, VARIANCE= 1.633931E 03,   CORRELATION= 0.630, R= 1.29176E 00, A= 6.77255E 03, A(NORM)= 2.00734E 04
X   1.029671E 04,   3.524965E 07, RSS(L) = 3.50P619E 11 INTO
SPLIT ON LRGST PLAC/SMSA PSU3I166,
    2 WITH CLASSES   3   4   5 .6
    3 WITH CLASSES   1   2

GROUP   3 , N =   1076, SUM W = 4.11590OE 04   SS(L)/TSS= 0.586, BSS/TSS= 0.020
Y MEAN= 7.401213E 04, VARIANCE= 1.89790RE 04,   CORRELATION= 0.596, R= 1.39794E 00, A= 7.05830E 03, A(NORM)= 2.14525E 04
X   1.212770E 04,   3.449557E 07, RSS(L) = 2.635197E 11 INTO
SPLIT ON DIST TO CNTR SMSA 31:58,
    4 WITH CLASSES   1   2
    5 WITH CLASSES   3   4   5

GROUP   4 , N =   791, SUM W = 2.65210OE 04   SS(L)/TSS= 0.350, BSS/TSS= 0.008
Y MEAN= 2.233470E C4, VARIANCE= 1.579482F C8,   CORRELATION= 0.584, R= 1.26258E 00, A= 7.23533E 03, A(NORM)= 2.02364F 04
X   1.195866E 04,   3.376765E 07, BSS(L) = 1.090070F 11 INTO
SPLIT ON RKT AGE HEAD GVICC9
    6 WITH CLASSES   2   3   4   5
    7 WITH CLASSES   6 .

GROUP   2*, N =   1012, SUM W = 4.041600E 04   SS(L)/TSS= 0.317, BSS/TSS= 0.0
Y MEAN= 8.606229E 04, VARIANCE= 1.047471E 08,   CORRELATION= 0.507, R= 9.60458E-01, A= 7.96266E 03, A(NORM)= 1.78532E 04
X   8.432055E 03   2.915349E 07

GROUP   6 , N =   718, SUM W = 2.58370OE 04   SS(L)/TSS= 0.295, BSS/TSS= 0.007
Y MEAN= 2.280399E 04, VARIANCE= 1.52083RF C8,   CORRELATION= 0.600, R= 1.34883E 00, A= 5.51837E 03, A(NORM)= 1.94048E 04
X   1.281533E 04,   3.008205E 07, RSS(L) = 9.535016E 10 INTO
SPLIT ON BKT AGE HEAD GVICC9
    8 WITH CLASSES   4   5
    9 WITH CLASSES   2   3

GROUP   5 , N =   285, SUM W = 1.16380OE 04   SS(L)/TSS= 0.214, BSS/TSS= 0.006
Y MEAN= 2.826706E C4, VARIANCE= 2.46067RF 08,   CORRELATION= 0.636, R= 1.65825F 00, A= 7.44527F 03, A(NORM)= 2.45198E 04
X   1.255667E C4,   3.620957E 07, BSS(L) = 7.965927E 10 INTO
SPLIT ON CURRENT REGION 0V472
   10 WITH CLASSES   4   2   2
   11 WITH CLASSES   1

GROUP   9*, N =   383, SUM W = 1.348000E 04   SS(L)/TSS= 0.167, BSS/TSS= 0.0
Y MEAN= 2.344R83E C4, VARIANCE= 1.657862F 08,   CORRELATION= 0.664, R= 1.68385E 00, A= 2.30735E 03, A(NORM)= 1.96455E 04
X   1.257920E 04   2.579814E 07

GROUP   8*, N =   335, SUM W = 1.23570OE 04   SS(L)/TSS= 0.126, BSS/TSS= 0.0
Y MEAN= 2.205899E 04, VARIANCE= 1.365040E 08,   CORRELATION= 0.551, R= 1.09275E 00, A= 7.77146E 03, A(NORM)= 1.90232E 04
X   1.30728RE 04   3.471758E 07

GROUP 11*, N =   97, SUM W = 5.11100OE 03   SS(L)/TSS= 0.119, BSS/TSS= 0.0
Y MEAN= 3.080915E 04, VARIANCE= 3.124820E 07,   CORRELATION= 0.698, R= 1.95977F 00, A= 5.73309E 03, A(NORM)= 2.59123E 04
X   1.275541E 04   3.968642E 07

GROUP 10*, N =   188, SUM W = 6.52700CE 03   SS(L)/TSS= 0.091, BSS/TSS= 0.0
Y MEAN= 2.627646E C4, VARIANCE= 1.870159E 08,   CORRELATION= 0.577, R= 1.36007E 00, A= 9.45323E 03, A(NORM)= 2.34575E 04
X   1.236937E 04   3.368021E 07

GROUP   7 , N =   73, SUM W = 3.684000E 03   SS(L)/TSS= 0.052, BSS/TSS= 0.007
Y MEAN= 1.904338E 04, VARIANCE= 1.891791E C8,   CORRELATION= 0.589, R= 1.87960E 00, A= 7.85839E 03, A(NORM)= 2.72121E 04
X   5.95C719E 03   1.858064E 07

198

```
SPLIT ON CURRENT REGION OV472    , RSS(I) =  8.890666E 10    INTO
       12 WITH CLASSES  4  3
       13 WITH CLASSES  2  1

GROUP 13*, N =  41,  SUM W =  2.14500E 03
Y MEAN= 2.171527E 04, VARIANCE= 7.569164E 08,  SS(L)/TSS= 0.040,  RSS/TSS= 0.0
X      5.96804E 03     2.050708E 07,  CORRELATION= 0.720,  B= 2.54792E 00,  A= 6.50690E 03,  A(NORM)= 3.27421E 04

GROUP 12*, N =  22,  SUM W =  1.539000E 03
Y MEAN= 1.531340E 04, VARIANCE= 7.585264E 07,  SS(L)/TSS= 0.008,  RSS/TSS= 0.0
X      5.92521E 03     1.649662E 07,  CORRELATION= 0.328,  B= 7.03581E-01,  A= 1.11504E 04,  A(NORM)= 1.83950E 04
```

A (NORM) is the value the subgroup regression one
predicts for V when X=grand mean of X. It is useful
for comparing levels free from X-effects.

100*RSS/TSS TABLE FOR 0-STEP LOOK-AHEAD
13 GROUPS, 8 PREDICTORS
< INDICATES LESS THAN 1 SPLITS WERE MADE

GROUP NUMBER (* INDICATES THE GROUP IS FINAL)

PREDICTOR	1	3	4	2*	6	5	9*	8*	11*	10*	7	13*	12*
1168	0.9	0.5	0.2	0.2	0.1	0.5	0.1	0.2	0.4	0.2	0.1	0.1	0.2
1009	1.7	1.3	0.8	0.4	0.7	0.4	0.1	0.0	0.4	0.1	*****	*****	*****
2002	0.0	0.4	0.3	0.3	0.2	0.1	0.1	0.1	0.1	0.0	0.2	0.2	0.1
1506	2.6	0.6	0.2	0.2	0.2	0.0	0.2	0.1	0.0	0.1	0.2	0.0	0.0
1438	0.6	2.0	0.2	0.1	0.1	0.1	0.2	0.0	0.3	0.3	0.4	0.2	0.0
1572	2.3	1.6	0.6	0.2	0.6	0.6	0.2	0.3	*****	0.4	0.7	0.1	0.1
2001	0.6	0.6	0.7	0.1	0.4	0.2	0.2	0.4	0.2	0.3	0.3	0.2	0.1
1499	0.9	0.0	0.7	0.2	0.5	0.3	0.5	0.1	0.0	0.1	0.1	0.0	0.1

Note how close some competing predictors came - indicating that another sample might give quite a different set of splits.

Most close runners-up, however, were used in later splits, e.g., V1572 in groups 5 and 7.

100*BSS/TSS TABLE FOR 0-STEP LOOK-AHEAD
13 GROUPS, 8 PREDICTORS

MAXIMUM BSS REGARDLESS OF ELIGIBILITY

GROUP NUMBER (* INDICATES THE GROUP IS FINAL)

PREDICTOR	1	3	4	2*	6	5	9*	8*	11*	10*	7	13*	12*
1168	0.9	0.5	0.2	0.3	0.1	0.5	0.1	0.2	0.4	0.2	0.2	0.1	0.3
1009	1.7	1.3	0.8	0.4	0.7	0.4	0.1	0.0	0.4	0.1*************************	0.3
2002	0.9	0.4	0.3	0.3	0.2	0.1	0.1	0.1	0.1	0.1	0.2	0.2	0.1
1506	2.6	0.6	0.2	0.2	0.2	0.0	0.2	0.1	0.0	0.0	0.2	0.2	0.1
1498	0.6	2.0	0.2	0.1	0.1	0.1	0.2	3.0	0.3	0.3	0.4	0.3	0.0
1572	2.3	1.6	0.6	0.2	0.6	0.6	0.2	0.3	0.3******	0.4	0.7	0.1	0.0
2001	0.5	0.6	0.7	0.1	0.4	0.2	0.2	0.4	0.2	0.3	0.3	0.2	0.1
1490	0.9	0.9	0.7	0.2	0.5	0.3	0.5	0.1	0.2	0.1	0.2	0.0	0.1

PROFILE OF CLASS MEANS AND SLOPES

REQUIRED ROOMS 23:12 , ETA = 0.024
GROUP

CLASS		1	3	4	2*	6	5	9*	8*	11*	10*
2	N	661	270	201	391	143	69	37	106	18	51
	YMEAN	1.762E 04	2.135E 04	2.029E 04	1.503E 04	2.124E 04	2.425E 04	2.328E 04	2.055E 04	2.473E 04	2.402E 04
	XMEAN	7.956E 03	6.928E 03	9.990E 03	6.588E 03	1.216E 04	9.760E 03	1.250E 04	1.205E 04	9.715E 03	1.002E 04
	SLOPE	1.069E 00	1.119E 00	1.054E 00	8.767E-01	1.169E 00	1.297E 00	2.230E 00	8.915E-01	1.519E 00	1.173E 00
3	N	557	292	225	265	214	67	128	86	33	34
	YMEAN	2.122E 04	2.532E 04	2.300E 04	1.644E 04	2.301E 04	3.252E 04	2.238E 04	2.246E 04	3.439E 04	3.007E 04
	XMEAN	1.090E 04	1.243E 04	1.218E 04	9.124E 03	1.243E 04	1.318E 04	1.213E 04	1.288E 04	1.301E 04	1.341E 04
	SLOPE	1.457E 00	1.588E 00	1.415E 00	9.424E-01	1.396E 00	1.379E 00	1.483E 00	1.338E 00	2.071E 00	1.710E 00
4	N	486	283	191	203	189	92	113	76	32	60
	YMEAN	2.256E 04	2.579E 04	2.304E 04	1.811E 04	2.321E 04	3.080E 04	2.419E 04	2.186E 04	3.377E 04	2.828E 04
	XMEAN	1.239E 04	1.363E 04	1.312E 04	1.088E 04	1.326E 04	1.456E 04	1.284E 04	1.384E 04	1.497E 04	1.424E 04
	SLOPE	1.499E 00	1.619E 00	1.361E 00	1.138E 00	1.371E 00	1.920E 00	7.899E-01	7.899E-01	2.103E 00	1.549E 00
5	N	225	126	93	99	91	33	57	34	7	26
	YMEAN	1.999E 04	2.398E 04	2.440E 04	1.595E 04	2.444E 04	2.287E 04	2.435E 04	2.462E 04	2.732E 04	2.041E 04
	XMEAN	1.156E 04	1.322E 04	1.328E 04	9.836E 03	1.355E 04	1.307E 04	1.588E 04	1.379E 04	1.241E 04	1.343E 04
	SLOPE	1.589E 00	1.560E 00	1.552E 00	1.442E 00	1.689E 00	1.593E 00	1.601E 00	1.873E 00	3.802E 00	6.452E-01
6	N	159	105	81	54	81	24	48	33	7	17
	YMEAN	1.998E 04	2.252E 04	2.313E 04	1.494E 04	2.313E 04	2.082E 04	2.063E 04	2.703E 04	1.807E 04	2.357E 04
	XMEAN	1.228E 04	1.330E 04	1.409E 04	1.026E 04	1.409E 04	1.111E 04	1.258E 04	1.645E 04	1.235E 04	9.883E 03
	SLOPE	1.377E 00	1.462E 00	1.348E 00	1.066E 00	1.348E 00	2.033E 00	2.135E 00	1.388E 00	1.527E 00	2.772E 00
	SLOPE	1.292E 00	1.398E 00	1.263E 00	9.695E-01	1.349E 00	1.658E 00	1.684E 00	1.093E 00	1.960E 00	1.360E 00

REQUIRED ROOMS 23:12 , ETA = 0.024
GROUP

CLASS		7	13*	12*
2	N	58	34	24
	YMEAN	1.940E 04	2.170E 04	1.318E 04
	XMEAN	5.687E 03	5.640E 03	5.761E 03
	SLOPE	1.688E 00	2.386E 00	7.064E-01
3	N	11	6	5
	YMEAN	2.226E 04	2.284E 04	2.310E 04
	XMEAN	8.036E 03	8.412E 03	7.575E 03
	SLOPE	2.183E 00	3.046E 00	2.632E-01
4	N	2	1	1
	YMEAN	1.143E 04	1.500E 04	8.000E 03
	XMEAN	3.299E 03	2.852E 03	3.726E 03
	SLOPE	-8.341E 00	0.0	0.0
5	N	2	0	2
	YMEAN	2.349E 04	0.0	2.349E 04
	XMEAN	4.864E 03	0.0	4.866E 03
	SLOPE	6.701E 01	0.0	6.692E 01
	SLOPE	1.880E 00	2.548E 00	7.036E-01

BKT AGE HEAD SV1009 , ETA = 0.049
GROUP

CLASS		1	3	4	2*	6	5	9*	8*	11*	10*
2	N	372	209	164	163	164	45	164	0	37	29
	YMEAN	1.987E 04	2.274E 04	2.072E 04	1.638E 04	2.072E 04	2.947E 04	2.072E 04	0.0	3.533E 04	2.535E 04
	XMEAN	1.083E 04	1.180E 04	1.148E 04	9.636E 03	1.148E 04	1.292E 04	1.148E 04	0.0	3.362E 04	2.234E 04
	SLOPE	1.778E 00	2.029E 00	1.680E 00	1.112E 00	1.680E 00	2.625E 00	1.680E 00	0.0	3.201E 00	1.784E 00
3	N	530	319	219	211	219	100	210	0	37	62

Statistical cross-tabulation printout (rotated). Rows per class block: YMEAN, XMEAN, SLOPE, N. Columns are GROUP categories (labels such as 1, 2*, 3, 4, 5, 6, 7, 8*, 9*, 10*, 11*, 12*, 13*). Values read left-to-right in image order.

RKT AGE HEAD GV1009 , ETA = 0.049 (GROUP)

CLASS	stat										
4	YMEAN	2.370E 04	2.761E 04	2.577E 04	2.577E 04	3.110E 04	2.577E 04	0.0	3.433E 04	3.795E 04	
	XMEAN	1.257E 04	1.370E 04	1.348E 04	1.348E 04	1.410E 04	1.348E 04	0.0	1.401E 04	1.419E 04	
	SLOPE	1.679E 00	1.708E 00	1.635E 00	1.635E 00	1.801E 00	1.635E 00	0.0	2.122E 00	1.322E 00	
	N	479	268	195	195	73	195	0	22	51	
5	YMEAN	2.134E 04	2.476E 04	2.334E 04	2.334E 04	2.805E 04	0.0	0.0	3.064E 04	2.631E 04	
	XMEAN	1.273E 04	1.415E 04	1.427E 04	1.427E 04	1.386E 04	0.0	0.0	1.500E 04	1.310E 04	
	SLOPE	1.224E 00	1.200E 00	1.128E 00	1.128E 00	1.401E 00	0.0	0.0	1.719E 00	1.126E 00	
	N	378	185	140	140	45	0	0	15	30	
6	YMEAN	1.908E 04	2.219E 04	2.037E 04	2.037E 04	2.738E 04	0.0	0.0	2.569E 04	2.862E 04	
	XMEAN	9.781E 03	1.156E 04	1.150E 04	1.150E 04	1.172E 04	0.0	0.0	1.066E 04	1.250E 04	
	SLOPE	1.124E 00	1.217E 00	1.061E 00	1.061E 00	1.603E 00	0.0	0.0	1.451E 00	1.664E 00	
	N	329	95	73	73	22	0	0	7	15	
	YMEAN	1.530E 04	1.877E 04	1.904E 04	1.376E 04	1.788E 04	0.0	0.0	1.489E 04	1.948E 04	
	XMEAN	4.926E 03	5.591E 03	5.951E 03	4.396E 03	4.397E 03	0.0	0.0	2.492E 03	5.414E 03	
	SLOPE	1.588E 00	1.888E 00	1.880E 00	1.220E 00	2.166E 00	0.0	0.0	9.892E 03	1.994E 00	
	SLOPE	1.292E 00	1.398E 00	1.263E 00	1.349E 00	1.658E 00	1.684E 00	1.093E 00	1.960E 00	1.360E 00	

SEX & MAR STATUS , ETA = 0.029 (GROUP)

Group headers: 7, 13*, 12* (left block); 1, 2*, 3, 4, 5, 6 (center); 8*, 9*, 10*, 11* (right block)

CLASS	stat	7	13*	12*	1	2*	3	4	5	6	8*	9*	10*	11*
1	N	73	41	32	1660	814	607	846	239	566	240	326	155	84
	YMEAN	1.004E 04	2.172E 04	1.532E 04	2.109E 04	1.470E 04	2.524E 04	2.340E 04	2.973E 04	2.364E 04	2.343E 04	2.381E 04	2.741E 04	3.262E 04
	XMEAN	5.951E 03	5.969E 03	5.925E 03	1.143E 04	9.475E 03	1.327E 04	1.312E 04	1.363E 04	1.366E 04	1.456E 04	1.294E 04	1.345E 04	1.386E 04
	SLOPE	1.880E 00	2.548E-01	7.036E-01	1.708E 00	1.019E 00	1.468E 00	1.339E 00	1.692E 00	1.400E 00	1.140E 00	1.708E 00	1.385E 00	1.994E 00
2	N	87	37	32	346	153	193	24	5	24	19	5	3	2
	YMEAN	1.443E 04	1.630E 04	1.583E 04	1.083E 04	1.360E 04	1.505E 04	1.844E 04	1.869E 04	1.739E 04	1.540E 04	3.447E 04	3.164E 04	6.600E 03
	XMEAN	6.390E 03	7.890E 03	7.940E 03	1.051E 04	5.450E 03	7.990E-01	1.051E 03	7.638E 03	7.638E 03	9.972E 03	1.333E 04	1.150E 04	4.035E 03
	SLOPE	1.505E 00	1.325E 00	7.990E-01	1.739E 00	1.325E 00		1.739E 00	3.230E 00	3.730E 00	9.414E-01	2.750E 00	7.661E 00	7.581E-01
3	N	41	152	128	52	76								
	YMEAN	1.580E 04	1.819E 04	1.773E 04	1.360E 04	1.747E 04	1.950E 04	1.725E 04	1.736E 04		2.089E 04	1.863E 04		
	XMEAN	4.926E 03	6.098E 03	6.191E 03	3.847E 03	7.049E 03	5.827E 03	6.829E 03	7.547E 03		5.957E 03	5.745E 03		
	SLOPE	1.588E 00	1.598E 00	1.459E 00	1.436E 00	1.521E 00	2.153E 00	1.448E 00	2.153E 00		2.302E 00	1.987E 00		
	SLOPE	1.292E 00	1.398E 00	1.263E 00	9.605E-01	9.605E-01	1.349E 00	1.349E 00	1.658E 00	1.658E 00	1.093E 00	1.684E 00	1.360E 00	1.960E 00

SEX & MAR STATUS , ETA = 0.029 (GROUP)

CLASS	stat	7	13*	12*
1	N	41	22	19
	YMEAN	2.080E 04	2.534E 04	1.523E 04
	XMEAN	7.391E 03	7.519E 03	7.235E 03
	SLOPE	2.018E 00	2.626E 00	7.455E-01
2	N	8	6	2
	YMEAN	1.202E 04	1.351E 04	6.000E 03
	XMEAN	4.209E 03	4.654E 03	2.785E 03
	SLOPE	1.215E-01	-1.765E-01	-5.536E-01
3	N	24	13	11

Overall / total (by table):

	I	II	III
YMEAN	1.841E 04	1.319E 04	1.737E 04
XMEAN	3.395E 03	3.631E 03	4.082E 03
SLOPE	2.683E 00	4.503E 00	1.101E 00
SLOPE	1.880E 00	2.548E 00	7.036E-01

LRGST PLAC/SMSA PSU31:66, ETA = 0.123
GROUP

CLASS	stat	1	2*	3	4	5	6	8*	9*	10*	11*
1	YMEAN	2.583E 04	0.0	2.583E 04	2.351E 04	3.014E 04	2.405E 04	2.267E 04	2.536E 04	2.732E 04	3.277E 04
	XMEAN	1.263E 04	0.0	1.263E 04	1.213E 04	1.354E 04	1.308E 04	1.288E 04	1.377E 04	1.343E 04	1.365E 04
	SLOPE	1.456E 00	0.0	1.456E 00	1.200E 00	1.632E 00	1.369E 00	9.675E-01	1.853E 00	1.298E 00	1.924E 00
	N	633	0	633	438	195	398	187	211	114	81
2	YMEAN	2.154E 04	0.0	2.154E 04	2.105E 04	2.363E 04	2.147E 04	2.137E 04	2.155E 04	2.461E 04	2.069E 04
	XMEAN	1.145E 04	0.0	1.145E 04	1.177E 04	1.011E 04	1.253E 04	1.329E 04	1.187E 04	1.067E 04	8.475E 03
	SLOPE	1.240E 00	0.0	1.240E 00	1.201E 00	1.672E 00	1.305E 00	1.266E 00	1.423E 00	1.580E 00	1.913E 00
	N	443	0	443	353	90	320	148	172	74	16
3	YMEAN	1.855E 04	1.855E 04	0.0	0.0	0.0	0.0	0.0	0.0	0.0	0.0
	XMEAN	1.028E 04	1.028E 04	0.0	0.0	0.0	0.0	0.0	0.0	0.0	0.0
	SLOPE	9.284E-01	9.284E-01	0.0	0.0	0.0	0.0	0.0	0.0	0.0	0.0
	N	222	222	0	0	0	0	0	0	0	0
4	YMEAN	1.846E 04	1.846E 04	0.0	0.0	0.0	0.0	0.0	0.0	0.0	0.0
	XMEAN	9.486E 03	9.486E 03	0.0	0.0	0.0	0.0	0.0	0.0	0.0	0.0
	SLOPE	8.726E-01	8.726E-01	0.0	0.0	0.0	0.0	0.0	0.0	0.0	0.0
	N	144	144	0	0	0	0	0	0	0	0
5	YMEAN	1.578E 04	1.578E 04	0.0	0.0	0.0	0.0	0.0	0.0	0.0	0.0
	XMEAN	8.460E 03	8.460E 03	0.0	0.0	0.0	0.0	0.0	0.0	0.0	0.0
	SLOPE	1.076E 00	1.076E 00	0.0	0.0	0.0	0.0	0.0	0.0	0.0	0.0
	N	200	200	0	0	0	0	0	0	0	0
6	YMEAN	1.394E 04	1.394E 04	0.0	0.0	0.0	0.0	0.0	0.0	0.0	0.0
	XMEAN	7.004E 03	7.004E 03	0.0	0.0	0.0	0.0	0.0	0.0	0.0	0.0
	SLOPE	8.637E-01	8.637E-01	0.0	0.0	0.0	0.0	0.0	0.0	0.0	0.0
	N	446	446	0	0	0	0	0	0	0	0
	SLOPE	1.292E 00	9.605E-01	1.398E 00	1.263E 00	1.658E 00	1.349E 00	1.093E 00	1.694E 00	1.360E 00	1.360E 00

LRGST PLAC/SMSA PSU31:66, ETA = 0.123
GROUP

CLASS	stat	7	12*	13*
1	YMEAN	2.000E 04	1.519E 04	2.375E 04
	XMEAN	6.010E 03	5.193E 03	6.646E 03
	SLOPE	2.043E 00	9.031E-01	2.582E 00
	N	40	19	21
2	YMEAN	1.782E 04	1.550E 04	1.932E 04
	XMEAN	5.875E 03	6.964E 03	5.171E 03
	SLOPE	1.475E 00	2.262E-01	2.427E 00
	N	33	13	20
	SLOPE	1.880E 00	7.036E-01	2.548E 00

DIST TO CNTR SMSA 31:58, ETA = 0.072
GROUP

CLASS	stat	1	2*	3	4	5	6	8*	9*	10*	11*
1	YMEAN	1.885E 04	1.643E 04	2.003E 04	2.003E 04	0.0	2.123E 04	2.065E 04	2.186E 04	0.0	0.0
	XMEAN	1.066E 04	9.618E 03	1.117E 04	1.117E 04	0.0	1.248E 04	1.257E 04	1.238E 04	0.0	0.0
	SLOPE	1.050E 00	8.008E-01	1.132E 00	1.132E 00	0.0	1.235E 00	1.142E 00	1.360E 00	0.0	0.0
	N	386	104	282	282	0	250	133	117	0	0
2	N	582	73	509	509	0	468	202	266	0	0

204

(Continuation — CLASS 3, 4, 5)

3 N	336	212	212	124						153
YMEAN	2.280E 04	2.343E 04	2.343E 04	1.855E 04	2.350E 04	0.0	2.172E 04	2.274E 04	0.0	0.0
XMEAN	1.210E 04	1.233E 04	1.233E 04	1.055E 04	1.239E 04	0.0	1.265E 04	1.333E 04	0.0	0.0
SLOPE	1.232E 00	1.309E 00	1.309E 00	8.077E-01	1.393E 00	0.0	1.823E 00	1.061E 00	0.0	0.0
4 N	245	55	55	190						26
YMEAN	2.504E 04	2.312E 04	2.312E 04	1.724E 04	0.0	2.975E 04	0.0	0.0	0.0	2.700E 04
XMEAN	1.176E 04	1.312E 04	1.312E 04	4.522E 03	0.0	1.312E 04	0.0	0.0	0.0	1.270E 04
SLOPE	1.571E 00	1.592E 00	1.592E 00	1.033E 00	0.0	1.592E 00	0.0	0.0	0.0	1.212E 00
5 N	539	18	18	521						7
YMEAN	1.733E 04	2.147E 04	2.147E 04	1.610E 04	0.0	2.147E 04	0.0	0.0	0.0	2.045E 04
XMEAN	8.911E 03	1.045E 04	1.045E 04	8.429E 03	0.0	1.045E 04	0.0	0.0	0.0	2.958E 03
SLOPE	1.205E 00	1.604E 00	1.604E 00	9.709E-01	0.0	1.604E 00	0.0	0.0	0.0	1.497E 00
SLOPE	1.597E 04	3.217E 04	3.217E 04	1.529E 04	0.0	3.217E 04	0.0	0.0	0.0	3.162E 04
	7.781E 03	1.277E 04	1.277E 04	7.573E 03	0.0	1.277E 04	0.0	0.0	0.0	1.233E 04
	1.114E 00	1.772E 00	1.772E 00	8.897E-01	0.0	1.772E 00	0.0	0.0	0.0	3.362E 00
SLOPE	1.292E 00	1.398E 00	1.263E 00	9.605E-01	1.349E 00	1.658E 00	1.684E 00	1.093E 00	1.960E 00	1.360E 00

DIST TO CNTR SMSA 31:58, ETA = 0.072

CLASS | GROUP

	7	12*	12*
1 N	32	15	17
YMEAN	1.427E 04	1.485E 04	1.375E 04
XMEAN	4.833E 03	4.616E 03	5.026E 03
SLOPE	7.088E-01	1.002E 00	5.502E-01
2 N	41	26	15
YMEAN	2.283E 04	2.554E 04	1.732E 04
XMEAN	6.834E 03	6.722E 03	7.067E 03
SLOPE	2.148E 00	2.655E 00	7.078E-01
SLOPE	1.880E 00	2.548E 00	7.036E-01

CURRENT REGION 0V472 , ETA = 0.063

CLASS | GROUP

	1	2*	3	4	5	6	7*	8*	9*	10*	11*	12*	13*
1 N	364	111	253	156	97	143	97	68	75	65	97		13
YMEAN	2.494E 04	1.786E 04	2.796E 04	2.597E 04	3.081E 04	2.608E 04	2.798E 04	2.514E 04	2.700E 04	2.798E 04	3.081E 04	0.0	
XMEAN	1.186E 04	9.464E 03	1.288E 04	1.295E 04	1.280E 04	1.375E 04	1.395E 04	1.392E 04	1.358E 04	1.395E 04	1.280E 04	0.0	
SLOPE	1.636E 00	9.931E-01	1.696E 00	1.487E 00	1.960E 00	1.712E 00	1.652E 00	1.458E 00	2.028E 00	1.652E 00	1.960E 00	0.0	
2 N	617	287	330	265	65	237	110	114	123	65			
YMEAN	1.988E 04	1.695E 04	2.277E 04	2.153E 04	2.798E 04	2.176E 04	1.266E 04	2.035E 04	2.327E 04	2.798E 04			
XMEAN	1.065E 04	8.735E 03	1.253E 04	1.219E 04	1.395E 04	1.310E 04	1.266E 04	1.350E 04	1.266E 04	1.395E 04			
SLOPE	1.150E 00	9.159E-01	1.255E 00	1.138E 00	1.652E 00	1.117E 00	1.517E 00	5.887E-01	1.517E 00	1.652E 00			
3 N	790	494	296	218	78	199	78	89	110	78			
YMEAN	1.595E 04	1.425E 04	1.936E 04	1.804E 04	2.296E 04	1.889E 04	2.296E 04	1.813E 04	1.933E 04	2.296E 04			
XMEAN	8.552E 03	7.451E 03	1.076E 04	1.074E 04	1.083E 04	1.159E 04	1.083E 04	1.150E 04	1.165E 04	1.083E 04			
SLOPE	1.179E 00	1.007E 00	1.411E 00	1.233E 00	1.615E 00	1.394E 00	1.615E 00	1.085E 00	1.688E 00	1.615E 00			
4 N	317	120	197	152	45	139	45	64	75	45			
YMEAN	2.133E 04	1.729E 04	2.462E 04	2.361E 04	2.771E 04	2.437E 04	2.771E 04	2.434E 04	2.439E 04	2.771E 04			
XMEAN	1.062E 04	9.448E 03	1.157E 04	1.141E 04	1.189E 04	1.223E 04	1.189E 04	1.220E 04	1.226E 04	1.189E 04			
SLOPE	9.404E-01	7.850E-01	8.984E-01	9.806E-01	6.205E-01	1.045E 00	6.205E-01	8.874E-01	1.272E 00	6.205E-01			
SLOPE	1.292E 00	9.605E-01	1.398E 00	1.263E 00	1.658E 00	1.349E 00	1.658E 00	1.093E 00	1.684E 00	1.658E 00	1.960E 00		1.360E 00

CURRENT REGION 0V472 , ETA = 0.063

CLASS		7	13*	12*	10*
1	N	13	13	0	0

YMEAN	2.497E 04	2.497E 04	0.0
XMEAN	5.911E 03	5.911E 03	0.0
SLOPE	2.704E 00	2.704E 00	0.0
2 N	28	28	0
YMEAN	1.995E 04	1.995E 04	0.0
XMEAN	6.001E 03	6.001E 03	0.0
SLOPE	2.504E 00	2.504E 00	0.0
3 N	19	0	
YMEAN	1.336E 04	0.0	1.336E 04
XMEAN	6.029E 03	0.0	6.029E 03
SLOPE	1.133E 00	0.0	1.133E 00
4 N	13		
YMEAN	1.799E 04	0.0	1.799E 04
XMEAN	5.785E 03	0.0	5.785E 03
SLOPE	9.983E-02	0.0	9.988E-02
SLOPE	1.880E 00	2.548E 00	7.036E-01

3-YR AVE $ INC   • ETA = 0.351   GROUP

CLASS	Stat	1	2*	3	4	5	6	9*	8*	11*	10*
	N	256	187	69	52	17	32	8	24	6	11
1	YMEAN	1.053E 04	1.020E 04	1.162E 04	1.078E 04	1.346E 04	9.618E 03	6.161E 03	1.020E 04	1.020E 04	1.687E 04
	XMEAN	1.923E 03	1.886E 03	2.049E 03	2.041E 03	2.066E 03	1.917E 03	2.554E 03	1.811E 03	2.113E 03	2.018E 03
	SLOPE	1.858E 00	1.051E 00	4.292E 00	2.234E 00	9.278E 00	-3.399E-02	3.335E 00	6.982E-01	-2.774E 00	1.362E 01
	N	257	158	99	79	20	60	77	33	3	17
2	YMEAN	1.323E 04	1.215E 04	1.566E 04	1.469E 04	1.966E 04	1.478E 04	1.403E 04	1.518E 04	2.469E 04	1.536E 04
	XMEAN	3.916E 03	3.925E 03	3.008E 03	3.845E 03	4.156E 03	3.931E 03	3.920E 03	3.937E 03	4.425E 03	4.027E 03
	SLOPE	-5.454E-01	-1.507E 00	9.737E-01	9.737E-01	4.815E 00	2.293E 00	2.848E 00	1.991E 00	-1.104E 00	4.945E-01
	N	386	204	182	127	55	115	68	47	16	39
3	YMEAN	1.408E 04	1.310E 04	1.558E 04	1.597E 04	1.469E 04	1.489E 04	1.464E 04	1.522E 04	1.161E 04	1.950E 04
	XMEAN	6.294E 03	6.284E 03	6.317E 03	6.317E 03	6.317E 03	6.434E 03	6.443E 03	6.443E 03	6.346E 03	6.152E 03
	SLOPE	-5.791E-01	8.110E-01	-3.003E 00	-3.314E 00	-2.365E 00	-1.075E 00	-1.826E 00	4.586E-01	-6.348E-01	-2.537E 00
	N	362	174	188	145	43	137	78	59	16	27
4	YMEAN	1.724E 04	1.571E 04	1.857E 04	1.701E 04	2.233E 04	1.688E 04	1.677E 04	1.702E 04	2.320E 04	2.211E 04
	XMEAN	8.424E 03	8.814E 03	8.834E 03	8.860E 03	8.723E 03	8.895E 03	8.963E 03	8.895E 03	8.657E 03	8.702E 03
	SLOPE	2.755E 00	2.340E 00	3.295E 00	2.575E 00	6.403E 00	2.081E 00	1.588E 00	2.836E 00	8.491E 00	7.543E 00
	N	497	202	295	217	78	205	126	79	27	51
5	YMEAN	2.259E 04	2.078E 04	2.387E 04	2.218E 04	2.822E 04	2.203E 04	2.226E 04	2.171E 04	3.073E 04	2.654E 04
	XMEAN	1.229E 04	1.225E 04	1.223E 04	1.223E 04	1.255E 04	1.205E 04	1.211E 04	1.244E 04	1.267E 04	1.247E 04
	SLOPE	1.297E 00	1.034E 00	1.459E 00	1.323E 00	1.109E 00	1.452E 00	1.591E 00	8.324E-01	7.364E-01	1.774E 00
	N	208	51	157	111	44	110	50	30	14	30
6	YMEAN	2.799E 04	2.346E 04	2.340E 04	2.678E 04	3.528E 04	2.675E 04	2.952E 04	2.432E 04	4.001E 04	3.194E 04
	XMEAN	1.718E 04	1.722E 04	1.717E 04	1.709E 04	1.736E 04	1.710E 04	1.695E 04	1.700E 04	1.724E 04	1.745E 04
	SLOPE	1.163E 00	4.369E-01	1.351E 00	1.066E 00	1.232E 00	1.106E 00	1.295E 00	1.116E 00	1.364E-01	1.708E 00
	N	122	36	86	60	26	59	26	33	13	30
7	YMEAN	3.904E 04	3.029E 04	3.995E 04	3.995E 04	4.783E 04	3.937E 04	4.435E 04	3.542E 04	5.221E 04	4.240E 04
	XMEAN	2.339E 04	2.341E 04	2.339E 04	2.444E 04	2.379E 04	2.341E 04	2.346E 04	2.346E 04	2.345E 04	2.309E 04
	SLOPE	2.255E 00	1.953E 00	2.370E 00	2.668E 00	1.507E 00	2.738E 00	1.911E 00	3.541E 00	1.044E 00	4.516E 00
	SLOPE	1.292E 00	9.605E-01	1.398E 00	1.263E 00	1.654E 00	1.349E 00	1.684E 00	1.033E 00	1.263E 00	1.340E 00

3-YR AVE $ INC   • ETA = 0.351   GROUP

CLASS	Stat	7	13*	12*
	N	20	12	8
1	YMEAN	1.130E 04	1.172E 04	1.053E 04
	XMEAN	2.066E 03	2.254E 03	1.805E 03
	SLOPE	3.618E 00	1.942E 00	4.657E 00

Computer printout — regression statistics (N, YMEAN, XMEAN, SLOPE).

Block A (columns 9 and 10)

Group	(measure)	col 1	col 9	col 10
2	N	19		
	YMEAN	1.461E 04	1.702E 04	1.219E 04
	XMEAN	3.770E 03	3.771E 03	3.769E 03
	SLOPE	-7.157E-01	5.199E 00	-3.598E 00
3	N	12	8	4
	YMEAN	2.110E 04	1.867E 04	2.601E 04
	XMEAN	5.762E 03	6.656E 03	5.976E 03
	SLOPE	-6.846E 00	-1.304E 00	-1.609E 01
4	N	8	4	4
	YMEAN	2.955E 04	4.126E 04	1.725E 04
	XMEAN	8.571E 03	8.917E 03	8.208E 03
	SLOPE	1.601E 01	1.033E 01	3.623E 00
5	N	12	7	5
	YMEAN	2.442E 04	3.079E 04	1.524E 04
	XMEAN	1.190E 04	1.169E 04	1.221E 04
	SLOPE	-2.274E-01	-7.225E-01	1.953E 00
6	N	1	0	0
	YMEAN	3.000E 04	0.0	3.000E 04
	XMEAN	1.539E 04	0.0	1.539E 04
	SLOPE	0.0	0.0	0.0
7	N	1	0	0
	YMEAN	7.500E 04	0.0	0.0
	XMEAN	2.500E 04	0.0	0.0
	SLOPE	0.0	0.0	0.0
	SLOPE	1.880E 00	2.548E 00	7.036E-01

RACE   GROUP   31:48, ETA = 0.030

CLASS	(measure)	1	3	4	2*	6	5	9*	8*	11*	10*
1	N	1626	775	537	851	476	238	243	233	94	144
	YMEAN	2.069E 04	2.498E 04	2.341E 04	1.649E 04	2.376E 04	2.862E 04	2.476E 04	2.276E 04	3.062E 04	2.699E 04
	XMEAN	1.056E 04	1.254E 04	1.243E 04	8.624E 03	1.324E 04	1.279E 04	1.295E 04	1.335E 04	1.288E 04	1.272E 04
	SLOPE	1.284E 00	1.390E 00	1.255E 00	9.332E-01	1.361E 00	1.641E 00	1.730E 00	1.103E 00	1.974E 00	1.310E 00
2	N	406	256	216	150	205	40	113	92	7	38
	YMEAN	1.178E 04	1.354E 04	1.313E 04	9.660E 03	1.441E 04	1.679E 04	1.471E 04	1.392E 04	2.338E 04	1.505E 04
	XMEAN	6.943E 03	8.400E 03	8.510E 03	5.228E 03	9.985E 03	7.543E 03	1.090E 04	8.539E 03	7.335E 03	7.594E 03
	SLOPE	8.872E-01	7.978E-01	7.580E-01	9.619E-01	7.158E-01	2.135E-01	9.324E-01	4.265E-01	1.670E 01	2.545E 00
3	N	56	45	38	11	37	7	27	10	1	6
	YMEAN	1.987E 04	2.109E 04	1.981E 04	1.553E 04	1.990E 04	2.827E 04	2.019E 04	1.873E 04	5.509E 04	1.828E 04
	XMEAN	9.594E 03	9.376E 03	9.541E 03	1.037E 04	9.842E 03	8.456E 03	1.027E 04	8.667E 03	1.882E 04	7.171E 03
	SLOPE	1.246E 00	1.385E 00	1.204E 00	1.163E 00	1.335E 00	7.530E 00	1.448E 00	7.994E-01	3.758E 00	3.716E 00
	SLOPE	1.232E 00	1.398E 00	1.263E 00	9.605E-01	1.349E 00	1.658E 00	1.684E 00	1.093E 00	1.966E 00	1.360E 00

RACE   GROUP   31:48, ETA = 0.030

CLASS	(measure)	7	13*	12*
1	N	61	37	24
	YMEAN	2.088E 04	2.316E 04	1.714E 04
	XMEAN	6.593E 03	6.352E 03	7.003E 03
	SLOPE	1.756E 00	3.778E-01	3.778E-01
2	N	11	4	7
	YMEAN	7.707E 03	8.232E 03	7.348E 03
	XMEAN	2.264E 03	2.382E 03	2.190E 03
	SLOPE	2.779E-01	6.028E 00	-2.058E-01
3	N	1	1	1
	YMEAN	2.000E 04	0.0	2.200E 04
	XMEAN	3.337E 03	0.0	3.337E 03

SLOPE 0.0   C.0   0.0

SLOPE 1.880E 00   2.548E CC   7.036F-01

..... END OF ANALYSIS .....

208

*****TIME IS   0:56:23
NO MORE RUN CARDS IN SETUP. STEP TERMINATED

Appendix VI

A Note on Partitioning for Maximum between Sum of Squares

11/10/62

by W. A. Ericson

1. The Problem

This note presents some results, both positive and negative, concerned with analysis of the following problem:

One is given k>2 sets of observations, where

$$\overline{x}_i, \quad i = 1, 2, \ldots, k$$

is the mean of the observations within the i'th set and

$$N_i, \quad i = 1, 2, \ldots, k$$

is the number of observations in that set. The problem is to partition these k sets of observations into two nonempty classes such that "between class sum of squares" is maximized. In other words, to find I, a set of any m (1≤m≤k) of the k indices i = 1, 2, ..., k, such that

$$N_I(\overline{x}_I - \overline{x})^2 + N_{\overline{I}}(x_{\overline{I}} - \overline{x})^2 \tag{1}$$

is maximized, where

$$N_I = \sum_{i \in I} N_i, \quad N_{\overline{I}} = \sum_{i \notin I} N_i,$$

$$\overline{x}_I = \frac{1}{N_I} \sum_{i \in I} N_i \overline{x}_i, \quad \overline{x}_{\overline{I}} = \frac{1}{N_{\overline{I}}} \sum_{i \notin I} N_i \overline{x}_i,$$

and $\overline{x}$ is the overall mean, i.e.,

$$\overline{x} = \frac{N_I \overline{x}_I + N_{\overline{I}} \overline{x}_{\overline{I}}}{N_I + N_{\overline{I}}}.$$

210

2. Previous Results

No literature search having been made, it is not known whether this problem has been researched by other investigators. This remains a point for further study.

3. Restatement and Assumptions

It is well-known that the problem outlined above is basically unchanged by the addition of the same arbitrary constant to each $\bar{x}_i$. It may thus be assumed without loss of generality that

$$\bar{x}_1 \geq \bar{x}_2 \geq \ldots \geq \bar{x}_k > 0 \tag{2}$$

Furthermore, it is easily seen that maximizing (1) by choice of I is equivalent to maximizing

$$f(I) \equiv \frac{(N_I \bar{x}_I)^2}{N_I} + \frac{(N_{\bar{I}} \bar{x}_{\bar{I}})^2}{N_{\bar{I}}} \tag{3}$$

4. A Negative Result

The following algorithm was suggested for finding I and its complement, $\bar{I}$, which maximizes (3):

a) Compute $f(I)$ for I taken, in turn to be $\{1\}$, $\{2\}$, ..., $\{k\}$.

b) Pick the maximum $f(I)$ over these I's. Suppose, e.g., $I = \{a\}$ maximizes $f(I)$ over the I's considered in (a).

c) Compute $f(I)$ for I taken in turn to be $\{a,1\}$, ..., $\{a, a-1\}$, $\{a, a+1\}$, ... $\{a, k\}$.

d) Choose that I, among those considered in (c) which maximizes $f(I)$, say $I = \{a,b\}$. If $f(\{a\}) > f(\{a,b\})$, stop and assert $I = \{a\}$ yields maximum value of (3), otherwise continue the process, looking next at $f(I)$ for I's of the form $\{a,b,i\}$, $i \neq a$, $i \neq b$, repeating steps (c) and (d) above.

This procedure does <u>not</u> lead invariably to the optimum or maximizing partition, I. That this is so is demonstrated by the following counterexample: Suppose $k = 5$ and the data are as shown below:

i:	1	2	3	4	5
$\bar{x}_i$:	3.1	3.0	2.0	2.0	1.0
N_i:	1	2	3	1	3

It is easily verified that

I	$\bar{I}$	f(I)
{1}	{2,3,4,5}	41.72111
{2}	{1,3,4,5}	42.85125
{3}	{1,2,4,5}	40.40142
{4}	{1,2,3,5}	39.31764
{5}	{1,2,3,4}	44.77285

Following the suggested algorithm we next look at $I = (5,i)$, $i = 1,2,3,4$, and obtain the following:

I	$\bar{I}$	f(I)
{5,1}	{2,3,4}	41.96916
{5,2}	{1,3,4}	40.84200
{5,3}	{1,2,4}	44.30250
{5,4}	{1,2,3}	44.25166

Each of these values of f(I) being less than f({5}), we conclude, as per the suggested algorithm, that I = {5} maximizes (3). This is not true since it is easily shown that

$$f(\{1,2\}) = 44.88904 > f(\{5\}) = 44.77285$$

5. The Basic Result

It will be proved in this section that (3) is maximized over all possible I's by I* where I* is that set $I_m \equiv \{1,2, ..., m\}$, $1 \le m < k$ for which $f(I^*) \ge f(I_m)$ for all m. Thus to find the maximizing partition one need only compute f(I) for the k -1 sets I_m and choose the maximum. Furthermore, I*, obtained in this fashion, maximizes (3) over <u>any</u> partition of the $N = \sum_1^k N_i$ <u>individual observations</u> into two sets (assuming each individual observation within any set equals the set mean $\bar{x}_i$ say).

The present proof of these assertions, while straightforward, involves considerable tedious algebra. Further study may yield more succinct and more tidy demonstrations. The present proof is given in two parts. We first state and prove the theoretical results, in some degree of generality and then make the necessary identifications to the problem stated in § 1 by which the assertions stated above become established.

We adopt the following notation: let

$$a_1 \geq a_2 \geq a_3 \geq \cdots \geq a_N \tag{4}$$

be any nonincreasing sequence of real positive numbers. Let P_m and P_n be <u>any</u> partition of the N a_i's, i.e., P_m is any set of m of the a_i's and P_n is the set of the remaining $n = N - m$ a_i's. Further, let H_m, L_m and M be respectively the set of the largest m a_i's, the set of the smallest m a_i's, and the $n - m$ middle a_i's. (It is assumed that $n \geq m$, hence M is null if $n = m$, otherwise not.) Thus

$$H_m = \{a_1, \ldots, a_m\}$$

$$L_m = \{a_{N-m+1}, \ldots, a_N\}$$

$$M = \{a_{m+1}, \ldots, a_{N-m}\}$$

The first result may then be stated as

<u>Theorem A</u>: At least one of the following is true:

a)
$$\frac{(\Sigma(H_m))^2}{m} + \frac{(\Sigma(M) + \Sigma(L_m))^2}{n} \geq \frac{(\Sigma(P_m))^2}{m} + \frac{(\Sigma(P_n))^2}{n}$$

b)
$$\frac{(\Sigma(L_m))^2}{m} + \frac{(\Sigma(M) + \Sigma(H_m))^2}{n} \geq \frac{(\Sigma(P_m))^2}{m} + \frac{(\Sigma(P_n))^2}{n} \quad ,$$

where $\Sigma(H_m) \equiv \sum\limits_{a_i \in H_m} a_i$, etc.

▼ <u>Proof</u>: The theorem is obviously true if either $\Sigma(L_m) = \Sigma(P_m)$ or $\Sigma(H_m) = \Sigma(P_m)$. We then consider the other cases, i.e., $\Sigma(H_m) > \Sigma(P_m) > \Sigma(L_m)$, and show that if (a) fails then (b) holds. Straightforward algebra[1] shows that if (a) is false, then

$$[m\Sigma(P_n) + m(\Sigma(L_m) + \Sigma(M)) - n(\Sigma(H_m) + \Sigma(P_m))] > 0. \tag{5}$$

---

[1]The major hint needed in going from (a) and (b) to (5) and (6) is to replace
$$[\Sigma(m) + \Sigma(L_m)]^2 \text{ by } [\Sigma(m) + \Sigma(L_m)] [\Sigma(P_n) + \Sigma(P_n) - \Sigma(H_m)]$$
and to replace
$$[\Sigma(P_n)]^2 \text{ by } [\Sigma(P_n)] [\Sigma(m) + \Sigma(L_m) + \Sigma(H_m) - \Sigma(P_m)] \quad \text{etc.}$$

Similarly, (b) is true if

$$[m\Sigma(P_n) \; + \; m(\Sigma(M) \; + \; \Sigma(H_m)) \; - \; n(\Sigma(L_m) \; + \; \Sigma(P_m))] \geq 0. \tag{6}$$

That (5) implies (6) is obvious, since the left side of (6) is greater than or equal to the left side of (5). ▲

The second main result is given by the following:

Theorem B: Suppose

$$a_1 \geq \ldots \geq a_m > a_{m+1} = \ldots = a_{m+n}$$

$$= a_{m+n+1} = \ldots = a_{m+n+\ell} > a_{m+n+\ell+1} \geq \ldots \geq a_{m+n+\ell+r}$$

where $m + n + \ell + r = N$, $m \geq 0$, $n > 0$, $\ell > 0$, $r \geq 0$, and $m + r \geq 1$. Then at least one of the following statements is defined and true:

d) $\dfrac{1}{m} \; (\Sigma_m)^2 + \dfrac{1}{n+\ell+r}((n+\ell)a + \Sigma_r)^2 \geq \dfrac{1}{m+n} (\Sigma_m + na)^2 + \dfrac{1}{\ell+r} (\ell a + \Sigma_r)^2$

or

d) $\dfrac{1}{m+n+\ell} (\Sigma_m + (n+\ell)a)^2 + \dfrac{1}{r} (\Sigma_r)^2 \geq \dfrac{1}{m+n} (\Sigma_m + na)^2 + \dfrac{1}{\ell+r} (\ell a + \Sigma_r)^2$,

where $a \equiv a_i$, $i = m + 1, \ldots, m + n + \ell$, $\Sigma_m \equiv \sum_{i=1}^{m} a_i$,

$\Sigma_r \equiv \sum_{i=1}^{r} a_{m+n+\ell+i}$.

▼ Proof: If $m = 0$, it is immediately verifiable that (d) is true. Likewise, if $r = 0$, then (c) is true. Suppose then that m, n, r, and ℓ are all positive. Straightforward algebra shows that (c) is equivalent to

c') $A \equiv (\Sigma_m)^2 - 2ma \; \Sigma_m \geq \dfrac{m(m+n)}{(n+\ell+r) \; (\ell+r)} \; (\Sigma_r)^2 - \dfrac{2mr \; (m+n)}{(n+\ell+r) \; (\ell+r)} \; a\Sigma_r$

$$+ \; \dfrac{m \; [(m+n)\ell - (\ell+r)n]^2 - m[(m+n)\ell^2 + (\ell+r)n^2]}{n(n+\ell+r) \; (\ell+r)} \; a^2 \; \equiv \; B$$

and (d) is equivalent to:

d') $A \equiv (\Sigma_m)^2 - 2ma \leq \dfrac{(m+n+\ell) \; (m+n)}{r(\ell+r)} \; (\Sigma_r)^2 - \dfrac{2(m+n+\ell) \; (m+n)}{(\ell+r)} \; a\Sigma_r$

$$- \; \dfrac{\{[(m+n)\ell - (\ell+r)n]^2 - r[(m+n)\ell^2 + (\ell+r)n^2]\}}{\ell \, (\ell+r)} \; a^2 \; \equiv \; C \quad .$$

To show that either (c) or (d) is true (or both) it suffices then to show that if (c') is false then (d') must be true. This is clearly established if the right side of the inequality in (c') is less than or equal to the right side of the inequality in (d'), i.e., if C - B ≥ 0. But some simple but tedious algebra shows that

$$C - B = \frac{(m+n) \ [(n+\ell+r) \ (m+n+\ell) \ - \ mr]}{r(n+\ell+r) \ (\ell+r)} \ [\Sigma_r - ra]^2$$

which is obviously nonnegative. ▲

To use these results for the problem stated in § 1 above and to establish the assertions at the beginning of the present section one need only identify the following nonincreasing sequence with those sequences of a_i's referred to above:

$$\underbrace{\overline{x}_1, \ \ldots, \ \overline{x}_1}_{N_1} \ , \quad \underbrace{\overline{x}_2, \ \ldots, \ \overline{x}_2}_{N_2} \ , \quad \underbrace{\overline{x}_3, \ \ldots, \ \overline{x}_3}_{N_3} \ , \quad \ldots, \quad \underbrace{\overline{x}_k, \ \ldots, \ \overline{x}_k}_{N_k} \ .$$

Then it is clear that Theorem A establishes the fact that for <u>any</u> partition of these $N = \sum_1^k N_i \ \overline{x}_i$'s into two sets of m and n = N - m elements respectively will yield a value of "between sum of squares," (3), no larger than that for either the partition consisting of the m largest $\overline{x}_i$'s and the N-m remaining or the m smallest $\overline{x}_i$'s and the N-m remaining. This result clearly includes the case where for every i = 1, ..., k all $N_i \ \overline{x}_i$'s are put in the same one of the two sets forming the partition, i.e., the case where the partition is of the k sets of means rather than of the N individual means.

Theorem B then closes the remaining loophole, viz., it may be that some partition, I, $\overline{I}$, of the k sets of means into $N_I =_{i\in I}\Sigma N_i$ and $N_{\overline{I}} = N - N_I$ observations, respectively, has a sum of squares, (3), which is no larger than that for the partition consisting, say, of the largest N_I individual $\overline{x}_i$'s and the $N_{\overline{I}}$ remaining $\overline{x}_i$'s. However, this latter partition may very easily split one set of N_i identical $\overline{x}_i$'s. Theorem B then says that for any partition of the N individual $\overline{x}_i$'s into the m largest and N - m remaining and where the partioning point occurs within one of the k sets of observations then there is another partition into largest and smallest $\overline{x}_i$'s where the partitioning point occurs <u>between</u> two of the k sets of $\overline{x}_i$'s and which has a between sum of squares no smaller than the original partition.

Theorems A and B then together demonstrate that to find the partition which maximizes (3) one need only look at the k - 1 partitions, I_m, where $I_m = \{1,2, \ldots, m\}$, $1 \le m < k$, and choose that one yielding the largest value of (3).

6. A Final Negative Result

It was further conjectured that perhaps (3), $f(\{I_m\})$, $m = 1, 2, \ldots, k - 1$, treated as a function of m was well-behaved in the sense of say concavity and that, e.g., if $f(\{I_1\}) > f(\{I_2\})$ then one might be able to stop and assert $I^* = I_1$, and thus not look at all $k - 1$ I_m's. This is not the case, however, as witnessed by the following counter example:

i	1	2	3	4	5
$\bar{x}_i$	3.000	2.01000	2.0010	2.0001	1.0000
N_i	1	1	1	1	2

here one finds the following values for $f(\{I_m\})$, $m = 1, 2, 3, 4$:

I_m	$f(\{I_m\})$
{1}	21.84
{1,2}	21.55
{1,2,3}	21.72
{1,2,3,4}	22.30

7. Conclusions

The above results indicate that to find the partition which maximizes the between sum of squares, (3), one need only compute (3) for the $k - 1$ partitions consisting of the first set of size N_1 and all the rest, the first two sets of size $N_1 + N_2$ and all the remaining, etc., and choosing that one which maximizes (3). Further the partition found in this manner maximizes (3) over all partitions of the $N = \sum_1^k N_i$ individual observations (assuming each observation within any one of the k sets equals the mean of that set). Finally it does not seem possible to improve on this technique, in the sense of reducing the computational burden.

PROBLEMS IN THE ANALYSIS OF SURVEY DATA, AND A PROPOSAL

JAMES N. MORGAN AND JOHN A. SONQUIST*

University of Michigan

Appendix VII

Most of the problems of analyzing survey data have been reasonably well handled, except those revolving around the existence of interaction effects. Indeed, increased efficiency in handling multivariate analyses even with non-numerical variables, has been achieved largely by assuming additivity. An approach to survey data is proposed which imposes no restrictions on interaction effects, focuses on importance in reducing predictive error, operates sequentially, and is independent of the extent of linearity in the classifications or the order in which the explanatory factors are introduced.

A. NATURE OF THE DATA AND THE WORLD FROM WHICH THEY COME

THE increasing availability of rich data from cross section surveys calls for more efficient methods of data scanning and data reduction in the process of analysis. The purpose of this paper is to spell out some of the problems arising from the nature of the data and the nature of the theories which are being tested with the data, to show that present methods of dealing with these problems are often inadequate, and to propose a radical new method for analyzing survey data. There are seven things about the data or about the world from which they come which need to be kept in mind.

First, there is a wide variety of information about each person interviewed in a survey. This is good, because human behavior is motivated by more than one thing. But the very richness of the data creates some problems of how to handle them.

Second, we are dealing not with variables for the most part, but with classifications. These vary all the way from age, which can be thought of as a variable put into classes, to occupation or the answers to attitudinal questions, which may not even have a rank order in any meaningful sense. Even when measures seem to be continuous variables, such as age or income, there is good reason to believe that their effects are not linear. For instance, people earn their highest incomes in the middle age ranges. Expenditures do not change uniformly with changes in income at either extreme of the income scale.

Third, there are errors in all the measures, not just in the dependent variable, and there is little evidence as to the size of these errors, or as to the extent to which they are random.

Fourth, the data come from a sample and generally a complex one at that. Hence, there is sample variability piled on top of measurement error. The fact that almost all survey samples are clustered and stratified leads to problems of the proper application of statistical techniques. Statistical tests usually assume simple random samples rather than probability samples. More ap-

---

* The authors are indebted to many individuals for advice and improvements. In particular, Professor L. J. Savage noticed that some interactions would remain hidden, and Professor William Ericson proved that locating the best combination of subclasses of a single code was simple enough to incorporate into the program. A Ford Foundation grant to the Department of Economics of the University of Michigan supported the author's work on some substantive problems which led to the present focus on methods. Support from the Rockefeller Foundation is also gratefully acknowledged.

Reprinted by permission of the Journal of the American Statistical Association, 58 (June 1963), pp. 415–35.

propriate tests have been developed for simple statistics such as proportions, means, and a few others.

Fifth, and extremely important, there are intercorrelations between many of the explanatory factors to be used in the analysis—high income goes along with middle age, with advanced education, with being white, with not being a farmer, and so forth. This makes it difficult to assess the relative importance of different factors, since their intercorrelations get in the way. Since many of them are classifications rather than continuous variables, it is not even easy to measure the extent of the intercorrelation. Measures of association for cross classification raise notoriously difficult problems which have not really been solved in any satisfactory way.[1]

Sixth, there is the problem of interaction effects. Particularly in the social sciences, there are two powerful reasons for believing that it is a mistake to assume that the various influences are additive. In the first place, there are already many instances known of powerful interaction effects—advanced education helps a man more than it does a woman when it comes to making money; and it does a white man more good than a Negro. The effect of a decline in income on spending depends on whether the family has any liquid assets which it can use up. Women have their hospitalizations at different ages than men. Second, the measured classifications are only proxy variables for other things and are frequently proxies for more than one construct. Several of the measured factors may jointly represent a theoretical construct. We may have interaction effects not because the world is full of interactions, but because our variables have to interact to produce the theoretical constructs that really matter. The idea of a family life cycle, unless arbitrarily created out of its components in advance, is a set of interactions between age, marital status, presence, and age of children.[2] It is therefore often misleading to look at the over-all gross effects of age or level of education. Where interaction effects exist, the concept of a main effect is meaningless, and it is our belief that in human behavior there are so many interaction effects that we must change our approach to the problems of analysis.

Another example of interaction effects appeared in the attempt to build equivalent adult scales to represent the differences in living expenses of families of different types. After many years of analysis, one of the most recent studies in this field has concluded "when its size changes, families' tastes appear to change in more complicated ways than visualized by our hypothesis."[3] More

---

[1] One seemingly appropriate measure for two classifications both being used to predict the same variable is one called lambda suggested by Goodman and Kruskal. With many kinds of survey data this measure, which assumes that an absolute prediction has to be made for each individual, is too insensitive to deal with situations where each class on the predicting characteristic has the same modal class on the other characteristic that is to be predicted. An effective and properly stochastic measure would be derived by assigning a one-zero dummy variable to belonging to each class of each of the two characteristics and then computing the canonical correlation between the two sets of dummy variables.

See Leo A. Goodman and William H. Kruskal, "Measures of association for cross classifications," *Journal of the American Statistical Association*, 49 (December, 1954), 732–64.

[2] John B. Lansing and James N. Morgan, "Consumer finances over the life cycle," in *Consumer Behavior*, Volume II, L. Clark (Editor) (New York: New York University Press, 1955).

See also Leslie Kish and John B. Lansing, "Family life cycle as an independent variable," *American Sociological Review*, XXII (October, 1957), 512–9.

[3] In other words family composition had different effects on different expenditures. F. G. Forsythe, "The relationship between family size and family expenditure," *Journal of the Royal Statistical Society*, Series A, vol. 123 (1961), 367–97, quote from p. 386.

recently in analyzing factors affecting spending unit income, it has become obvious that age and education cannot operate additively with race, retired status, and whether the individual is a farmer. The attached table illustrates this with actual average incomes for a set of nonsymmetrical groups. The twenty-one groups account for two-thirds of the variance of individual spending unit incomes, whereas assuming additivity for race and labor force status even with joint age-education variables produces a regression which with 30 variables accounts for only 36 per cent of the variance. A second column in the

TABLE 1. SPENDING UNIT INCOME AND THE NUMBER IN THE
UNIT WITHIN VARIOUS SUBGROUPS

Group	Spending unit average (1958) income	Number in unit	Number of cases
Nonwhite, did not finish high school	$ 2489	3.3	191
Nonwhite, did finish high school	5005	3.4	67
White, retired, did not finish high school	2217	1.7	272
White, retired, did finish high school	4520	1.7	72
White, nonretired farmers, did not finish high school	3950	3.6	87
White nonretired farmers, did finish high school	6750	3.6	24
The Remainder			
0–8 grades of school			
18–34 years old	4150	3.8	72
35–54 years old	4670	3.8	240
55 and older—not retired	4846	2.2	208
9–11 grades of school			
18–34 years old	5032	3.7	112
35–54 years old	6223	3.4	202
55 and older—not retired	4720	2.1	63
12 grades of school			
18–34 years old	5458	3.3	193
35–54 years old	7765	3.8	291
55 and older—not retired	6850	2.0	46
Some college			
18–34 years old	5378	3.0	102
35–54 years old	7930	3.8	112
55 and older—not retired	8530	2.0	36
College graduates			
18–34 years old	7520	3.8	80
35–54 years old	8866	2.9	150
55 and older—not retired	10879	1.8	34

Source: 1959 Survey of Consumer Finances.

table gives the average number of people in the unit, and it can be seen that this particular breakdown is not particularly useful for analyzing the number of people in a unit. On the other hand, if each group were to be used to analyze expenditure behavior, income, and family size are likely to operate jointly rather than additively.

In view of the fact that intercorrelation among the predictors on the one hand and interaction effects on the other are frequently confused, it seems useful to give a pictorial example indicating both the differences between them and the way in which they operate when both are present. Our concern is not with statistical tests to distinguish between them, but with the effects of ignoring their presence.

Chart I shows pictorially three cases, real but exaggerated. First, there is a case where the two explanatory factors, income and education, are correlated with one another, but do not interact. Second, a case where income and being self-employed interact with one another but are not correlated, and third, a situation where income and asset holdings are correlated with one another and also interact in their effect on saving. The ellipsoids represent the area where most of the dots on a scatter diagram would appear. In the first case, it is clear that a simple relation between income and saving would exaggerate the effect of income on saving by failing to allow for the fact that high income people have more education, and that highly educational people also save more. An ordinary multiple regression, however, using a dummy variable representing high education would adequately handle this difficulty. In the second case there is no particular correlation, we assume, between income and being self-employed, but the self-employed have a much higher marginal propensity to save than other people. Here, the simple relationship between income and saving becomes a weighted compromise between the two different effects that really exist. A multiple correlation would show no effect of being self-employed and the same compromise effect of income. Only a separate analysis for the self-employed and the others would reveal the real state of the world. In the third case, not only do the high-asset people have a higher marginal propensity to save, but they also tend to have a higher income. Multiple correlation clearly will not take care of this situation in any adequate way. It *will* produce an "income effect" which can be added to an "asset effect" to produce an estimate of saving. Here the income effect is an average of two different income effects. The estimated asset effect is likely to come out closer to zero than if income had been ignored. Of course, where interactions exist, there is little use in attempting to measure separate effects.

Finally, there are logical priorities and chains of causation in the real world. Some of the predicting characteristics are logically prior to others in the sense that they can cause them but cannot be affected by them. For instance, where a man grows up may affect how much education he gets, but his education cannot change where he grew up. We are not discussing here the quite different analysis problem where the purpose is not to explain one dependent variable but to untangle the essential connections in a network of relations.

In dealing with a single dependent variable representing some human behavior, we might end up with at least three stages in the causal process—early childhood and parental factors, actions and events during the lifetime, and current situational and attitudinal variables. If this were the end of the problem we could simply run three separate analyses. The first would analyze the effects of early childhood and parental factors. The second would take the residuals from this analysis and analyze them against events during a man's lifetime up until the present, and the third would take the residuals from the

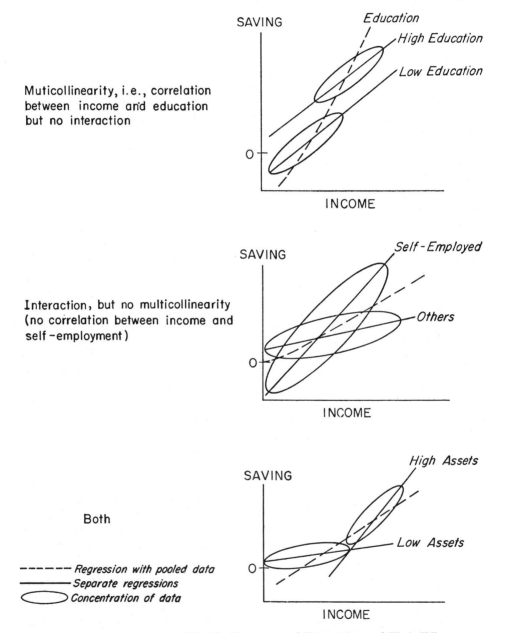

CHART I. Combinations of Multicollinearity and Interaction and Their Effects.

second analysis and analyze them against current situational and attitudinal variables. But the real world is not even that simple, because some of the same variables which are logically prior in their direct effects may also tend to mediate the effect of later variables. For instance, a man's race has a kind of logical priority to it, but at the same time it may affect the way other things such as the level of his education operate to determine his income.

This is an impressive array of problems. Before we turn to a discussion of current attempts to solve these problems and to our own suggestions, it is essential to ask first what kind of theoretical structure is being applied and what the purposes of analysis are.

B. NATURE OF THE THEORY AND PURPOSES OF ANALYSIS

Perhaps the most important thing to keep in mind about survey data in the social sciences is that the theoretical constructs in most theory are not identical with the factors we can measure in the survey. The simple economic idea of ability to pay for any particular commodity is certainly a function not only of income but of family size, other resources, expected future income, economic security, and even extended family obligations. A man's expectations about his own economic future, which we may theorize will affect his current behavior, might be measured by a battery of attitudinal and expectational questions or by looking at his education, occupation, age, and the experience of others in the same occupation and education group who are already older. The fact that the theoretical constructs in which we are interested are not the same as the factors we can measure, nor even simply related to them, should affect our analysis techniques and focus attention on creating or locating important interaction effects to represent these constructs.

Second, there are numerous hypotheses among which a selection is to be made. Even if the researcher preferred to restrict himself to a single hypothesis and test it, the intercorrelations among the various explanatory factors mean that the same result might support any one of several hypotheses.[4] Hence, comparisons of relative importance of predictors, and selecting those which reduce predictive errors most, are required.

When we remember that there are also variable errors of measurement, the problem of selecting between alternative hypotheses becomes doubly difficult, and ultimately requires the use of discretion on the part of the researcher. Better measurement of a factor might increase its revealed importance.

Finally, researchers may have different reasons why they wish to predict individual behavior. Most will want to predict behavior of individuals in the population, not just in the sample, which makes the statistical problem somewhat more complicated. But some may also want to focus on the behavior of some crucial individuals by assigning more weight to the behavior of some rather than others. Others may want to test some explanatory factors, however small their apparent effect, because they are important. They may be important because they are subject to public policy influences or because they

---

[4] For an excellent statement of the application of this problem to the economists' concern with the permanent income hypothesis versus the relative income hypothesis, see Jean Crockett, "Liquid assets and the theory of consumption" (New York: National Bureau of Economic Research, 1962) (mimeographed).

are likely to change over time, or because they are crucial to some larger theoretical edifice. The nature of these research purposes thus combines with the nature of the data and their characteristics to make up the problem of how to analyze the data.

C. THE STRATEGY CHOICE IN ANALYSIS

One can think of a series of strategies ranging from taking account of only the main effects of each explanatory classification separately or jointly, to trying to take account of all possible combinations of all the classifications at once. Even if there were enough data to allow the last, however, it would not be of much use. The essence of research strategy then consists of putting some restrictions on the process in order to make it manageable. One possibility is to cut the number of explanatory factors utilized, and another is to restrict the freedom with which we allow them to operate.[5] One might assume away most or all interaction effects, for instance, and keep a very large number of explanatory classifications. Still further reduction in the number of variables is possible, if one assumes linearity for measured variables or, what amounts to the same thing builds arbitrary scales, incestuously derived out of the same data in order to convert each classification into a numerical variable. Clearly, the more theoretical or statistical assumptions one is willing to impose on the data, the more he can reduce the complexity of the analysis. A difficulty is that restrictions imposed in advance cannot be tested. There seems some reason to argue that it would be better to use an approach which developed its restrictions as it went along. In any case keeping these problems in mind we turn now to a summary of how analysis problems in using survey data are currently being handled and some of the difficulties that present methods still leave unsolved.

D. HOW PROBLEMS IN ANALYSIS ARE CURRENTLY BEING HANDLED—AN APPRAISAL

We take the seven problems in section A in the same order in which they are presented there plus the major problem in section B, that of theoretical constructs not measured directly by the factors on which we have data. The first problem was the existence of many factors. The simplest procedure has been to look at them one at a time always keeping in mind the extent to which one factors is intercorrelated with others. Another technique, particularly with attitudes, has been to build indexes or combinations of factors either arbitrarily or with the use of some sort of factor analysis technique.[6] The difficulty is that the first of these is quite arbitrary, and the second is arbitrary in a different sense, in that most mechanical methods of combining factors are based on the intercorrelations between the factors themselves and not in the way in which they may affect the dependent variable. It is quite possible for two highly correlated factors to influence the dependent variable in opposite ways. Building a combination of the two only on the basis of their intercorrelation would create a factor which would have no correlation at all with the dependent

[5] For a discussion of alternative strategies made while commenting on a series of papers, see James Morgan, "Comments," in *Consumption and Saving*, Volume I, I. Friend and R. Jones (Editors.) (Philadelphia: University of Pennsylvania Press, 1960), pp. 276–84.

[6] Charles Westoff and others, *Family Planning in Metropolitan America* (Princeton: Princeton University Press, 1961).

variable. With highly correlated attitudes, however, some such reduction to a few factors may be required and meaningful.

With the advent of better computing machinery, the problem of multiple factors has frequently been handled by using multiple correlation techniques. The use of these techniques, of course, required solving the second problem, that arising from the fact that in many cases we have classifications rather than continuous variables. This has been done in two ways, first, by building arbitrary scales. For instance, one could assign the numbers one, two, three, four, five, and six to the six age groups in order. Or if age were being used to predict income, one could assign a set of numbers representing the average income of people in those age groups.[7] But unless machine capacity is extremely limited, a far more flexible method which is coming into favor is to use what have been called dummy variables.[8] The essence of this technique is to assign a dummy variable to each class of a characteristic except one. It is called a dummy variable because it takes the value one if the individual belongs in that subclass or a zero if he does not. If ordinary regression procedures are to be used, of course, dummy variables cannot be assigned to every subclass of any characteristic, since this would overdetermine the system. However, at the Survey Research Center we have developed an iterative program for the IBM 7090, the output of which consists of coefficients for each subclass of each characteristic, the set for each characteristic having a weighted mean of zero. This means that the predicting equation has the over-all mean as its constant term, and an additive adjustment for each characteristic, depending on the subclass into which the individual falls on that characteristic. This is the standard analysis of variance formulation when all interactions are assumed to be zero. Of course, the coefficients of dummy variables using a regular matrix inversion routine can easily be converted into sets of this sort. There remain two difficulties with this technique. One is the problem of interaction effects, which are either assumed away or have to be built in at the beginning in the creation of the classes. A second arises from the nature of the classifications frequently used in survey data. Even though association between, say, occupation and the incidence of unemployment faced by an individual is not terribly high, the occupation code generally includes one or two categories such as the farmers and the retired who, by definition, cannot be unemployed at all. When dummy variables are assigned to these classes, it may easily occur that there is a perfect association between a dummy variable representing one of these peculiar (not applicable) groups in one code and a dummy variable representing something else in another classification (not unemployed). If the researcher omits one of each such pair of dummy variables in a regression routine, he is all right.

A third problem, that of errors in the data, is generally handled by not re-

---

[7] For an example see Jerry Miner, "Consumer Personal Debt—An Intertemporal Analysis," in *Consumption and Saving*, Volume II, I. Friend and R. Jones (Editors) (Philadelphia: University of Pennsylvania Press, 1960), 400–61.

[8] Daniel Suits, "The Use of Dummy Variables in Regression Equations," *Journal of the American Statistical Association*, 52 (December, 1957), 548–51.

T. P. Hill, "An Analysis of the Distribution of Wages and Salaries in Great Britain," *Econometrica*, 27 (July, 1959), 355–81.

jecting hypotheses too easily and by attempting to use some judgment in the assessment of relative importance of different factors or different hypotheses keeping in mind the accuracy with which the variables have probably been measured.

The fact that the data come from a sample has frequently been ignored. As the analysis techniques become more complicated, it becomes almost impossible to keep the structure of the sample in mind too. However, there is some reason to believe that the clustering and stratification of the sample become less and less important the more complex and more multivariate the analysis being undertaken.[9]

What about intercorrelations among the predictors? The main advantage of multivariate techniques like multiple regression is that they take care of these intercorrelations among the predictors, at least in a crude sense. Indeed, if one compares an ordinary subclass mean with the multivariate coefficient of the dummy variable associated with belonging to that subclass, the difference between the two is the result of adjustments for intercorrelations. Where these differences seem likely to be the result of a few major interrelations, some statement as to the factors correlated with the one in question (and responsible for the attenuation of its effect on the multivariate analysis) are often given to the reader. It is, of course, true that where intercorrelations between two predictors are too high, no analysis can handle this problem, and it becomes necessary to remove one of them from the analysis.

Perhaps the most neglected of the problems of analysis has been the problem of interaction effects. The reason is very simple. The assumption that no interactions exist generally leads to an extremely efficient analysis procedure and a great reduction in the complexity of the computing problem. Those of us who have looked closely at the nature of survey data, however, have become increasingly impressed with the importance of interaction effects and the useful way in which allowing for interactions between measured factors gets us closer to the effects of more basic theoretical constructs. Where interaction effects have not been ignored entirely, they have been handled in a number of ways. They can be handled by building combination predictors in the first place, such as combinations of age and education or the combination of age, marital status, and children known as the family life cycle.[10] Sometimes where almost all the interactions involve the same dichotomy, two separate analyses are called for.[11] Interactions are also handled by rerunning the analysis for

---

[9] Actually there are no formulas available for sampling errors of many of the statistics from complex probability samples. Properly selected part-samples can be used to estimate them by a kind of hammer-and-tongs procedure, but this is expensive. See Leslie Kish, "Confidence intervals for clustered samples," *American Sociological Review*, 22 (April, 1957), 154–65. So long as the samples are representative of a whole population the basic statistical model is presumably the "fixed" one, see M. B. Wilk and O. Kempthorne, "Fixed, mixed, and random models," *Journal of the American Statistical Association*, 50 (December, 1955), 1144–67.

See also L. Klein and J. Morgan, "Results of alternative statistical treatments of sample survey data," *Journal of the American Statistical Association*, 46 (December, 1951), 442–60.

[10] Guy Orcutt and others, *Microanalysis of Socioeconomic Systems* (New York: Harper and Brothers, 1961).

[11] For instance, hospital utilization was studied separately for men and women in Grover Wirick, Robin Barlow, and James Morgan, "Population survey: Health care and its financing," *Hospital and Medical Economics*, Volume I, Walter McNerney (Editor) (Chicago: American Hospital Association, 1962).

Participation in recreation was studied separately for those with and without paid vacations; see Eva Mueller and Gerald Gurin, *Participation in Outdoor Recreation: Factors Affecting Demand Among American Adults* (U.S. (U.S.G.P.O., ORRRC Study Report 20, 1962.)

some subgroup of the population. In a recent study of factors affecting hourly earnings, for instance, the analysis was rerun for the white, nonfarmer males only, to test the hypothesis that some of the effects like that of education were different for the non-whites, women, and farmers.[12] A difficulty with this technique, of course, is that if one merely wants to see whether the interaction biases the estimates for the whole population seriously, one reruns the analysis with the group that makes up the largest part of the sample. But if one wants to know whether there are different patterns of effects for some small subgroup, the analysis must be run for that small subgroup.

Another method of dealing with interaction effects is to look at two- and three-way tables of residuals from an additive multivariate analysis. This requires the process, often rather complicated and expensive, of creating the residuals from the multivariate analysis and then analyzing them separately.[13] Where some particular interaction is under investigation, an effective alternative is to isolate some subgroup on a combination of characteristics such as the young, white, college graduates. It is then possible to derive an estimate of the expected average of that subgroup on the dependent variable by summing the multivariate coefficients multiplied by the subgroup distributions over each of the predictors. Comparing this expected value with the actual average for that subgroup indicates whether there is something more than additive effect. It is only feasible to do this with a few interactions, just as it is possible to put in cross product terms in multiple regressions in only a few of the total possible cases. Consequently, most of these methods of dealing with interaction effects are either limited, or expensive and time-consuming.

Still another technique for finding interactions is to restrict the total number of predictors, use cell means as basic data, and use a variance analysis looking directly for interaction effects.[14] Aside from the various statistical assumptions that have to be made, this turns out to be a relatively cumbersome method of dealing with the data. It requires a good deal of judgment in the selecting of the classes to avoid getting empty cells or cells with very small numbers of cases,

---

[12] James Morgan, Martin David, Wilbur Cohen, and Harvey Brazer, *Income and Welfare in the United States* (New York: McGraw-Hill, 1962).

Malcolm R. Fisher, "Exploration in savings behavior," *Bulletin of the Oxford University Institute of Statistics*, 18 (August, 1956), 201–77.

[13] James Morgan, "An analysis of residuals from 'normal' regressions," in *Contributions of Survey Methods to Economics*, L. Klein (Editor) (New York: Columbia University Press, 1954).

[14] F. Gerald Adams, *Some Aspects of the Income Size Distribution* (unpublished Ph.D. dissertation, The University of Michigan, 1956); and a summary, "The size of individual incomes: Socio-economic variables and chance variation," *Review of Economics and Statistics*, XL (November, 1958), 394–8.

James Morgan, "Factors related to consumer savings" in *Contributions of Survey Methods to Economics*, L. Klein (Editor) (New York: Columbia University Press, 1954).

Mordechai Kreinin, "Factors associated with stock ownership," *Review of Economics and Statistics*, XLI (February, 1959), 12–23; "Analysis of liquid asset ownership," *Review of Economics and Statistics*, XLIII (February, 1961), 76–80.

M. Kreinin, J. Lansing, J. Morgan, "Analysis of life insurance premiums," *Review of Economics and Statistics*, XXXIX (February, 1957), 46–54.

Robert Ferber has pointed out that using the highest order interaction as "error" may hide significant main effects or lower-order interaction effects, and that the heteroscedasticity of means based on subcells of different sizes may make the tests nonconservative. He has made use of the more complex method of fitting constants which provides an exact test for interactions but assumes that the individual observations are all independent. Since this assumption is not correct for most multistage samples the results of this method are also nonconservative. See Robert Ferber, "Service expenditures at mid-century," in *Consumption and Saving*, Volume I, I. Friend and R. Jones (Editors) (Philadelphia: University of Pennsylvania Press, 1960), pp. 436–60.

and the unequal cell frequencies lead to heterogeneity of variances which makes the F-test nonconservative. Sometimes interaction effects are considered important only when they involve one extremely important variable. In the case of much economic behavior, current income appears to be such a variable. In this case one can rely on covariance techniques, but these techniques tend to become far too complex when a large number of other factors are involved. Also, as more and more questions arise about the meaning of current income as a measure of ability to pay, the separation of current income for special treatment becomes more doubtful.

Finally, it is also true that if we restrict the number of variables, multiple regression techniques, particularly using dummy variables, can build in almost all feasible interaction effects. One way to restrict the number of variables is to make an analysis with an initial set and run the residuals against a second set of variables. However, unless there is some logical reason why one set takes precedence over another, this is treacherous since the explanatory classifications used in the second set will have a downward bias in their coefficients if they are at all associated with the explanatory classifications used in the first set.[15]

All these methods for dealing with interaction effects require building them in somehow without knowing how many cases there are for which each interaction effect could be relevant. The more complex the interaction, the more difficult it is to tell, of course.

The problem of logical priorities in the data and chains of causation can be handled either by restricting the analysis to one level or by conducting the analysis sequentially, always keeping in mind that the logically prior variables may have to be reintroduced in later analyses on the chance that they may mediate the effects of other variables. In practice, very little analysis of survey data has paid much attention to this problem. Perhaps the reason is that only recently has anyone been able to handle the other problems so that a truly multivariate analysis was possible. And it is only when many variables begin to be used simultaneously that the problem of their position in a causal structure becomes crucial.

Finally, there is the problem remaining from section B that the constructs of theories do not have any one-to-one correspondence with the measures from the survey. Sometimes this problem is handled by building complex variables that hopefully represent the theoretical construct. The life cycle concept, for instance, has been used this way. In a recent study, a series of questions that seemed to be asking evaluations of occupations were translated into a measure which was (hopefully) an index measure of achievement motivation.[16] More commonly, the analyst has been constrained to interpret each of the measured characteristics in terms of some theoretical meaning which it hopefully has. This is often not very satisfactory. In the case of liquid assets, the amount of

---

[15] James Morgan, "Consumer investment expenditures," *American Economic Review*, XLVIII (December, 1958), 874–902, Appendix, 898–901.

Arthur S. Goldberger and D. B. Jochems, "A note on stepwise least squares," *Journal of the American Statistical Association*, 56 (March, 1961), 105–11.

[16] Morgan, David, Cohen, and Brazer, *Income and Welfare in the United States*. (New York: McGraw-Hill Book Company, Inc., 1962).

these assets a man has represents both his past propensity to save and his present ability to dissave, two effects which could be expected to operate in opposite directions. In general, the analysis of survey data has been much better than this summary of problems would indicate. Varied approaches have been ingeniously used, and cautiously interpreted.

E. PROPOSAL FOR A PROCESS FOR ANALYZING DATA

One way to focus on the problems of analyzing data is to propose a better procedure. The proposal made here is essentially a formalization of what a good researcher does slowly and ineffectively, but insightfully on an IBM sorter. With large masses of data, weighted samples, and a desire for estimates of the reduction in error, however, we need to be able to simulate this process on large scale computing equipment. The basic idea is the sequential identification and segregation of subgroups one at a time, nonsymmetrically, so as to select the set of subgroups which will reduce the error in predicting the dependent variable as much as possible relative to the number of groups. A subgroup may be defined as membership in one or more subclasses of one or more characteristics. If more than one characteristic is used, the membership is joint, not alternative.

It is assumed that where the problem of chains of causation and logical priority of one variable over another exists, that this problem will be handled by dividing the explanatory variables or predictors into sets. One then takes the pooled residuals from an analysis using the first set of predictors and analyses these residuals against the second set of predictors. The residuals from the analysis using this second set could then be run against a third set. In practice, we might easily end up with three states—early childhood or parental factors, actions and events during the lifetime, and current situational and attitudinal variables.

The possibilities of interactions between variables in different stages can be handled by reintroducing in the second or third analyses, factors whose simple effects have already been removed, but which may also mediate the effects of factors at one of the later stages, that is, nonwhites may have their income affected by education differently from whites.

Temporarily setting aside these complications, we turn now to a description of the process of analysis using the variables from any *one* stage of the causal process. Since even the best measured variable may actually have nonlinear effects on the dependent variable, we treat each of the explanatory factors as a set of classifications. As we said, our purpose is to identify and segregate a set of subgroups which are the best we can find for maximizing our ability to predict the dependent variable. We mean maximum relative to the number of groups used, since an indefinitely large number of subgroups would "explain" everything in the sample. To be more sophisticated, if we use a model based on the assumption that we want to predict back to the population, there is an optimal number of subgroups. However, as an approximation we propose that with samples of two to three thousand we arbitrarily segregate only those groups, the separation of which will reduce the total error sum of squares by at least one per cent and do not even attempt further subdivision unless the group to be divided has a residual error (within group sum of squares) of at least two per cent of the total sum of squares. This restricts us to a *maximum* of fifty-one groups. It is just as arbitrary as the use of the 5 per cent level in significance tests and perhaps should be subject to later revision on the basis of experience.

We now describe the process of analysis in the form of a series of decision rules and instructions. We think of the sample in the beginning as a single group. The first decision is what single division of the parent group into two will do the most good. A second decision has then to be made: Which of the two groups we now have has the largest remaining error sum of squares, and hence should be investigated next for possible further subdivision? Whenever a further subdivision of a group will not reduce the unexplained sum of squares by at least one per cent of the total original sum of squares, we pay no further attention to that subgroup. Whenever there is no subgroup accounting for at least two per cent of the original sum of squares, we have finished our job. We turn now to a more orderly description of this process.

1) Considering all feasible divisions of the group of observations on the basis of each explanatory factor to be included (but not combinations of factors) find the division of the classes of any characteristic such that the partitioning of this group into two subgroups on this basis provides the largest reduction in the unexplained sum of squares.

Starting with any given group, and considering the various possible ways of splitting it into two groups, it turns out that a quick examination of any possible subgroup provides a rapid estimate of how much the error variance would be reduced by segregating it:

The reduction in error sum of squares is the same size (opposite sign) as the increase in the explained sum of squares.

For the group as a whole, the sum of squares explained by the mean is

$$N\overline{X}^2 = \frac{(\sum X)^2}{N} \tag{1}$$

and the total sum of squares (unexplained by the mean) is

$$\sum (X - \overline{X})^2 = \sum X^2 - \frac{(\sum X)^2}{N} . \tag{2}$$

If we now divide the group into two groups of size N_1 and N_2 and means $\overline{X}_1$ and $\overline{X}_2$, what happens to the explained sum of squares?

$$\text{Explained sum of squares} = N_1\overline{X}_1^2 + N_2\overline{X}_2^2. \tag{3}$$

The division which increases this expression most over $N\overline{X}^2$ clearly does us the most good in improving our ability to predict individuals in the sample.

Fortunately we do not even need to calculate anything more than a term involving the subgroup under inspection, since N and $\sum X$ remain known and constant throughout this search process.

$$N_2 = N - N_1 \qquad\qquad (4)$$

$$\sum X_2 = \sum X - \sum X_1 \qquad\qquad (5)$$

$$\therefore \text{ explained sum of squares} = N_1\left(\frac{\sum X_1}{N_1}\right)^2 + (N - N_1)\left(\frac{\sum X_2}{N - N_1}\right)^2$$

$$= \frac{(\sum X_1)^2}{N_1} + \frac{(\sum X - \sum X_1)^2}{N - N_1}.$$

The number of cases (or proportion of sample) and the sum of the dependent variable for any subgroup are enough to estimate how much reduction in error sum of squares would result from separating it from the parent group.

If it seems desirable, a variance components model which takes account of the fact that we really want optimal prediction of members of the population not merely of the sample, can be used. Indeed, the expression for the estimate of the explained, or "between" component of variance in the population turns out to be

$$\hat{\sigma}_B^2 = \frac{\left(\dfrac{N-1}{N-2}\left[\dfrac{(\sum X_1)^2}{N_1} + \dfrac{(\sum X - \sum X_1)^2}{N - N_1}\right] - \dfrac{\sum X^2}{N-2}\right)}{N - \dfrac{N_1^2 + N_2^2}{N}} \qquad (7)$$

which, though it looks formidable, contains only one new element and that is a term from the total sum of squares of the original group which is constant and can be ignored in selecting the best split. The expression in the brackets is the explained sum of squares already derived. N, $\sum X$, and $\sum X^2$ are known and constant. The denominator is an adjustment developed by Ganguli for a bias arising from unequal N's. Where N_1 equals N_2, the denominator becomes equal to N_1. The more unequal the N's, the smaller the denominator, relative to an arithmetic mean of the N's. The ratio of the explained component of variance to the total is rho, the intraclass correlation coefficient. Hence, in using a population model, we are searching for the particular division of a group into two that will provide the largest rho.[17] Computing formulas for weighted data or a dummy (one or zero) dependent variable can be derived easily.

(2) Make sure that the actual reduction in error sum of squares is larger than one per cent of the total sum of squares for the whole sample, i.e., $>.01\ (\sum X^2, -N\bar{X}^2)$ (If not select the next most promising group for search for possible subdivision, etc.)

(3) Among the groups so segregated, including the parent, or bereft ones, we now select a group for a further search for another subgroup to be split off. The selection of the group to try is on the basis of the size of the unexplained

---

[17] R. L. Anderson and T. A. Bancroft, *Statistical Theory in Research* (New York: McGraw-Hill Book Company, 1952).

M. Ganguli, "A note on nested sampling," *Sankhya* 5 (1941), 449–52.

For an example of the use of rho in analysis see Leslie Kish and John Lansing, "The family life cycle as an independent variable," *American Sociological Review*, XXII (October, 1957), 512–4.

sum of squares within the group, or the heterogeneity of the group times its size, which comes to the same thing. It may well *not* be the group with the most deviant mean.

In other words, among the groups, select the one where

$$\sum X_{ij}^2 - N_i \overline{X}_i^2 \text{ is largest.}$$

If it is less than two per cent of the total sum of squares for the whole sample, stop, because no further subdivision could reduce the error sum of squares by more than two per cent. If it is more than two per cent, repeat Step 1.

Note that the process stops when no group accounts for more than two per cent of the error sum of squares. If a group being searched allows no further segregation that will account for one per cent, the next most promising group is searched, because it may still be possible that another group with a smaller sum of squares within it can be profitably subdivided.

Since only a single group is split off at a time, the order of scanning to select that one should not affect the results. Since an independent scanning is done each time, the order in which groups are selected for further investigation should not matter either, hence our criterion is a pure efficiency one.

Chart II shows how the process suggested might arrive at a set of groups approaching those given earlier in Table 1. The numbers are rough estimates from Table 1.

Note on Amount of Detail in the Codes

The search for the best single subgroup which can be split off involves a complete scanning at each stage of each of the explanatory classifications, and within each classification of all the feasible splits. This is not so difficult as it seems, for within any classification not all possible combinations of codes are feasible. If one orders the subclasses in ascending sequence according to their means (on the dependent variable), then it can be shown that the best single division—the one which maximizes the explained sum of squares—will never combine noncontiguous groups.

Hence, starting at either end of the ordered subgroups, the computer will sequentially add one subgroup after another to that side and subtract it from the other side, always recomputing the explained sum of squares. By "explained" we mean that the means of the two halves are used for predicting rather than the over-all mean. Whenever the new division has a higher explained sum of squares, it is retained, otherwise the previous division is remembered. But in any case, the process is continued until there is only one subgroup left on the other side, to allow for the possibility of "local maxima."

The machine then remembers the best split, and the explained sum of squares associated with it, and proceeds to the next explanatory characteristic. If upon repeating this procedure with the subclasses of that characteristic, a still larger explained sum of squares is discovered, the new split on the new characteristic is retained and the less adequate one dropped.

The final result will thus be the best single split, allowing any reasonable

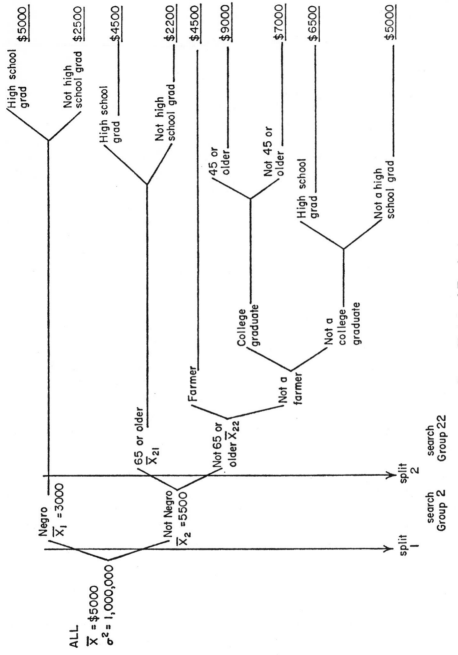

CHART II. Annual Earnings.

combination of subclasses of a single category, to maximize the explained sum of squares. It is easy to see that this choice will not depend on the order in which factors are entered, but may depend on the amount of detail with which they are coded. The number of subclasses probably should not vary too much from one factor to the next.

The authors are planning to try out such a program under a grant from the National Science Foundation. Data which have already been analyzed using dummy variable multiple regressions will be re-analyzed to see whether the new program provides new insights.

DISCUSSION

What is the theoretical model behind this process? Instead of simplifying the analysis by arbitrary or theoretical assumptions that restrict the number of variables or the way in which they operate, this process essentially restricts the complexity of the analysis by insisting that there be a large enough sample of any particular subgroup so that we can be sure it matters, and by handling problems one at a time. This is essentially what a researcher does when first investigating a sample using a sorter and his own judgment. It is assumed that the sample being used in a situation like this is a representative probability sample of a large important population. It is possible that there may be subgroups of the population whose behavior is of more importance than that of other subgroups, in which case it would be easily possible to weight the data to take account of this fact. It may be that there are certain crucial characteristics, the importance of which must be investigated. In this case, either lower admission criteria could be used or an initial arbitrary division of the sample according to this characteristic could be made before starting.

Why not take all possible subsets, in other words, all possible combinations of characteristics, and then start combining subcells where the means are close to one another? The simple reason is that there are far too many possible subsets, and since this is a sample, the means of these subsets are unstable and unreliable estimates. It is true, however, that this is the only way one would avoid all possibility of failing to discover interaction effects. Let us take a simple example of a stituation where the method we propose would fail to discover interaction effects. Suppose we have males and females, old and young, in the following proportions who go to the hospital each year, young females eight per cent, young males two per cent, old females two per cent, old males eight per cent. Assuming half the population is male and half the population is old, the old-young split would give means of five and five per cent, and the male-female split would give means of five and five per cent. Thus we would never discover that it is young females and old males who go to the hospital. One way out of this difficulty which would also vastly increase the efficiency of the machine processes would be to set up a relatively arbitrary division of the sample into perhaps ten groups to start with, groups which are known to be important and suspected to be different in their behavior. The only problem with this is that the remaining procedures will not be invariant with respect to which initial groups were selected.

Previous Work of a Similar Nature

One can never be sure that there does not exist previous work relevant to any "new" idea. William Belson has suggested a sequential, nonsymmetrical division of the sample which he calls "biological classification," for a different purpose, that of matching two groups on other characteristics used as controls so that they can be compared.[18] His procedure is restricted to the case where the criterion can be converted to a one-zero division, and the criterion for subdivision is the best improvement in discrimination. The method takes account of the number of cases, i.e., focuses on improvement in prediction, not on levels of significance. We have proposed this same focus. No rules are provided as to when to stop, or in what order to keep searching, though an intelligent researcher would intuitively follow the rules suggested here.

Another approach to the problem as been suggested and tried by André Danière and Elizabeth Gilboy. Their approach attempts to keep numerical variables whenever there appears to be linearity, at least within ranges, and to repool groups whenever there does not appear any substantial nonlinearity or interaction effect. The method is feasible only where the number of factors is limited. The pooling both of groups and of ranges of "variables" makes it complicated.[19] In practice, they found it useful to restrict the number of allowable interaction effects.

There are also studies going on in the selection of test items to get the best prediction with a limited set of predictors. But the prediction equation in these analyses always seems to be multiple regression without any interaction effects.[20] Group-screening methods have been suggested whereby a set of factors is lumped and tested and the individual components checked only if the group seems to have an effect. These procedures, however, require knowledge of the direction of each effect and again assume no interaction effects.[21] These group-screening methods are largely used in experimental designs and quality control procedures. It is interesting, however, that they usually end up with two-level designs, and our suggested procedure of isolating one subgroup at a time has some similarity to this search for simplicity.

The approach suggested here bears a striking resemblance to Sewall Wright's path coefficients, and to procedures informally called "pattern analysis." The justification for it, however, comes not fron any complicated statistical theory, nor from some enticing title, but from a calculated belief that for a large range of problems, the real world is such that the proposed procedure will facilitate understanding it, and foster the development of better connections between theoretical constructs and the things we can measure.

One possible outcome, for those who want precise measurement and testing,

18 William A. Belson, "Matching and prediction on the principle of biological classification," *Applied Statistics*, VIII (1959), 65–75.

19 André Danière and Elizabeth Gilboy, "The specification of empirical consumption structures, in *Consumption and Saving*, Volume I, I. Friend and R. Jones (Editors) (Philadelphia: University of Pennsylvania Press, 1960), pp. 93–136.

20 Paul Horst and Charlotte MacEwan, "Optimal test-length for multiple prediction, the general case," *Psychometrika*, 22 (December, 1957), 311–24 and references cited therein.

21 G. S. Watson, "A Study of the group-screening method," *Technometrics*, 3 (August, 1961), 371–88.

    G. E. P. Box, "Integration of techniques for process control," *Transactions of the Eleventh Annual Convention of the American Society for Quality Control, 1958.*

is the development of new constructs, as combinations of the measured "variables," which are then created immediately in new studies and used in the analysis. The family life cycle was partly theoretical, partly empirical in its development. Other such constructs may appear from our analysis, and then acquire theoretical interpretation.

F. WHAT NEEDS TO BE DONE?

It may seem that the procedure proposed here is actually relatively simple. Each stage involves a simple search of groups defined as a subclass of any one classification and a selection of one with a maximum of a certain expression which is easily computed. It turns out, however, that the computer implications of this approach are dramatic. The approach, if it is to use the computer efficiently requires a large amount of immediate access storage which does not exist on many present-day computers. Our traditional procedures for multivariate analysis involve storing information in the computer in the form of a series of two-way tables, or cross-product moments. This throws away most of the interesting and potentially fruitful interconnectedness of survey data, and we only recapture part of it by multivariate processes which assume additivity. The implications of the proposed procedure are that we need to be able to keep track of all the relevant information about each individual in the computer as we proceed with the analysis.

Only an examination of the pedigree of the groups selected by the machine will tell whether they reveal things about the real world, or lead to intuitively meaningful theoretical constructs, which had not already come out of earlier "multivariate" analyses of the same data.

It may prove necessary to add constraints to induce more symmetry, such as giving priority to seriatim splits on the same characteristic, since this might make the interpretation easier. Or we may want to introduce an arbitrary first split, say on sex, to see whether offsetting interactions previously hidden could be uncovered in this way.

Most statistical estimates carry with them procedures for estimating their sampling variability. Sampling stability with the proposed program would mean that using a different sample, one would end up with the same complex groups segregated. No simple quantitative measure of similarity seems possible, nor any way of deriving its sampling properties. The only practical solution would seem to be to try the program out on some properly designed half-samples, taking account of the original sample stratification and controls, and to describe the extent of similarity of the pedigrees of the groups so isolated. Since the program "tries" an almost unlimited number of things, no significance tests are appropriate, and in any case the concern is with discovering a limited number of "indexes" or complex constructs which will explain more than other possible sets.

It seems clear that the procedure takes care of most of the problems discussed earlier in this paper. It takes care of any number of explanatory factors, giving them all an equal chance to come in. It uses classifications, and indeed only those sets of subclasses which it actually proves important to distinguish. The results still depend on the detail with which the original data were coded.

Differential quality of the measures used remains a problem. Sample complexities are relatively unimportant since measures of importance in reducing predictive error are involved rather than tests of significance, and one can restrict the objective to predicting the sample rather than the population. Intercorrelations among the predictors are adequately handled, and logical priorities in causation can be.

Most important, however, the interaction effects which would otherwise be ignored, or specified in advance arbitrarily from among a large possible set, are allowed to appear if they are important.

There is theory built into this apparently empiristic process, partly in the selection of the explanatory characteristics introduced, but more so in the rules of the procedures. Where there is one factor of supreme theoretical interest, it can be held back and used to explain the differences remaining within the homogeneous groups developed by the program. This is a severe test both for the effect of this factor and for possible first-order interaction effects between it and any of the other factors used in defining the groups.

Finally, where it is desired to create an index of several related measures, such as attitudinal questions in the same general area, the program can be restricted to these factors and to five or ten groups, and will create a complex index with maximal predictive power.

Reprinted from the JOURNAL OF THE AMERICAN STATISTICAL ASSOCIATION
June, 1963, Vol. 58
pp. 415-434

The above listed volumes are published by the Institute for Social Research. For information about prices and available editions write to: Sales Fulfillment Section, Institute for Social Research, The University of Michigan, Box 1248, Ann Arbor, Michigan 48106.